THE

Unlisted Securities Market

THE
Unlisted Securities Market

ROGER BUCKLAND
and
EDWARD W. DAVIS

CLARENDON PRESS · OXFORD
1989

Oxford University Press, Walton Street, Oxford OX2 6DP
Oxford New York Toronto
Delhi Bombay Calcutta Madras Karachi
Petaling Jaya Singapore Hong Kong Tokyo
Nairobi Dar es Salaam Cape Town
Melbourne Auckland
and associated companies in
Berlin Ibadan Nicosia

Oxford is a trade mark of Oxford University Press

Published in the United States
by Oxford University Press, New York

British Library Cataloguing in Publication Data
Buckland, Roger
The unlisted securities market
1. Great Britain. Unlisted securities
markets
I. Title II. Davis, Edward W. (Edward
Willmore, 1941–)
332.64′2
ISBN 0–19–828526–4

Library of Congress Cataloging in Publication Data
Buckland, Roger.
The unlisted securities market/Roger Buckland and Edward W. Davis.
Bibliography: p. Includes index.
1. Over-the-counter markets—Great Britain. 2. Over-the-counter markets—United States. 3. Over-the-counter markets—France.
I. Davis, Edward W. II. Title.
HG5432.B78 1989 332.64′3—dc19
88–32232 CIP
ISBN 0–19–828526–4

Phototypeset by Cotswold Typesetting Ltd, Gloucester

Printed and bound in
Great Britain by Biddles Ltd,
Guildford and King's Lynn

To our fathers
Frank and Ted

Foreword

The Stock Exchange's introduction of the Unlisted Securities Market in 1980 was a very important event in Britain's commercial history. It made it possible for younger and less mature companies to come to the stock market for new capital. When it started there were 11 companies which immediately took advantage of it and there were many sceptics who thought it would not succeed. In the event, over 80 companies came to the market in the first year and nearly 700 have now done so. A large number of these companies have grown and thus greatly helped the progress of the British economy in terms of products, services, and jobs. In addition to this the new market did a lot to alter attitudes to risk among investors who, during the 1960s and 1970s, had become averse to risk owing to the economic and fiscal policies pursued by governments during those decades. It is significant that other stock exchanges throughout the world have tried to copy our lead.

Sir Nicholas Goodison

Acknowledgements

The research for this book was carried out at Aston University with the aid of a grant from the Economic and Social Research Council. Mr Jonathan Liu has been invaluable in data collection, Ms Gail Russell indispensable in the preparation of the manuscript. Our editor, Andrew Schuller, and copy editor, Connie Wilsack, have patiently coped with our delays and our manuscript. While remaining responsible for all that follows, the authors are grateful for the help of colleagues, including Professors Ian Davidson, Jack Revell, and Geoffrey Whittington; and for the comments of anonymous referees and reviewers. Dr Sue Wright has prepared the index for us, and we must thank our wives, Lorna and Mary, for many suggestions and endless support. Our appreciation is also extended to Peat Marwick McLintock for permission to use data produced in their survey of the Over-the-Counter Market. To Sir Nicholas Goodison for kindly writing a preface to our work, our thanks are also due. For such various help, whether financial support or advice received, the authors wish to record their considerable gratitude.

Contents

List of Abbreviations x

1. Introduction 1

2. Access to the New Issue Market: Small Firms and the Issuing Process 5

3. Financial Analysis of the Quotation Decision 21

4. New Entrants to British Equity Markets 37

5. The Significance of Administrative Costs 53

6. Debt Management by Companies Entering the Unlisted Securities Market 64

7. The Pricing of New Issues on the USM 91

8. Secondary Markets: Alternatives and Parallels 112

9. Firms' Quotation Experience: The Implications for Corporate Policy 135

10. Epilogue 148

Appendix 153

References 168

Index 173

Abbreviations

BES	Business Expansion Scheme
COB	Commission d'Operation de Bourse
NASDAQ	National Association of Securities Dealers Automated Quotation System (USA)
NASDIM	National Association of Securities Dealers and Investment Managers (UK)
OL	Official List
OTC	Over-the-Counter Market
USM	Unlisted Securities Market

1

Introduction

The Stock Exchange and the Birth of the Unlisted Securities Market

The central theme of this book is that of innovation by the Stock Exchange to provide greater access to its markets for smaller firms. In 1977–8 several witnesses to the Wilson Committee (1979: para. 37) raised the question of the need for a lower-tier market in the securities of companies that, while falling short of full quotation, could still benefit from improved marketability. A three-tier market had been well established in the USA for many years. There, the Over-the-Counter (OTC) market arose on the basis of essentially decentralized transactions in the securities of companies unable or unwilling to obtain a quotation on the New York or American stock exchanges. In 1971 the National Association of Securities Dealers Automated Quotation System (NASDAQ) was established, providing a computerized information system for dealers making markets over the counter in various securities. The remarkable success of the US OTC, which in the ten years to the end of 1985 virtually doubled its share of trading on US stock exchanges, is reflected in the attraction it holds for companies. An undeniable influence here has been the fact that reporting requirements and costs increase with progression towards full quotation. In addition, in the UK an independent example of financial innovation had arisen in the form of sponsorship of a market in unlisted securities [illegible] a firm of licensed dealers, Granville and Co. (then called M. J. H. Nightingale & Co.). The basis of this market was that of matching transactions by which buyers could be put in touch with sellers and each charged a commission. Although the sums of funds transferred or raised may have been small, they were important: first, in stimulating recognition of the need for such a market; and second, in providing an alternative ongoing basis for quotation outside the recognized Stock Exchange.

The reaction of the Stock Exchange itself was to publish a brochure in December 1977, emphasizing the existence of Rule 163(2) of the Exchange, which allowed bargains to be transacted between matched buyer and seller, subject to specific approval from the Stock Exchange. The intent of this provision was that of allowing a limited degree of marketability for companies which did not otherwise meet the Stock Exchange qualifications for a full listing. Under this dispensation, however, there was no formal relationship between the Stock Exchange and the company, which benefited by its freedom from disclosure requirements and by the virtually automatic approval given for individual transactions. Within a relatively short period an expanding number of companies had sought sanction for trading under Rule 163(2), now Rule 535(2), with effect from 1 January 1985.

The growth of this unlisted market raised not only problems of regulation but questions of principle as well. For there was a clear anomaly, in that members of the Stock Exchange were able to deal in the shares of companies which had no obligation to adhere to its rules, a situation which could only be prejudicial to the ultimate authority of the Exchange. The dilemma was posed by the need to encourage the growth of small and medium-sized businesses alongside, but less than consistent with, the need for formally explicit relationships between the Exchange and the companies whose securities were quoted under Rule 163(2) (see Wilson 1980: paras. 1177–81). The Stock Exchange's substantive response to the disquiet being voiced took the form of a consultative document, published in December 1979, which emphasized a commitment to a policy of 'making its capital raising markets as widely available as possible on terms and conditions necessary to ensure public confidence in the market' (Stock Exchange 1979). Within a year the Stock Exchange opened the Unlisted Securities Market.

An Outline of this Book

The objective of this book is to examine certain aspects of the process of obtaining a quotation by firms entering the USM, the Official List, or the OTC. Our interest lies in the experience of companies which are joining an organized secondary market for the first time. This event, which may or may not be accompanied by a sale of shares, represents a separate interest from that of the question of the efficiency of secondary stock markets. We are not, therefore, investigating hypotheses of 'weak' or 'strong' market efficiency of the USM. While these are, of course, of considerable interest in themselves (see, e.g. Firth 1977; Keane 1983), this research does not address them. In this book our focus rests upon the nature of the issuing process together with the characteristics at entry and experience of firms obtaining a first quotation, and comparisons in this respect between the USM and the Official List, and to a lesser extent with the OTC.

The very justification for the USM in the first instance depends on the extent to which it has lowered barriers to entry for firms which otherwise would not have obtained a listing. This extends towards consideration of cost in its widest interpretation, embracing not just the significance of administrative expenses but how, for example, changes in reporting regulations, or the nature of institutional competition for new issues, were reflected in the experience of USM entrants. While the main justification for any new issue market must be that of issuing or transferring equity on behalf of shareholders or the firm, we should not forget that the need to raise additional equity must be seen in relation to alternative capital sources and in particular bank borrowing, dependence on which may indeed have propelled the firm towards obtaining a quotation. In this sense, therefore, the issuing process must be considered to represent an opportunity for transformation, not just of new for old shareholders, but of the composition of the financial structure of the firms themselves.

In Chapter 2 we examine the reasons behind the decline in the attraction of the traditional new issue market in the 1960s and 1970s. We do so in the context of a review of the processes which new entrants encountered on seeking quotation, and the extent to which these have in the past constituted a significant barrier to entry. Upon this essentially institutional framework of the new issue market process we proceed in Chapter 3 to conduct a general discussion of various theories which impact upon our research, setting out the implications of quotation for the value of an equity, the significance of secondary markets, and a consideration of alternate ways in which one can interpret the incidence of costs. The advantage of quotation to the general capital position of the firm is also considered. The chapter concludes with a statement of the methodology adopted in this research.

The succeeding chapters, 4 to 7 inclusive, are generally concerned with the evidence gathered from our survey of new issue market performance. So Chapter 4 provides an outline profile of the financial characteristics of new entrants to the USM and the Official List. The main purpose is to consider the extent to which the introduction of the USM is associated with a materially different type of client company, whether its new entrants are smaller, have shorter trading histories or lower quality of accounting records than firms admitted to the Official List. In Chapter 5 we investigate the most obvious element of fixed cost, the expenses involved in the administration and marketing of the issue.

The question of the influence of financial structure on the decision of the firm to obtain a quotation is examined in Chapter 6. The capital constraints encountered by small firms have been the subject of long-standing debate in the UK, originating with the report of the Macmillan Committee (1931) and continuing beyond the report of the Bolton Committee (1971). Chapter 6 reviews the debt management behaviour of companies following quotation in relation both to their motives in this respect and to their financial structure as published on admission to quotation.

In Chapter 7 we provide evidence on the management of new issue pricing, seeking to examine whether systematic influences identified in previous research continue to affect new entrants to the USM. Further, given that USM companies can be expected to be different from companies entering the Official List, we seek to know whether such differences are reflected in the relative pricing behaviour of the USM *vis-à-vis* the Official List markets. In Chapter 8 we introduce a comparative analysis of the OTC market in the UK, and the French Second Marché, to put into perspective the development of the USM in the UK. While the experience of the US OTC market may be said to have provided an important stimulus to the debate about the necessity for such a market in the UK, it is in many respects significantly different from the USM. A more relevant comparison is with the OTC market in Britain and with the French Second Marché as representative of but one overseas example. In Chapter 9 we bring together our findings in terms of a general summary of our results and analysis of their implications for both corporate and wider public policy. Finally, in Chapter 10, we conclude our analysis with a short epilogue in which we consider the potential impact of both Stock Exchange deregulation and the events of the general 1987 collapse in share prices in the context of the future development of the market.

2

Access to the New Issue Market: Small Firms and the Issuing Process

Introduction

There are two main objectives in this chapter. The first is to trace the reasons behind the decline in the use of the traditional (London) new issue market and the second is to illustrate the nature of the issuing process. So we need to examine how various formal and informal Stock Exchange processes have in the past affected firms' resort to the new issue market in order to appreciate their significance in the development of the USM.

In Section I we begin our review of access to the new issue market by small firms by a short description of the underlying reasons which compel firms to go public and proceed to consider the reasons for the market's relative unattractiveness in the 1960s and 1970s. This inevitably involves consideration of the nature of the issuing process and of Stock Exchange requirements to that effect. In Section II we concentrate upon the procedures required to obtain admission to the market, with reference to the incidence of costs incurred in association with different methods of issue and with the extent of economies of scale. This shift in emphasis towards the process by which new firms enter the market is continued when we examine the role of institutional advisers to USM entrants.

I Access to the New Issue Market: The Quotation Decision and the Motives of Firms

The question of the motives of the firms themselves in seeking a stock market quotation is important, not least because conventional economic theory accords the new issue market a primary function in organizing the supply of new capital. Table 2.1 bears witness to the remarkable success of the USM in raising 'new money' for companies. The motives which firms themselves provide may be found in the prospectuses which they are required to publish on quotation. This evidence is found in past surveys of companies seeking a full Stock Exchange quotation in the 1960s, while for those companies using the USM in the 1980s this is indicated in Table 2.2.

In effect, obtaining a stock market quotation is a necessary stage in the long-

TABLE 2.1 Funds raised on the USM and the Listed Market (£m)

	Unlisted Securities Market				Listed market: net amount raised[b]
	Raised on entry				
	For share-holders	For company	Raised by rights issues	Amount for company[a]	
1980[c]	1.5	11.1	1.5	12.6	243.0
1981 year	24.2	51.0	12.0	63.0	1,832.0
1982 year	31.9	50.2	35.4	85.6	1,167.0
1983 year	72.8	123.0	56.4	179.4	2,812.0
1984 year	84.9	110.6	66.1	176.7	1,721.0
Q1	18.7	28.3	20.4	48.7	153.0
Q2	29.6	41.7	22.4	64.1	596.0
Q3	16.8	22.4	7.8	30.2	653.0
Q4	19.8	18.2	15.5	33.7	319.0
1985 Q1	10.5	34.0	27.8	61.8	1,199.0
Q2	23.4	49.0	21.4	70.4	2,035.0
Q3	22.0	55.6	18.9	74.5	1,252.0

[a] The sum of second and third columns.
[b] Issues less redemptions by UK listed companies.
[c] Nov./Dec. only.
Source: Bank of England Quarterly Bulletin, Dec. 1985.

TABLE 2.2 USM companies: First and Second Stated Reasons for Issue

Reasons offered	First stated reason		Second stated reason	
	No. of companies	%	No. of companies	%
Cash for shareholders	55	16.8	36	11.0
Repaying loans	41	12.5	11	3.4
Working capital	35	10.7	41	12.5
Fixed capital	45	13.8	30	9.2
Capital market access	75	22.9	34	10.4
Acquisitions	25	7.6	42	12.8
Other (transfers from R163)	35	10.7	7	2.1
No reason offered	16	4.9	126	38.5
Total number of companies	327		327	

term growth of successful, independent enterprises. Possible advantages include increased liquidity of the company's shares, enabling existing shareholders to sell stock more readily if they seek to meet tax obligations or to diversify their wealth portfolios. But the company may also benefit from easier access to the capital market, which, in turn, may lead to an increased capacity to raise debt, particularly bank borrowing. Lenders are more likely to be tolerant of higher levels or of longer periods of borrowing if the borrower is able to fund such liabilities by a new issue of equity. Cursory examination of Table 2.2 indicates that such motives continue to matter for USM companies.[1] 'Access' to secondary markets is most frequently recorded, particularly for Stock Exchange Introductions, where information is most scanty. However, almost 28% of entrants cite 'cash for shareholders', and a substantial number of entrants cite new money for fixed and working capital: in Chapter 6 we concentrate upon this aspect in particular. Firms may also be attracted by the fact that further growth will now be facilitated by the ability of the company to offer its equity as part of any consideration in takeovers. Beyond this we may consider as a possible influence the potential value to be derived from an enhancement of the company's status as a result of a stock market quotation, as discussed further in Ch. 3.

The decline of new issue markets in the 1970s

Given the attractions of a stock market quotation we need to ask why the number of companies seeking quotation fell significantly during the 1970s. During the late 1960s and early 1970s approximately fifty companies a year obtained a quotation upon the London Stock Exchange, but in contrast, in the eight years preceding the formation of the USM, between 1972 and 1979, new admissions fell to well under half this rate (see Fig. 2.1). By comparison, in the five and a half years of USM operation up to the end of June 1986, Stock Exchange sources indicate that 470 companies had obtained a quotation on the USM (of which 119 firms had departed, for reasons illustrated in Table 2.3).

Two reasons may be put forward to explain this phenomenon. First, the general behaviour of the economy in the period of the mid- to late 1970s did not provide a sympathetic climate for small business flotation. We may note that the number of UK-registered companies with equity quoted on the London Stock Exchange fell from 3,816 in 1955 to 2,052 at the end of 1979, in which year over half the equity capitalization of the market was represented by the fifty largest companies (see also Wilson 1980: appendices paras. 3.292–318). Further, during the 1970s the UK stock market experienced its greatest volatility since 1945. The impact of the first oil shock of 1973 upon

[1] Prospectus declarations of motive may be biased by vendors' or management's signalling activity, of course (see e.g. ch. 6). The cited reasons are more diverse than those recorded in survey-based research (see e.g. Ghandi 1964; Ray and Hutchinson 1983).

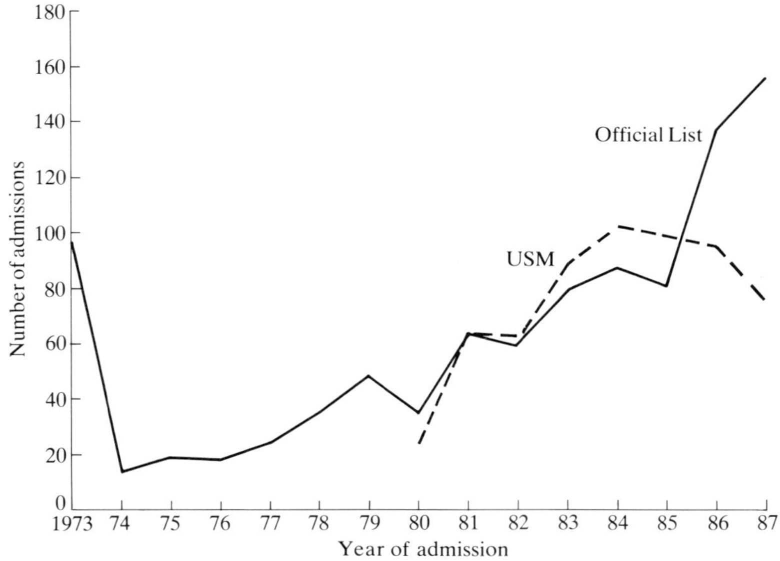

FIG. 2.1 Admissions to the London Stock Exchange, 1973–1985.
Source: Stock Exchange Yearbook.

Stock Exchange values and the prospects for market entrants should not be underestimated, as is evident from the steep fall in the graph of Fig. 2.1. Existing companies' values had been damaged, while world recession had sent equity prices into long-term decline. The UK's index of equity prices, the *Financial Times* All-Share, collapsed from 220 in December 1972 to 66 in December 1974.

TABLE 2.3 USM Entrants and Summary History: Population November 1980 to December 1987 and Sample November 1980 to March 1985

	All entrants		UK entrants	
	Nov. '80–Dec. '87	%	Nov. '80–Mar. '85	%
All entrants	604	100.0	327	100.0
Transfers to official list	108	17.9	41	12.5
Failed/withdrawn	28	4.6	6	1.8
Taken over/merged	98	16.2	22	6.7
No change and continuing at end of period	370	61.3	258	78.9

Source: Stock Exchange Quarterly and *Stock Exchange Fact Sheet.*

A second substantial factor underlying the case for reform, was the burden on small firm entrants deriving from the combination of Stock Exchange regulations alongside economies of scale in the issuing process. The conditions imposed by the Stock Exchange for admission to listing, incorporated in the Listing Agreement to which all entrants must adhere, represented a considerable barrier (as distinct from a mere cost) to many new companies (Wilson, 1980: paras. 759–61). In this context we may cite the general requirement that 25% of the shares of a quoted company be in public hands before dealing starts, which proportion itself had only recently been reduced from the previous level of 35% applicable during the 1960s. Notwithstanding their role in investor protection, the requirements of the Listing Agreement formed a barrier to new entrants. In addition, continuing disclosure requirements for listed companies exceeded those applicable to unquoted companies, which had only to meet the minimum criteria specified in companies acts. Such requirements were exacting enough, but were compounded by requirements such as the publication and expensive advertisement of a prospectus, whose high fixed costs inevitably militated against smaller firms.

The exclusion of small firms

Table 2.4 records the mean net assets of companies obtaining a quotation on the London new issue market between 1965 and 1971. Significantly, it is found that the mean size of firm for the 172 companies which came to the market with Offers for Sale during this period was £1.66m, some six times the size of the

TABLE 2.4 Mean Size of Companies Using Offers for Sale and Placings for New Listings on the London Stock Exchange, 1965–1971 (£000)

Year	Mean net assets		Mean size of issue[a]	
	Offers for Sale	Placing	Offers for Sale	Placing
1965/6	1,264	260	738	145
1966/7	597	380	425	136
1967/8	662	320	592	173
1968/9	776	373	771	221
1969/70	2,564	417	1,306	287
1970/1	4,420	829	1,188	272

[a] Prospectus values.
Source: Davis *et al.* (1974: 16).

Bolton Committee's 'small firm': although a more meaningful comparison would be based on a mean of £0.84m, after excluding three very large firms which went to the market late in this period. In numerical terms, 131 of these 172 firms had net assets of less than £1.0m, 87 had net assets of under £0.5m, while 28 reported net assets of under £0.25m, which at this time corresponded to the upper limit of the Bolton Committee's size definition of a small firm. In the case of Placings, the mean net assets of companies coming to the market for the first time over this period was £0.43m, considerably lower than that for Offers for Sale. The relative attraction of Placings for smaller firms wishing to make relatively small issues reflects the lower cost basis of administrative expenses and is echoed by the corresponding preference of contemporary USM companies for this method of issue.

A finance gap may be considered to arise where the marginal return on investment opportunities open to small firms exceeds their marginal costs of capital, but where profitable investment is blocked by a lack of funds arising from the reluctance of capital suppliers to finance such activity. This can happen, for example, when the duration of the capital requirement is too long, or when the amount is too small to warrant an issue of long-term equity. It has generally been argued that a gap would exist if the cost of funding small firms, defined as the riskless rate of interest together with an adjustment for a difference in risk plus transaction costs, was greater than the cost of capital to large firms.

Research into the existence of such a gap and its interpretation has so far proved inconclusive. Stoll and Curley (1970) argued that capital costs of small and large firms are indistinguishable, whereas Davis *et al.* (1974: ch. 5) produced results which suggest that small firms may be required to offer higher returns than otherwise similar, but larger enterprises. It may also be speculated that any returns differentials are small in relation to transactions costs or methods of risk specification (see e.g. Stoll and Waley 1983, Roll 1981); while the question of small firm's access to funding, at whatever price, could be considered to be the true reflection of a 'gap'.

In wider-ranging official or institutional analyses of financing 'gaps', opinion as to the existence, size and significance of the disadvantage to small firms also varies (Curran 1986). The Bolton Committee, following extensive research into the financing of small firms, concluded that there was 'no institutional deficiency in the finance market, that while there are some differences in the basis on which small firms and large can raise money, these are mostly functions of inherent cost and scale differences' (Bolton 1971: para. 19.13). Addressing the same issue in the context of the 1970s, the Wilson Committee envisaged that institutional changes might counteract such differences, a finding which was to lead to the innovation of the USM. In its investigations of institutional 'short-termism' the CBI concluded that the 'gap' is attitudinal and educational rather than financial (CBI 1987).

II Procedures for Gaining Admission to Quotation

An essential prerequisite for obtaining a quotation is that the company must be examined to establish whether its structure and operations are suitable for secondary trading in its shares. Legal titles to its assets must be verified, with rigorous separation of corporate from owner's activities.

Contractual obligations and rights must be documented and if necessary changed to conform with the General Undertaking (USM) or Listing Agreement (Official List) required by the Stock Exchange of all new entrants. Further, capital structures may need to be revised, as may relationships with subsidiaries or associate companies; this may involve modifications to anomalous classes of stock. In addition, all aspirants to a Stock Exchange quotation are required to publish a prospectus providing detailed accountant's reports of the firm's business and history, which must be presented to potential investors in every case of sales of shares.

It is with the significance of such costs as a barrier to entry that the question of what actually comprises a gap in the provision of capital is commonly confused. Arguably, it was economies of scale in the issuing process which constituted the original Macmillan Gap of the 1930s, which have persisted since and which the USM was intended to overcome. This can be illustrated most readily by discussion of exactly what representative costs are incurred as a result of obtaining a stock market quotation, making use of previous research to demonstrate the existence of scale economies. Issue costs will vary with the method of issue adopted, so the discussion must proceed from a basic definition of the methods of issue and the services employed by firms seeking a stock market quotation.

Methods of issue

When a company has no present intention of seeking new capital by an issue of new shares but wishes simply to obtain a quotation for shares already in existence, it will, if possible, resort to a *Stock Exchange Introduction*. This method allows trade in shares which are already held by the public. To use an Introduction, the firm will have to ensure that there is already some minimum distribution of ownership. The Introduction is favoured by its separation of *quotation* from *sale* of shares. The needs for information of a wide shareholding group are already being met, and little further 'investor education' need be accomplished at the time of quotation.

In contrast with the Introduction are those methods of issue that entail the offer of shares at a stated price and in which the issuing house is retained to advise upon the appropriate valuation. Methods which involve share sales must be used when the Stock Exchange cannot be persuaded that existing patterns of shareholding could sustain a market. For companies seeking admission to a full Stock Exchange quotation, the most popular method of issue is that of the *Offer for Sale*. Here the company sells shares to an issuing house or broker at a fixed price, who in turn sells the shares on the market, again at a fixed price, with receipts normally being guaranteed by demand from underwriters. The difference between the prices at which the issuing house buys and sells represents the fee for its services. The Offer for Sale has the potential for mobilizing very large equity investment (the Offer for Sale in British Telecommunications plc in November 1984 attracted applications for some £10b of equity, for example). On the other hand it does imply uncertainty in price-setting, and the City has for many years also used a variation, the *Offer for Sale by Tender*, where applications are invited at or above a minimum price. On receipt of applications the issuing house can then establish a 'striking price' where all shares are sold, but at a price consistently close to the eventual market price. The issuing house leaves only sufficient unsatisfied demand to promote an active market in the early days of the quotation.

Offers for Sale are relatively cumbersome to administer and rely upon the generation of demand from independent third parties. Alternatively, the shares may be placed with individuals or institutions who hold them. We may distinguish between a *Stock Exchange Placing* in which there is a public quotation of the shares, and a *Private Placing* in which there is no immediate application for quotation. Private Placings bear a close resemblance to venture capital arrangements, whereby firms place part of their equity with institutional investors who do not have any present requirement for public quotation of the shares. All Placings, however, offer favoured treatment to the investing clients of the particular issuing house or broker. To guard against abuse of this privilege, prior to 1986 the Stock Exchange had restricted the maximum size of Placings to £3m for any one security. While the original intention was that Placings were a suitable means of marketing securities for which public interest was likely to be slight, the method has become, particularly through the USM, the most popular means of flotation. Not least of the attractions to the issuer is the fact that a Placing allows a sponsor to put stock into firm hands, avoiding the uncertainty associated with a public offer.

The next main attraction of the Placing method of issue is that the administrative costs are lower, in particular because the advertising requirements of the Stock Exchange are much less than those imposed for Offers for Sale and other public issues. It is therefore not surprising to find that, within the category of fixed price methods of issue, Placings have been most favoured by companies using the USM. From Table 2.5 it is immediately clear that very few current entrants to the Official List, whether by direct entry or transfer from the USM, make use of Placings, whereas by contrast approximately two-thirds of all entrants to the USM use this method of issue. For companies entering the Official List, the relatively low proportion of companies using the Offer for Sale, in comparison with the proportion doing so in the London new issue market of the 1960s, may be accounted for by the very existence of the USM.

TABLE 2.5 Methods of Entry to UK Quoted Markets, November 1980–March 1985

	USM entrant	USM transfer	Official List entrant	Official List transfer[a]	Total
Placing	215	—	10	1	226
Offer for Sale	26	—	37	2	65
Offer by Tender	10	—	26	—	36
Introduction	33	31	11	38	113
Other method	30	2	3	2	37
All methods	314	33	87	43	477

[a] These issues will also be included in the numbers of USM entrants.

But we need now to consider how administrative costs in general for companies seeking a full quotation are subject to significant scale economies. We can do so first by reference to Table 2.6, which is derived from the Wilson Committee's investigation. It sets out a schedule of typical costs of an issue to raise £2m by sale of ordinary shares and calculates costs as a percentage of proceeds of issue. It compares the administrative costs incurred by a company coming to the market for the first time with the costs of a subsequent issue of similar size, either placed or issued to shareholders by means of a rights issue. Such estimates can be compared with those suggested for contemporary issues on the Official List and the USM by the accountants Peat, Marwick, Mitchell (PMM 1985) or Newell (1985), as reported in Chapter 5. The comparison highlights the possibilities for lowering entry costs to quotation through such second-tier mechanisms. Second, we can illustrate how smaller companies, which during the 1960s and 1970s were able to issue much smaller amounts than £2m, would have been particularly affected by the fixed charges involved. Fig. 2.2 shows how issues involving Offers for Sale of less than £0.25m in the late 1960s, for example, would have incurred administrative costs approaching 15% of the size of issue. By contrast, issues over £1m during that period would have incurred costs much lower as a percentage of issue, with values approximating those represented in the estimates of the Wilson Committee (Davis *et al.* 1974: 20).

Market pricing costs and small firms

A further cost element creating potential significant barriers for smaller firms arises from the process of flotation of the company's shares by means of a fixed price Offer for Sale or Placing. Both the company and its advisers will wish to obtain the maximum possible valuation per share consistent with securing a full subscription and an 'orderly' equilibrium price in the market. Full subscription is a minimum criterion, and successful issuing therefore depends

TABLE 2.6 Typical Costs of Issues to Raise £2m by Ordinary Shares (£)

	New issues prospectus of Offer for Sale	Further issues	
		Placing	Rights
Capital duty at 1%	20,000	20,000	20,000
Advertising	25,000	—	—
Accountancy fees[a]	20,000	4,000	4,000
Legal fees	15,000	4,000	4,000
Listing fees	2,400[b]	1,200	1,200
Receiving banker's/registrar's fees	15,000	2,000	5,000
Printers			
Extel card	2,000	—	—
Allotment letters	2,000	1,500	1,500
Share certificates	1,500	1,000	1,000
Offer for Sale	10,000	—	—
Circular	—	4,000	4,000
Underwriting commission at $1\frac{1}{4}$%	25,000	—	25,000
Broker's commission at $\frac{1}{4}$%	5,000	5,000	5,000
Issuing house $\frac{1}{2}$%[c]	10,000	10,000	10,000
Total cost of issue	152,900	52,700	80,700
As % of proceeds	(7.6%)[d]	(2.6%)	(4.0%)

[a] These figures may be higher, depending on the amount of work to be done.

[b] This figure relates to the fee for bringing a company to the market for the first time. Since the percentage of the company's equity offered on the first occasion is normally a minimum of 35%, total market capitalization in this example would be about £5.7m. The 35% minimum is imposed to ensure an adequate spread of shareholdings. (This minimum has since been reduced to 25%.)

[c] This figure can rise to $\frac{3}{4}$%. The issuing house may also charge fees for pre-issue corporate finance work.

[d] This figure appears high because it relates to the expense of a company's first quotation (see *b*). Because of the need for a full prospectus, advertising, legal, accountancy, and printing fees are inevitably higher than for a company already listed. The figure here is a percentage of the new money being raised, but as a proportion of the market capitalization of the company is only 2.7%.

Source: Wilson (1978), iii. 257.

upon some level of excess demand necessary to ensure that this occurs. The risks involved in this process inevitably reflect those which face the investor in previously unquoted equity, particularly for issues by smaller companies. First, the company is relatively unknown; second, if the company is small, it will be vulnerable to the greater specific risks associated with small firm performance; third, the size of the issue involved may mean that the amount of shares on offer is so small as to inhibit economic investment by institutional investors. Scale economies involved in the purchase and sale of securities imply minimum levels of transaction for funds managers which may amount

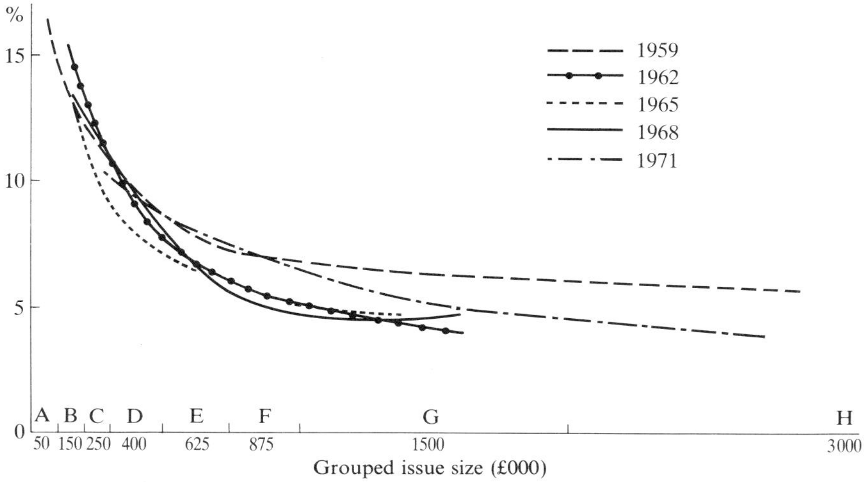

FIG. 2.2 Comparison of conventional costs (as percentage of issue size) in size groupings, uncorrected for inflation, 1959–1971, triannually. (The mean points of the size groupings are numbered for each year considered.)
Source: Davis *et al.* (1974: 21).

to a large percentage of a small issue. This in turn may increase the risks involved in purchasing smaller firms' equity by reducing the scope for efficient transactions in their securities.

Under such circumstances, one way of ensuring full subscription is by offering the purchaser a price incentive in the form of an introductory discount setting the issue price of the new share below what it is expected to make in equilibrium in normal trading. Any such discount enables new shareholders to purchase a share in profits at a preferential price compared with the intrinsic value to existing shareholders. Indeed, shareholders who market a portion of their holdings at this time subsidize those who retain their shares. Consequently the firm's objective should be to minimize any such discount to the level necessary to persuade investors to buy the previously unquoted shares. This transfer of wealth in effect represents a market cost of the transition from unquoted to quoted status. While brokers and issuing houses appear in general to aim for around 10%, actual measurement of the discount can produce results which appear to depend on a number of factors. These will include such obvious influences as the period of measurement involved and the level and volatility of stock market activity, as well as structural systematic influences which are of greater concern. (For a fuller discussion of the pitfalls involved in such measurement see Davis *et al.* 1974.)

Of particular relevance here is the association of fixed-price, advisory methods of issue with smaller companies whose flotation depends upon the retention of institutional underwriters' goodwill. The fixing of the issue price to reduce the risk of the issue being undersubscribed therefore matters, not just to the issuing company and its shareholders but also to the underwriters. Issuing houses acting as advisers to small firms may be disposed towards conservative pricing partly to protect underwriters. The consequence for small firms, which the Bolton Committee considered 'may be very important', can be readily ascertained from Fig. 2.3 and from Table 2.7, which illustrates the relationship between the scale of discount and firm size for a sample of 172 issues by Offer for Sale made by firms seeking a full quotation on the Stock Exchange between 1966 and 1971, according to the state of stock market activity at the time of quotation.

The performance of the markets' institutions in minimizing the cost of wealth transfers during the issuing process has been found in the past to be erratic and to vary greatly according to the method of issue and the general level of equity market behaviour. When equity prices in general were unstable and falling (a 'bear' market), new issues have been subject to a more volatile reception, with higher proportions of issues left with underwriters and discounts on value more unstable and unpredictable (see especially Buckland *et al.* 1981 and Davis *et al.* 1974: 56). Barriers to entry particularly to small firms using fixed-price issuing methods, were known to be high, and there is widespread agreement that such penalties choked off new private sector entrants to equity markets in the 1970s (see e.g. Vaughan *et al.* 1977; Touche Ross, 1986; PMM 1986*a*). Of particular relevance here is the association of

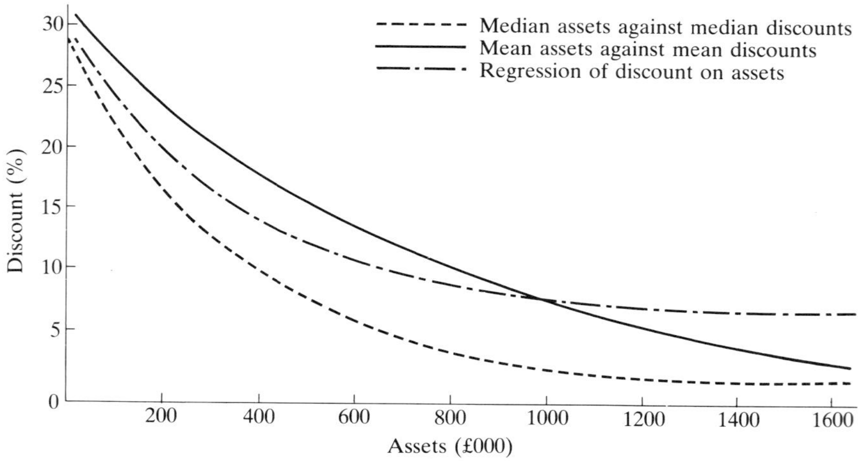

FIG. 2.3 The size–discount relationship (offers for sale and other issues) in a stable or steadily rising stock market.
Source: Davis and Yeomans (1976: 38).

TABLE 2.7 Mean Revealed Discount on All Offers for Sale, by Market Volatility States and Net Assets Groupings[a]

Mean discount % / Size of sample / Standard deviation	Volatility[b] Stable	Bull	Bear	All levels	Df/F ratio[c]
£0–250,000	24.90	15.70	−1.48	7.84	2+25
	6	6	16	28	
	14.20	21.28	18.53	21.02	5.20*
£250–500,000	17.51	1.94	0.91	7.91	2+56
	24	15	20	59	
	19.02	11.12	12.68	17.04	7.96*
£500,000–1m	11.26	3.17	13.99	9.17	2+41
	18	15	11	44	
	15.28	7.69	19.85	14.95	2.05
Over £1m	8.04	6.46	3.54	6.72	2+38
	19	14	8	41	
	10.38	25.49	12.21	16.94	0.19
All sizes	13.80	5.21	5.13	8.88	2+169
	67	50	55	172	
	16.07	17.01	15.62	16.72	5.80*
Df/F	3+63	3+46	3+51	3+168	
	2.50	1.04	2.24	0.14	

[a] Net assets (last balance sheet).
[b] Volatility indicates stable or rising markets (1); bull market (2); bear market (3, 4). See Davis *et al.* (1974) for a full description.
[c] Values of F significant at better than the 5% level are indicated by an asterisk.
Source: Davis *et al.* (1974), 30.

this 'cost' with the Stock Exchange's requirement on the minimum proportion of equity to be issued. Clearly, the obligation to offer 25% of equity implies a correspondingly greater risk on this account than that of the 10% now conceded as a normal minimum for USM entrants.

The role of advisers to USM entrants

In embarking upon this costly process entrants need to buy advice from sponsors (either broking firms or specialized issuing houses) not just on the fundamental valuation to be placed upon the company but on associated questions of methods, timing, and marketing of the issue. Corresponding to the administrative expenses incurred by firms are the revenues of advisers to USM entrants. The USM has played a major role in restoring income for those financial institutions active within the new equity issue market, and it has been particularly influential for broking firms. These have largely taken over the traditional 'issuing house' role, previously assumed for Official List entry by the merchant banks within the Issuing Houses Association. Peat, Marwick, Mitchell's compilation of data on professional advisers to USM entrants highlighted the importance of broking firms and the concentration of business within institutions (PMM 1985 and 1986*a*). From the USM's inception to March 1985 the 20 most active sponsors of issues captured 184, or 53%, of the sponsoring business in this market. Not only is this more concentrated than was the case for Official List business in the past (see e.g. Buckland and Yeomans 1977), but only 7 of these 20 firms are specialized 'issuing houses' independent of the broking function, with 3 of the top 5 being stockbroker sponsors.

While the business from the quotation and issue itself is small in relation to the income from corporate clients as a whole,[2] business at this stage will be very influential in securing allegiance and income in the long-term of emergent corporate clients. This is reflected not only in brokers' eagerness to promote the USM, but also in the competition amongst accounting partnerships to become USM 'specialists'. Notable here are Peat, Marwick, Mitchell, which in addition to publishing reviews of the market's development, runs annual USM conferences. Its promotion, specialized department, and rapid expansion in the area made it the reporting accountants for 67 of these USM issues, almost double the number of the nearest competitor.

Even if one accepts that new issue business is small in relation to overall City income from corporate clients, the USM has stimulated remarkable resurgence in its size and importance. The decline of new issues for the Official List in the 1970s was accompanied by a slump in the income for issuing houses over that period. Since 1980, however, such income has grown very rapidly indeed. Table 2.8 shows that, in the period covered by this sample, the fee income from new entrants to the Stock Exchange's equity markets totalled £83.5m in 1980 prices,[3] of which £34.4m (40%) was earned through USM work. Further, USM fee incomes have risen from £4.8m per year in 1981 to £10m per year in 1985 (from 1st quarter business and at 1980 prices). Table 2.6 also showed that, despite the smaller size (and hence fees) of USM entrants, and despite the economies of fees entailed in the simplified issuing procedures, the scale of USM business is, for the City institutions, approaching that of the Official List. Indeed, if the very large fee incomes from privatization entrants were excluded, the USM is of equivalent importance in income terms.

[2] Brokers would argue that it is commission on share trading which makes sponsoring profitable or not while Kleinwort Benson would maintain that even their extensive income from privatization issues hardly covers their costs in provision of complex advice and services.

[3] Fees and expenses as disclosed in issue prospectuses and notices of introductions. Figures disclosed will in general be understatements of expenses incurred and exclude any price discounting, managerial, or compliance costs of quotation and issue.

TABLE 2.8 Real Fee Incomes from Equity Issuing, November 1980 to March 1985 (£000, 1980 prices)

	1980 Nov.–Dec.	1981	1982	1983	1984	1985 Jan.–Mar.	Total
USM	1,550	4,846	6,012	8,977	10,883	2,226	34,440
Official List	827	5,334	11,207	9,563	17,360	4,783	49,073
Total	2,376	10,180	17,219	18,539	28,193	7,009	83,516

Conclusion

The decline in the new issue market from the 1960s to the 1970s was significantly affected by the nature of the issuing process itself, not least by the economies of scale inherent in administrative and market pricing costs. The introduction of the USM has been associated with a significant relaxation in entry requirements. Under the original proposal by the Stock Exchange facilitating the introduction of the USM, to allow an orderly market in securities, companies were to have been allowed to have offered 15% of their equity to the general public compared with 25% for a full listing. This minimum stipulation was reduced to 10%. At the same time USM companies would no longer be required to produce a formal accounting prospectus, including auditor's certificates, before entry, but only a table of financial statistics.

In this chapter we have provided an explanation of the reasons behind the decline in the traditional new issue market which led to the birth of the USM. A contributing factor has been the elements of the issuing process, which we have considered in detail. We now need to examine the underlying theoretical arguments which affect our interpretation of new issue market performance and which will serve together with our illustration of process in providing a framework for subsequent appraisal of the evidence on USM performance.

3

Financial Analysis of the Quotation Decision

Introduction

The distinctive essence of the new issue market is that of a corporate transformation process in which the raising of capital, while important, is not necessarily the prime event which takes place. Rather, firms themselves are changing status, since following quotation, wider opportunities exist for secondary sale and purchase of their equity. The finance of growth may be facilitated by an enhanced capacity not only to use equity to finance acquisitions but also to raise debt capital from lenders now conscious that the firm's quotation affords it the opportunity to fund borrowings by new equity issues in the future.

In this chapter, therefore, we need to discuss the general themes which affect our understanding of the new issue market process. The area addressed in Section I is that of a detailed analysis of the effect of quotation on equity value, which leads on to the justification for secondary equity markets. This clarifies the link between quoted status, secondary trading, and the value of a firm's equity. Section II establishes the changes in search and transactions costs which are brought about during the process of quotation and discusses the central place of quotation in the formation of investors' expectations about returns on firms' assets. The efficiency of this transformation process is a central concern of this book, and Section II discusses the theoretical framework behind transactions and market pricing costs which affect the new issue market. Extending beyond this Section III considers the system impacts of equity quotation, in terms of the implication of quotation for firms' debt finance. Finally, Section IV sets out the methodology adopted in this research, as well as a description of the data involved.

I Quotation, Secondary Trading, and the Value of Equity

The quotation decision is one which almost exclusively affects the financing of the firm. Just as firms can choose to invest in different projects and, by managing these in diverse ways, alter the earnings available from the cash which is invested, so they can select different financing instruments, whose sale will generate the cash for investment. Owners can be made better off by judicious selection of low-cost financial assets such that, in the correct combination with other assets, the overall or average cost of the cash attracted is minimized. Thus, the cost of financial assets (or required returns) is important in the financial structure of firms, as is the mixture of different financial assets.

Equity holders can be regarded as equating the value of the rewards expected from ownership of a share with the amount that they would either be prepared to accept for selling the share on to a third party, or be prepared to pay for an additional share in the same business. In its most general form, this valuation can be written as:

$$\text{Price} = \sum_{t=0}^{T} \frac{\alpha_t \times \text{net benefit}_t}{(1+r)^t} \tag{3.1}$$

where benefits, normally dividends, accrue over future periods $t=0, \ldots T$; r is a constant rate of discount, and α_t are certain equivalence factors applied to the uncertain benefits expected from ownership.[1]

To incorporate the possibilities of secondary trades (that is, not involving the firm itself), all the variables in (3.1) might be subscripted by i to indicate that they are expectations, certain equivalents, and hence are values or prices which are specific to the individual. Trades in equities are then explicable in terms of the existence of two individuals, j and k, where j holds the equity and k does not. Individual k will buy from j as long as, first, the equity is more valuable to k than it is to j, or

$$\sum_{t=0}^{T} \frac{\alpha_{t,k} \times \text{net benefit}_{t,k}}{(1+r_k)^t} > \sum_{t=0}^{T} \frac{\alpha_{t,j} \times \text{net benefit}_{t,j}}{(1+r_j)^t} \tag{3.2}$$

and, second, the cost of making the trade is less than the extent of the inequality in individual valuations.

Equities are created by firms as assets whose returns will arise until the demise of the firm in take-over, in voluntary or involuntary liquidation, or never. From (3.2), we can envisage occasions when equities also may be traded secondarily: that is, from the equity-holder to a third party such as k above, when the firm itself is not directly involved. By such a transaction the right to the risky future stream of benefits can be exchanged for other valuable rights (commonly for cash, or for other equity rights). Such secondary trading is fundamental to the importance of the secondary equity markets in general and

[1] While (3.1) is expressed in certain equivalents, it could as easily be expressed in terms of risk-adjusted discount factors. The former presentation, however, allows the retention of an initial simplifying assumptions that r is constant over time periods.

Hence:

$$\frac{1}{\prod^{t} (1+r_{t,i})} = \frac{1}{(1+r_i)^t} \text{ for any } i, t$$

to the USM in particular. From (3.1) it is seen that the value of equity is influenced by the expectations of its owner. Clearly, the potential exchange value of an equity will be influenced similarly, but by the expectations of others. Where these diverge from that of the owner (because benefits, certain equivalence factors, or discount rates vary), there is the potential that the equity's value in exchange may exceed the discounted value of dividends anticipated by its owner. From (3.2) it is clear that there may be circumstances in which equities are traded. This alters the perception of the equity's value; and for equity-holder j, (3.1) then becomes

$$\text{Value} = \sum_{t=0}^{T} \frac{\alpha_{t,j} \times \text{net benefits}_{t,j}}{(1+r_j)^t} + \frac{1}{(1+r_j)^T} \sum_{t=T}^{T'} \frac{\alpha_{t,k} \times \text{net benefits}_{t,k}}{(1+r_k)^t} \tag{3.3}$$

for some $k \neq j$, where k is any buyer, T is the time of disposal and T' is the demise of the firm. The consideration of transactions costs of disposal is deferred at this stage. Rational equity-holders will choose k, T such that (3.3) is maximized.

The justification for secondary equity markets

The introduction of the new variables of k and T leads to several propositions concerning the effects of quotation. Since potential trades increase the value of equity (or at worst do not diminish it[2]) expectations of the existence of secondary markets increase the value of all equities, even when not presently traded or tradeable. Thus, if T is restricted to some future range $T \geq t'$ (where t' may be contingent upon, say, profits growth, market sentiment, or age of the firm), then (3.3) is constrained, but remains higher than value would under conditions of no trade (3.1). Further, gradations of secondary tradeability will constrain (3.3) below its maximum; the maximum value in exchange among a subset of potential buyers I'' will always be at least the maximum of the (narrower) subset $I' \subset I''$. Finally, individual secondary trades will be subject the vagaries of stochastic searching, paralleling the problems of optimal stopping analysed extensively in the job search literature (see e.g. McKenna 1985).

The relationship of the USM to these propositions is threefold. Firstly, the marketplace of the USM brings together numbers of prospective traders—potential ks in the fashion of (3.3) above—whose presence will increase the value of equities by affording a larger set of possible transactions. Secondly, by admitting equities to the USM in advance of their qualification for alternative markets (and notably the Official List), the new market changes the

[2] Since $T = \infty$ can be elected, where value in (3.3) $\geq$ value in (3.1).

restrictions upon equity-holders' choice of disposal times *T*, again increasing the value of their equities. Thirdly, records of trades within the market will provide information for transactors with which their search routines and stopping rules can be enhanced.

If the accession to quotation is considered first, then valuable benefits will accrue to shareholders when their shares become quoted. Further, however, anticipation of quotation—even the potential for quotation—will increase the value of unquoted shares to their holders, the more so the closer is the anticipated date of quotation.

Not only do these considerations provide the rationale for the creation of stock exchanges and other secondary trading arrangements, but they underlie the oft-repeated comments and criticisms that 'gaps' have appeared in venture capital provision in the United Kingdom. When there are barriers to entry to secondary markets, shareholders are deterred from investing in unquoted equity and will tend towards heavier investment in equities which are already quoted, or in other, more secure financial assets such as property, gilts, or term-lending.

The impact of tradeability upon equity value is illustrated in Fig. 3.1. Otherwise identical equities (that is, identical streams of risky future dividends about which investors hold homogeneous expectations) are distinguished solely by the anticipated marketing arrangements for the share. For ease of presentation, the differential valuation bases are exaggerated: annual returns for this risk class of equity are assumed to be 10% on a full quoted market, rising to 20% for the equivalent but unquoted equity.

Fig. 3.1. shows the effects which quotation arrangements may have upon equity. The existence of future quotation implies trajectories of changing value, lettered *A* to *F*. Prospects even of distant quoted market access lift the value of unquoted shares (compare *F* with *B*, for example); and the closer is the prospect of (some) access, the greater is the differential (compare *E* with *B*, for example). So, for example, companies trading under the Stock Exchange's Rule 535(2) intending to seek a listing on the Official List find that information about their prospective debut impacts upon their current 'unquoted' share price (Tait 1986). Moreover, if barriers to secondary market access are relaxed (*B* and *C*) or a second-tier market is introduced (*C* to *D* or *E*), then the investor in unquoted shares will anticipate more rapid accretion of value as well as higher present values. Indeed, even were the eventual accession to full listing improbable, the prospect of a second-tier listing retains a powerful influence on equity values (compare *F* with *E* in this instance).

II New Issue Market Channelling Efficiency

The implications of information and transactions costs

Secondary markets' direct beneficial impact upon equity values have so far

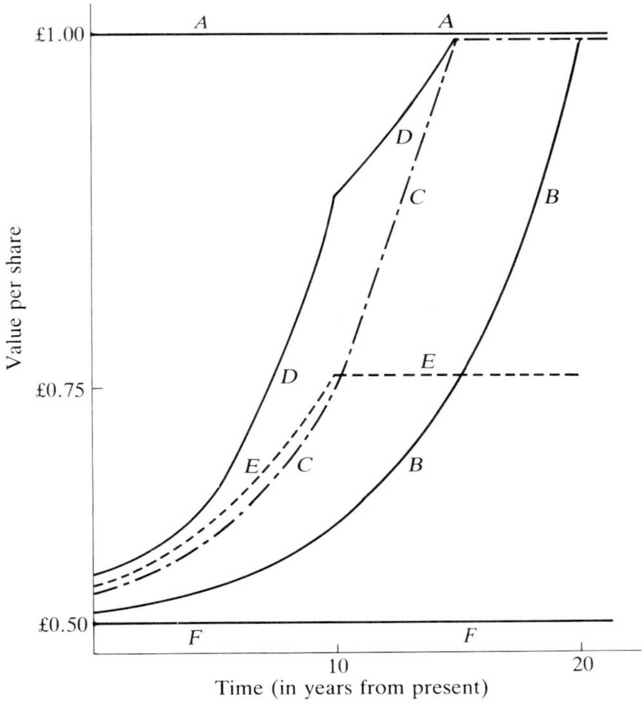

Dividends constant at £0·10 per share; required returns (unquoted) 20% p.a.; (USM quoted) 14% p.a.; (quoted) 10% p.a. Transactions costs are zero.

1. Equity in company *A* quoted on London Stock Exchange Official List.
2. Equity in company *B* gains first quotation on Official List after 20 years.
3. Equity in company *C* gains first quotation on Official List after 15 years.
4. Equity in company *D* gains quotation on USM after 10 years, Official List after 15 years.
5. Equity in company *E* quoted on USM from year 10 onwards.
6. Equity on company *F* never gains a quotation.

FIG. 3.1 Trajectories of equity value for identical businesses under different secondary market conditions.

been analysed in isolation from the penalties involved in firms' accession to quoted status. Whereas tradeability necessarily increases the value of otherwise identical potential future dividend streams, there are offsetting penalties in terms of the transactions costs of supporting the market and the potential loss of control to predators.

The limiting factor is, of course, that of the costs of generating and sustaining a secondary market. Without stock exchanges, an individual equity owner *j* must bear the costs of finding some other individual, *k*, whose valuation of the equity exceeds his or her own. This is costly in four major ways. First, share transfer has to be paid for; second, k must be located from the set I of potential buyers; third, k must be provided with information on the share's benefits and with sufficient information to produce the set of $\alpha_{t,k}$; fourth, j must engage in a bilateral bargaining game to apportion the potential gains from the trade between j and k.

These costly activities not only diminish the value of traded equity to both buyers and sellers, but they render the prospective value in trade more uncertain and risky. Situations can readily be envisaged where distributions of prospective values in trade net of transactions costs lie partly or wholly below the non-traded value. In general, the higher the prospective transactions costs, the fewer will be the subset of individuals, k, to whom equity value net of purchase costs exceeds the value of dividends to j gross of selling costs. Thus, the higher are prospective search costs, the more uncertain are the gains in bilateral bargaining and the rarer are trades.

Returning to (3.3) above, the impact of transactions costs can be entered as follows in the value of equity to j, given the possible trade with individual k:

$$\text{Value} = \sum_{t=0}^{T} \frac{\alpha_{t,j} \times \text{net benefits}_{t,j}}{(1+r_j)^t} + \frac{1}{(1+r_j)^T} \sum_{t=T}^{T'} \frac{\alpha_{t,k} \times \text{net benefits}'_{t,k}}{(1+r_k)^t} - \sum_i \text{costs}_{t,i} \qquad (3.4)$$

where 'costs' comprise
search costs $_{t,i}$ = representing the search and inform and bargain costs for individual i, which must include at least $i = j, k$; plus transactions costs T, i representing the costs of transfer from j to k at the time of disposal; and T is the period of expected transfer from j to some k.

In the absence of markets, any holder j hoping to take advantage of trading opportunities will need to incur search costs in order to find some individuals, k, and disposal times, T, where the value of the equity to k after time T is greater than it then is to j. The anticipated size of these costs varies with T, with the choice of the numbers of k to search, and with any contribution to costs incurred by prospective buyers. Clearly, however, unless the disparity of evaluation of underlying dividends from an equity is large, the costs of generating bilateral trades will inhibit secondary trading in all save extreme circumstances (such as distress sales from investors' estates, for example, or the transfer of large, perhaps controlling blocks of equity in acquisitions and take-overs).

In an organized market-place, the existence of many buyers/offerees lowers bargaining costs and hence the potential value in trades is enhanced; likewise, economies of search by agents/market-makers enhance value in trades, and the dissemination of common information has a similar effect. Additionally, specialist market-makers can eliminate bargaining costs by their recontracting and contingent sale activity. Thus, secondary markets lower transactions costs in total and also shift important elements of them away from the seller *j* to the firm, or even to market participants as a whole. As a result more individuals *k* become attractive as purchasers, and thus equity values increase.

Private equity trades, on the other hand, remain rare and costly for the investor in unquoted equity, who appears in a perpetually weak position as seller. The seller bears the incidence of all elements in (3.4), and the resulting illiquidity of equity investment in firms may seriously hamper firms' raising of capital. This constitutes the core problem of small firm financing identified by both the Macmillan and Bolton Committees of Enquiry. While such financing 'gaps' can be alleviated by the presence of specialized venture capital institutions, the seller remains in a position of uncertainty and powerlessness. Indeed, the growth of institutional venture capital might be ascribed to financial institutions' comparative advantage in profitably exploiting the inadequacies of the 'market' in unquoted equity. Competition between venture capital providers does, of course, improve the chance of the individual investor to participate in bargaining positions, but the institutional buyer is but a poor surrogate for a true secondary market in which all traders are effectively price-takers.

Restructuring of costs and the stimulation of trading

The existence of an authentic secondary market fundamentally changes the cost structure of equity trading. The first and most prominent change is the generation of market-makers, or pricing intermediaries, whose innovatory skills enable them to liaise between sellers and buyers of equities. In a market of competing market-makers, buyers and sellers need not engage in any direct contact. Equally important, however, is the support for trading given by the changed incidence of costs and the availability of information. Whereas with unquoted equities the transactions costs fall upon the seller individually, in a true secondary market transactions costs are met primarily by the firm's shareholders in common. That is, the market is supported by periodic fees paid by the firm, is informed at the firm's expense, and entry to the market is financed by the firm as a whole. Although transaction fees are charged to sellers or buyers, these cover only marginal costs and not the unit costs of trades. The content and release of information is controlled by the market in order to reduce asymmetries between traders and between prospective buyers and sellers.

This alteration of the cost structure transforms the position for the equity-holders. They now face only the marginal costs of trades, which enhances the value of individual trades and boosts trading volume. As activity increases, so the uncertainty which besets the market-makers' function diminishes and the 'free' information upon equity values, derived from recorded trades, increases.

Secondary equities markets are clear examples of dual tariff pricing and, as with all dual tariff pricing, twin conditions must be met for secondary trading to occur successfully. Transaction costs (including here the buy/sell spread of market-makers) must be such that individuals find trade beneficial; and the fixed costs borne by the firm as a whole must be outweighed by the benefits to shareholders who do not trade equity. These latter costs occur not only through the periodic fees and information provision entailed by membership of secondary markets, but by the once-and-for-all entry costs themselves. Not only, therefore, must one be concerned with the marginal costs of trading (whose structure in the UK has since Autumn 1986 been radically altered in response to the Office of Fair Trading's strictures on restrictive practices), but great importance must be attached to the costs of and barriers to entering the market. This book concentrates on the USM's role in redefining the conditions of access to secondary markets and determines how much those conditions have changed in relation to entry to the traditional Official List.

Quotation and the formation of expectations

In discussing the cost advantages of organized markets, it has been noted that trading itself produces information about values. In the extreme, an efficiently trading equities market produces a market clearing price which can be taken as the best available measure of an equity's value at that time. The UK Stock Exchange's Official List is one market-place which has been shown to be technically efficient in such a way (see e.g. Firth 1977).

Generally, one can consider the process of secondary trading as producing relevant information by which investors' opinions and expectations are formed. There are significant complexities, however. Firstly, an exchange will seek to codify and regulate participants' release and provision of information. This is done, on the one hand, to ensure common access to relevant data: material plans and events, periodic reports on activity, and matters relating to managerial competence; and, on the other hand, to control the 'language' of the market. By regulating the participants and the information released about them, an exchange seeks to enhance the information content of data: participants produce comparable data on compatible key areas.

Such codification and regulation, over and above the statutory requirements of the companies acts, can be entered as a justification for market entry barriers: investors are 'protected' against participants whose data could degrade the common information content of the market as a whole. Secondly, however, there exists a hierarchy of information separate from that of market price. While the market-clearing price of an equity is a powerful indicator of value, it is not the only one. This is particularly important at the time of first quotation, when the information in entrants' prospectuses is offered to underpin the (as yet untested) price of the equity. At the point when a price is being established, prospectus signals of intent, financial status, profitability, and management probity can be expected to influence investors' expectations. In the context of the growing literature on informational asymmetry and the signalling nature of prospectus information, of issue method, or of financial policy, the information presented by entrants is central to their transition to quoted status (see e.g. Leland and Pyle 1977; Ross 1977; Downes and Heinkel 1982; Heinkel and Schwartz 1986; and Franke 1987). In making commitments to potentially costly, second-best policies, vendors attempt to convey some insider knowledge (Downes and Heinkel 1982: 2). As part of this study we shall investigate the significance of information content as well as undertake more conventional analyses of entry barriers and entry costs.

The pricing efficiency of the new issue market: the origins of discounts on new issues

In Chapter 2 we considered how the pricing of firms' equities could generate elements of underpricing or market discount, which in itself could serve as a substantial additional cost to the shareholders of previously unquoted companies. Here we examine the theoretical arguments affecting our understanding of this process. It could be argued that the strongest test of the efficiency of new equity markets would be the equivalence of issue and market price and the adoption of issue methods appropriate to attaining that goal (an argument well presented in Ibbotson 1975: 262–6). There are, however, several directions down which one can pursue measurement of pricing efficiency beyond such a purist's standpoint. One long-established argument is that of the price: pressure hypothesis, by which it is argued that the market's capacity to absorb volumes of equity is related to the capital gain offered by the seller: the bigger is the volume, the larger must be the discount offered to the buyer. While this hypothesis is reflected in most institutional commentary upon new equity issue markets, particularly in terms of the financial press and broker opinion, there is little other than impressionistic opinion in its favour. Practitioners continue to be guided by it: in the conservative pricing of massive privatization issues, for example. Yet there is no decisive evidence in its support. It would suggest that bigger issues necessitate bigger discounts, but the results of tests for Official List issues over 1965–71 show positive coefficients on (the logarithm of) issue size only in the case of Tenders. For Placings and Offers for Sale, tests show significant but negative coefficients (see Davis *et al.* 1974: 46).[3]

However, while the price: pressure hypothesis provides one rationale for discounting, it is not the only one. It is possible to argue that the essence of quoted status is that uncertainty over valuation is resolved by the Exchange's

[3] Empirical research is equivocal as to whether there is any price: pressure effect during issuing. For the USA, Scholes (1972) and more recently Bhagat *et al.* (1985) have forcefully shown that discounts are not needed for sizeable 'secondary' issues, but it is clear that discounts do exist for new, 'unseasoned' issues (see e.g. Ibbotson 1975; and, in the UK, Davis *et al.* 1974).

provision of the signal of a market-clearing price. On the assumption that quotation is valuable in itself, then the investor, in a state of ignorance preceding this price signal, is in a position where the share's value is lower than it becomes once trading, and information provision, has begun.

By this argument, the issue prospectus is seen as a mechanism by which prospective investors are provided with such alternative (but inefficient) information as may stand in for a market-clearing price within an 'efficient' market. In so far as the value and reliability of this prospectus information is less than the collective wisdom of investors in the market, then equities must be less valuable before trading than they are afterwards; and there will be a discount on the new equity issue. Stemming from such an argument are the hypotheses that pricing discounts should be related to the firm's characteristics contained in the prospectus: for example, prospective yields, industry, profits records, and financial structure (see e.g. Keeley 1986: 117).

This argument also confirms the importance of considering the reliability of prospectus information, both as an indication of the value of prospectus information in itself and in terms of whether and how price discounts are linked to the information offered. While our main interest is with the latter, it is worth repeating that the prospectus offered by admissions to quotation is subject to substantial debate in terms of the incremental value of its information content within the general question of financial reporting and capital market efficiency.

The use of options theory to explain new issue price behaviour

New equity issuing can also be approached as an exchange of options between the firm and its shareholders. The investor secures an option on a risky equity value by paying the certain issue price; conversely, the firm secures options upon future retentions of earnings from any newly issued shares, plus access to future equity capital. The option elements of new issue pricing have been most extensively analysed by Dimson (1979), who showed that discounts were associated with the resolution of risk during the marketing process.

Option elements point up the links between discounting and risk, raising the possibility that any relationships found between prospectus information and discount may be reflections of an underlying link between discount and issue risk, thence to the underlying characteristics of the business depicted in prospectus information. Here the links between discounts, prospectus values, and firm risk will be explicitly investigated.

The significance of the institutions in new issue management

Finally, there are good reasons to suggest that discounts will vary in line with the issuer's concern with managing the share register rather than with maximizing receipts. Once again, this argument rests on the value of options, with the issuing firm putting a positive value on the creation of a shareholder base which will prove resistant to predators; receptive to the firm's future issues, acquisitions, and investments; and will comprise sufficiently firm holders of shares that the share price remains stable without the market becoming illiquid. The precise combination of these features will be difficult to generalize and difficult to attain, but discounting, along with the choice of issue method, is one of the major levers in attaining such register objectives.[4] Further, and more widely, the pressures of register management can be observed in the choice of issue methods. Whereas an Offer for Sale by Tender minimizes the issuing house/broker's control over initial shareholders, the Placing gives opportunities for very close control. Issuing brokers will strive, in a Placing, to blend an appropriate mix of clients who will be firm, long-term holders with clients who are expected to be active aftermarket traders. By judicious choice of clients for these 'mobile' newly issued shares, the broker can look forward to an active, but not overheated, aftermarket and a firm evaluation of the newly traded equity; to, in their eyes, a 'success' of the process of flotation; and to continuing commission fee income from the secondary trade in the equity.

'True' versus 'Recorded' discount: the broker's influence

In addition to their role in actively pursuing goals of register management and of exciting trading in issue after-markets, the actions of issuing houses and brokers undermine analysis of new issue discounting. Essentially, a high (or low) discount can arise either because there is a (lesser) need for discounting or because the issue price has been set too low (high) in false anticipation of the discount truly required. Hence the measured, recorded discounts may be related to risk measures, or to other issue and entrant characteristics, merely because advisers treat these as signals, not because investors do.

Although competition between brokers and advisers will operate to squeeze out some such divergence of recorded from necessary issue discounting, the main empirical defence against the bias is through comparison of issue methods. The Tender, with its reliance upon investors' presentation of demand prior to pricing and its freedom from massively oversubscribed and unsatisfied demand can be and is taken here as the reference subsample. When links to pricing and discounting can be shown for Offers for Tender, these are unlikely to be influenced by advisers' errors. For fixed-price Offers for Sale, the extent of advisers' underpricing can be gauged to some extent from the level of subscription.[5] The position is least secure for Placings, where there are few external signs to show whether discounts measured were (*a*) necessary to sell

[4] It is of particular importance for the privatization issues amongst Official List entrants in this sample, where the seller (government) pursues an objective of fragmented equity ownership in addition to objectives of receipts maximization and of the provision of a shareholder base to underpin the firms' future capital-raising activities. Closer analysis of these privatization issues can be found in Buckland and Davis (1984) and in Buckland (1987).

[5] Although, of course, subscription levels will be unstable as stags (speculative applicants), chase any perceived excess discounting by raising application levels in anticipation of these being subsequently scaled down. See Buckland *et al.* (1981) for an analysis.

the shares, (*b*) necessary to meet secondary, register, and option-related objectives of issuers, or (*c*) distorted by advisers' witting or unwitting misconception of the equity's worth.

III The System Impacts of Equity Quotation: The Significance for Firms' Debt Finance

A knowledge of equity values is not only important for the current and prospective holders of firm's equities, but also has far-reaching implications for the implied costs of other elements in corporate financing—and in particular the ability to raise debt capital. While this matters for all firms, it is more likely to be of consequence for relatively smaller, high-growth firms, which should be considered prime candidates for the USM. Surveys of issues on the London Stock Exchange in both the 1960s and 1970s again support the observation that the dominant role of the new issue market in this period was less one of raising new capital for expansion than the secondary function of transferring shares already in existence. Where new money was involved in equity issues, its prime purpose was to reduce levels of debt (Davis *et al.* 1974), and for small firms in particular there was evidence of a more systematic dependence on bank borrowing than for larger firms. From the lender's standpoint it should, of course, be emphasized that smaller firms record on average more volatile trading performance, are usually more vulnerable in the market, and are less liquid than larger firms, with generally lower levels of asset cover. The most important small firm—the high technology, high growth enterprise—suffers virtually by definition from a capital constraint. For the very process of capital formation is at once more expensive, and more protracted, than in areas of older, less sophisticated technology. In consequence its capital requirement depends to an even greater extent upon an adequate supply of long-term risk capital, whereas in the past the more routine trading and even investment activities of less capital-intensive small firms could more easily have been accommodated within the traditional scope of bank lending. In this context, the fact of quotation impacts upon the whole financial position of the firm.

Put simply, the creditors of firms which have secondarily traded equity possess relatively sound bases for evaluating the security and performance of the firms to which they have lent capital. The more efficient is the market within which equities are traded, the less uncertainty remains about the earnings expectations of the firm. The better is the quality of information provided by equities markets, the lower will be the agency costs faced by lenders. One would expect, therefore, that creditors' capitalization rates on lending would be lowered where equities are quoted,[6] and also that the volume

[6] They may also be unstable, of course. Depressed equity prices will be seen as a powerful signal against continued or further lending; and false signalling from an inefficient market may damage an otherwise sound company.

of lending available to quoted firms would increase in comparison with identical unquoted ones. Since secondary markets are capable of exploitation by participants for less costly primary issues of equity (either by new public or rights issues of equity, or by the offering of equity in the financing of corporate acquisitions), lenders' security is further enhanced by the improved opportunities for expanding the firm's equity base. It follows that one indirect test of the efficiency of secondary equities markets lies in changes in entrants' access to and costs of other, debt-based financial markets. Other things being equal, one would anticipate that firms with quoted equities would diminish their recourse to 'tied' finance (borrowing on overdraft from their clearing bank, borrowing from suppliers, or other trade relationships) in favour of borrowing from disinterested sources, once agency costs can be reduced by the knowledge of equity value.

We shall therefore analyse the movements in corporate gearing for USM entrants, using the Official List market as a control, to determine whether debt behaviour is materially affected by entry. This situation is, of course, complicated by the probability that entry may itself have been triggered by accumulated, pent-up financing imbalances. Immediate shifts in the capital structure of entrants may reflect the circumstances of their entry rather than their exploitation of the benefits of quotation. This problem, which occurs when quotation forms part of a process whereby entrants seek to move towards their 'norm', or 'target', financial structure (see e.g. Hutchinson *et al.* 1988; Marsh 1982), is discussed in Chapter 6.

One peculiarity of any benefits from the lowering of non-equity capital costs is that remaining shareholders share equally with trading shareholders in the added value to the firm. Indeed, any such advantages offer a once-and-for-all increase in the prospective dividends of the firm when quoted and the remaining, non-trading shareholders will benefit from this process as much as those who sell.[7] Another peculiarity is that systematic influences upon the costs of other capital sources are confined to equity quotation. While secondary markets in corporate debentures and other corporate debt (primarily by trade bill discounting) exist, they will enhance the value only of those particular instruments and they have little or no systematic impact upon costs elsewhere. This asymmetry arises wholly from the nature of equity quotation as an information mechanism. While debt markets can signal changes in default anticipations, investors can usually glean such information more easily from the shifting equity values in those same firms.

This central position of the firm's equity value gives added weight to the importance of Chapter 6, which deals with entrants' debt management and the information they provide at the time of issue. An efficient market's evaluation of an equity's value constitutes unbiased information to debt-holders as well as

[7] It can be argued, indeed, that large discounts at the time of quotation impose penalties upon the sellers *vis-à-vis* those who remain as shareholders, raising the problem of how such sellers are to be compensated for their sacrificial role.

to prospective equity traders. The prospectus, on the other hand, contains relatively inefficient information, generated by management and controlled only by auditors and listing particulars. The extent to which such prospectus information is biased, or is contradicted by entrants' behaviour, will both distort investors' acceptance of the entrant and degrade investors' attitudes to market information.

IV Methodology and Data

In our sample we considered in detail 327 USM companies, representing all those UK-domiciled companies which came to the USM in the period between its inception and the end of the first quarter of 1985. Included within this group were those firms which in this period transferred to quotation upon the main Stock Exchange and those which were subsequently acquired, failed or had their quotation suspended. In addition, we considered the 118 UK companies which had recourse to a full Stock Exchange listing (on the Offical List) over the same time period, including within this group 35 companies which transferred from the USM to the Official List and 7 entrants generated by privatization issues. As a result we can make some preliminary comparisons of the effects of the USM by reference to the criteria originally envisaged as justification for its foundation, and with features of those firms considered suitable for a full Stock Exchange listing on the Official List.

The data sources used for analysis were the accounts and other relevant information presented in companies' prospectuses prior to quotation, together with details derived from accounts and other company information in the period following listing. We thus combined information as represented to potential investors upon quotation with data on certain features of the company's post-issue performance. Aside from the public nature of prospectus data, it offered the advantage of control and oversight by the Exchange's Quotations Department. Thus, in addition to being the common basis of investors' attitudes to the newly quoted equity, prospectus information is recently audited, subjected to stringent legal scrutiny, timely, and commensurate. The analysis here does not consider the influence of other, informal sources of information, such as press comment or institutional reports upon individual new issues. It does, on the other hand, explore the potential influence of market-wide shifts in equities.

The methodology adopted was cross-sectional, comparing entrant with entrant. There were, of necessity, considerations of time within the design, but these were to facilitate consistency of observations between entrants. Thus, in studying the movement of an entrant's share price during quotation, contemporaneous shifts in the broader equities index were employed as a bench-mark: only abnormal price movements were used as information in the research. Similarly, entrants' characteristics, in terms of size, borrowing, profits, and other measures, were compared in the real terms of 1980 pounds rather than in current prices.

Wherever possible, company characteristics were compared on ordinal scales rather than by cardinal or ratio scaling. Ratio comparisons, in particular, are exposed to potential collinearity with size measures. (See e.g. Whittington 1980 or Lee 1985, who advocate regression approaches to descaling for inter-company comparisons, rather than the traditional balance sheet ratio proportionality approach. Such an approach would be problematic here as the examples studied vary with respect to the type of industry, the time periods considered, and company size.)

For some variables, however, information is presented explicitly in ratio form—particularly by prospectus measures of company gearing, taken here as the ratio of total corporate book debt to total book assets. In so far as the properties of firms' gearing ratios have been analysed, it would appear that scaling biases are inconclusive, if present at all.[8]

Prospectus information on yields and price:earnings ratios was also taken as it stood, without attention to scaling bias. Here, although it is known that yields ratios correlate with company size (see e.g. Davis *et al.* 1974: ch. 5), a deviation from the assumption of proportionality would require both that that is true and significant and that investors interpret prospectus information about yields efficiently in the face of non-proportionality.

With these caveats as to time and to the proportionality of ratio measures in the data, the study proceeded by a cross-sectional analysis of all entrants to the USM from its inception in November 1980 until the cut-off date at end March 1985. The data set thus generated, described fully in Chapter 4, comprised information on entrants' policy and accounting history (as recorded in their audited prospectus), their entry (as recorded by the Stock Exchange Daily Official List and the financial press), and their activity in financing markets for the subsequent three years (drawn from the Extel USM company cards service and the risk measurement service of the London Business School).[9]

The above data were analysed statistically to test support for various hypotheses. These included, for example, the bases of the pricing of previously unquoted shares, the existence of any discounting on new issues and the presence of any systematic influences on such discounts, together with the existence of scale economies in issuing costs and the presence of any interactions between company characteristics and later behaviour in financial markets. The main vehicle for this analysis was the SPSS (versions 9 and X) package of statistical techniques, installed on Aston University's mainframe Harris and VAX machines. This package permitted layers of analysis to be

[8] McDonald and Morris (1984) and Berry and Nix (1988) confirm this: 'the intercept term is not consistently significant' (McDonald and Morris 1984: 94); 'For TD/TA (gearing as measured here) there appears to be no evidence of a significant intercept term' (Berry and Nix 1988: 8).

[9] The data set is now lodged with the ESRC Data Archive at the University of Essex, England.

built up, from frequencies and means comparisons, through simple and partial correlation analysis to multiple regression techniques and to more sophisticated procedures such as factor analysis.

The principle followed throughout this study was to apply minimally sophisticated methods which succeed in tests of the hypotheses, while confronting such tests with further statistical method to determine whether confirmatory (or otherwise) results were spurious. Thus, populations and samples from populations were compared, wherever possible by non-parametric methods (to avoid presumptions of normality in the distribution(s) of variables); and where axes of differentiation were uncovered, the possibilities of multicollinearity were explored.

This technique is particularly helpful in such heterogeneous samples, where the diverse effects of time, industry, motives, and issue method can be expected to interact in a complex and non-linear fashion.[10] The design was also compatible with previous studies of new issue markets. Thus, additionally, two control samples of new issue market entrants were employed, to test hypotheses concerning, first, the distinctiveness of USM entrants, their performance, and behaviour; and, second, the relative performance of the USM market-place in providing quotations, when compared with the alternatives. The most crucial control sample was that of the contemporaneous entrants to the Official List, with all entrants to that market included and the same data recorded as for the USM sample. This allowed direct comparison of USM performance and USM entrants with the pre-existing and competing market that had been regarded as failing small firms, growing businesses, and the economy. It also implied that any USM entrant which transferred to the Official List before the end of March 1985 became a member of the control sample, providing detailed information on these Official List entrants which were then used to confront the experience and nature of the 'raw' entrants to the Official List.

With this design, therefore, we could examine USM entrants, USM *vis-à-vis* Official List entrants and USM–Official List transfers *vis-à-vis* Official List entrants. The data were also collected to be consistent with the samples of new entrants studied in the ESRC project on small firms and the capital market, covering Official List entrants between April 1965 and March 1971 (Davis *et al.* 1974), and with the extended sample (to 1975) of Offers for Sale on the Official List studied by Buckland *et al.* (1981).

[10] Note, for example the problems of heteroscedasticity in analysis of pooled samples reported by Davis *et al.* (1974): chapter 4, appendix.

4

New Entrants to British Equity Markets

Introduction

In this chapter we are concerned with summary classification of the characteristic company entering the USM and with contrasting this with corresponding features of companies joining the Official List. The original justification for the USM was that of provision of an equity trading facility more suited to the needs of smaller firms. To this end we examine simple differences which exist between USM and Official List companies, in terms of size, industrial distribution, and profit performance, to consider how far physical barriers to entry to the new issue market have been reduced. Any relaxation of regulations for entry to the USM should be reflected in a lower average size, for example, or shorter or more volatile profits records of entrants. Another barrier to Official List entry, arising from a formal regulation to this effect, was the prescription of a minimum proportion of equity to be issued. On this count, we should expect that relaxation of this significant deterrent would be reflected in a lower average proportion of equity being marketed in the USM than for companies admitted to the Official List. A relevant factor here is the extent to which this was related to the amount of new equity capital raised by firms, which indeed must be considered an important criterion for the primary role of the new issue market.

Entry barriers in the new issue market: access for small firms

As a starting point to our analysis of USM companies, we consider the size characteristics of the companies entering the USM. We should expect that USM companies would on average be smaller than new entrants to the Official List, on the basis of earlier criticisms of the latter market's suitability for smaller firms. In fact, as Table 4.1 indicates, the market capitalization of firms entering the USM, while undoubtedly and statistically highly significantly lower than Official List companies in terms of mean size, nevertheless entails a significant measure of overlap.

Thus, while over two-thirds of USM entrants involved market capitalizations of less than £7.5m, one-fifth of Official List entrants fell into this category also. When we consider firms with market capitalizations of under £15m we find that 90% of USM entrants fell within this category compared with about half the entrants to the Official List, whether by direct entry or transfer from

TABLE 4.1 Grouped Market Capitalization of Companies by Entry Status

Count Row % Column % Total %	USM entrant	From OTC or 163[a]	OL entrant	USM transfer	Row total
Under £2.5m	70	7	7	1	85
	82.4	8.2	8.2	1.2	19.2
	23.8	21.9	8.6	2.9	
	15.8	1.6	1.6	0.2	
£2.5–£7.5m	135	7	12	4	158
	85.4	4.4	7.6	2.5	35.7
	45.9	21.9	14.8	11.4	
	30.5	1.6	2.7	0.9	
£7.5–£15m	60	7	24	14	105
	57.1	6.7	22.9	13.3	23.8
	20.4	21.9	29.6	40.0	
	13.5	1.6	5.4	3.2	
Over £15m	29	11	38	16	94
	30.9	11.7	40.4	17.0	21.3
	9.9	34.4	46.9	45.7	
	6.5	2.5	8.6	3.6	
Column total	294	32	81	35	442
	66.5	7.2	18.3	7.9	100.0

Chi square = 100.82 with 9 degrees of freedom. Significance = 0.0000. Missing = 3.

Average Entrant (1980 £)[b]

	USM entrant	From OTC or 163	OL entrant	USM transfer	Row total
Mean (£000)	7,324.96	17,929.61	24,871.35	27,045.16	12,676.65
No. of firms	294	32	74	35	435
SD	9,471.47	27,538.55	31,925.14	25,100.61	18,381.01

$F = 27.16$, significance = 0.0000; K–W chi square = 84.07, significance = 0.0000.[c]

[a] Companies transferring from OTC markets or from quotation under Rule 163.
[b] Data for OL entrants exclude 7 privatization issues.
[c] The F test compares means parametrically, the Kruskal–Wallis (K–W) test non-parametrically.

the USM. In terms of numbers there were almost as many USM entrants with market capitalization above £15m (29) as those directly entering the Official List (38), although in percentage terms the significance of the former was much less (9.9%) than that of the latter (46.3%).

While the mean sizes of market capitalization were clearly greater for Official List companies, it would be misleading to presume that size alone, represented by market capitalization, inevitably ordained which market was the automatic choice; but it is nevertheless clear that market capitalizations were decidedly lower for USM entrants than for admissions to the Official List. This is, of course, what we should expect.[1]

Although equity capitalization is one measure of size, it is not the only available one, nor always the most relevant. As it excludes the influence of debt-financed assets it may not be a good proxy for the size of the issue being made (as opposed to the size of the firm being quoted). One size measure which is unaffected by gearing is that of total assets. Table 4.2 shows how our interpretation is affected by a shift to the balance-sheet book value of total assets as the size measure. The relative frequency of firms with total assets below £2.5m is much greater for USM than Official List companies, while, in contrast with the market capitalization measure, the incidence of USM companies with total assets greater than £7.5m is sharply reduced. This suggests that part of the overlap in firm sizes stems from the relatively high P:E ratios (and hence market capitalizations) in the early years of the USM; and that when measured by book assets, nearly all the smaller firms have chosen the USM in preference to the Official List. Table 4.2 also highlights that firms transferring from the USM to the Official List are characteristically larger. Firms which take this indirect route are unlikely to be motivated by avoidance of scale barriers.

We also considered, as a possible size proxy, a classification based upon the gross proceeds of the issues concerned. This indicates the volume of capital available to the market and may, for institutional investors concerned with the illiquidity of small lines of stock, matter almost as much as the size of the firm making the issue. Obviously the much smaller market capitalizations which are feasible on the USM, coupled with the much lower public holdings requirement (10%), may mean that extremely small issues could be put on the market. From Table 4.3 we can in fact observe that, while only 7% of share issues on the Official List were of less than £1m, nearly 50% of USM share issues fall under that threshold. While the 'overlap' remains, here in the range of £1–5m size of issue, the differences between the two markets are stark, striking, and significant.

Industrial classification of issues: capital for new technologies

Of obvious relevance is the industrial distribution of the USM population. From Table 4.4 we can see that the largest industrial category represented is management services. This could reflect back upon the discussion of size measures above, as there is much less likelihood for such businesses to have

[1] One aspect which biases this comparison is the prohibition of 'large' issues from use of the Placing method of issue. When the Placing was limited to a maximum of a £3m issue and where a minimum of 10% of equity was required to be placed, the effective maximum size of a firm utilizing the Placing method was £30m. Any larger firm was necessarily obliged to use the more expensive Offer for Sale method.

TABLE 4.2 Grouped Total Assets of Companies, by Entry Status

Count Row % Column % Total %	USM entrant	From OTC or 163[a]	OL entrant	USM transfer	Row total
Under £2.5m	152	6	10	2	170
	89.4	3.5	5.9	1.2	38.5
	52.1	18.8	12.2	5.7	
	34.5	1.4	2.3	0.5	
£2.5–£7.5m	110	14	28	15	167
	65.9	8.4	16.8	9.0	37.9
	37.7	43.8	34.1	42.9	
	24.9	3.2	6.3	3.4	
£7.5–£15m	20	9	14	11	54
	37.0	16.7	25.9	20.4	12.2
	6.8	28.1	17.1	31.4	
	4.5	2.0	3.2	2.5	
Over £15m	10	3	30	7	50
	20.0	6.0	60.0	14.0	11.3
	3.4	9.4	36.6	20.0	
	2.3	0.7	6.8	1.6	
Column total	292	32	82	35	441
	66.2	7.3	18.6	7.9	100.0

4 out of 16 (25.0%) of the valid cells have expected cell frequency less than 5.0. Chi square = 132.73 with 9 degrees of freedom. Significance = 0.0000. Missing = 4.

Average Entrant (1980 £)[b]

Mean (£000)	4,196.32	8,256.80	16,320.19	13,132.23	7,310.55
No. of firms	294	32	75	36	437
SD	7,064.11	6,393.47	27,326.92	15,813.56	14,374.51

$F = 18.40$, significance = 0.0000; K–W chi square = 104.10, significance = 0.0000.[c]

[a] Companies transferring from OTC markets or from quotation under Rule 163.
[b] Data for OL entrants exclude 7 privatization issues.
[c] The F test compares means parametrically, the Kruskal–Wallis (K–W) test non-parametrically.

substantial tangible asset backing. However, what is also clear is that there are no marked differences between the industrial categories of USM new entrants and Official List new entrants, even when the latter are adjusted to exclude transfers and privatization issues.

This is a somewhat surprising refutation of a very widespread belief (cf. e.g. Bannock and Doran 1987: 13; PMM 1985) that the USM has been crucial in

TABLE 4.3 Grouped Gross Proceeds of Share Issues, by Entry Status (excluding Introductions)

Count Row % Column % Total %	USM entrant	From OTC or 163[a]	OL entrant	USM transfer	Row total
Under £200th	8	0	0	0	8
	100.0	0.0	0.0	0.0	2.3
	3.1	0.0	0.0	0.0	
	2.4	0.0	0.0	0.0	
£200th–£400th	36	0	1	0	37
	97.3	0.0	2.7	0.0	11.0
	13.8	0.0	1.4	0.0	
	10.7	0.0	0.3	0.0	
£400th–£1m	83	0	4	0	87
	95.4	0.0	4.6	0.0	25.8
	31.8	0.0	5.6	0.0	
	24.6	0.0	1.2	0.0	
£1–£5m	122	2	34	2	160
	76.3	1.3	21.3	1.3	47.5
	46.7	100.0	47.9	66.7	
	36.2	0.6	10.1	0.6	
Over £5m	12	0	32	1	45
	26.7	0.0	71.1	2.2	13.4
	4.6	0.0	45.1	33.3	
	3.6	0.0	9.5	0.3	
Column total	261	2	71	3	337
	77.4	0.6	21.1	0.9	100.0

Chi square = 97.86 with 12 degrees of freedom. Significance = 0.0000. Missing = 2.

Average Entrant (1980 £)[b]

Mean (£000)	1,658.29	2,918.04	8,182.09	5,848.82	2,969.24
No. of firms	261	2	64	3	330
SD	3,725.63	2,133.82	12,367.98	5,390.44	6,868.50

$F = 18.07$, significance = 0.0000; K–W chi square = 98.39, significance = 0.0000.[c]

[a] Companies transferring from OTC markets or from quotation under Rule 163.

[b] Data for OL entrants exclude 7 privatization issues.

[c] The F test compares means parametrically, the Kruskal–Wallis (K–W) test non-parametrically.

TABLE 4.4 Entry Status, by Industrial Classification

Count Row % Column % Total %	USM entrant	From OTC or 163	OL entrant	USM transfer	Row total
Distribution and other	79	8	23	2	112
	70.5	7.1	20.5	1.8	25.2
	26.8	25.0	28.0	5.6	
	17.8	1.8	5.2	0.4	
Communications and leisure	30	2	4	3	39
	76.9	5.1	10.3	7.7	8.8
	10.2	6.3	4.9	8.3	
	6.7	0.4	0.9	0.7	
Traditional manufacturing	26	3	11	5	45
	57.8	6.7	24.4	11.1	10.1
	8.8	9.4	13.4	13.9	
	5.8	0.7	2.5	1.1	
Electronics and process industries	58	0	20	8	86
	67.4	0.0	23.3	9.3	19.3
	19.7	0.0	24.4	22.2	
	13.0	0.0	4.5	1.8	
Energy and mineral exploration and extraction	12	15	4	5	36
	33.3	41.7	11.1	13.9	8.1
	4.1	46.9	4.9	13.9	
	2.7	3.4	0.9	1.1	
Management services	90	4	20	13	127
	70.9	3.1	15.7	10.2	28.5
	30.5	12.5	24.4	36.1	
	20.2	0.9	4.5	2.9	
Column total	295	32	82	36	445
	66.3	7.2	18.4	8.1	100.0

6 out of 24 (25.0%) of the valid cells have expected cell frequency less than 5.0. Minimum expected cell frequency = 2.589. Chi square = 90.19 with 15 degrees of freedom. Significance = 0.0000. Missing = 0.

promoting new technologies and novel industrial groupings to quoted status. While it is true that the 'typical' USM entrant is different from the historical Official List norm, it is no more different than are contemporary Official List entrants: the latter are equally likely to be in the fields of computer software, computer service bureaux, public relations and 'people' businesses. The Official List is equally populated by entrants in electronics or in new technology processing. Table 4.4 expands upon this, distinguishing the industrial distribution of quotations by the entry status of the companies. It can be seen that USM entrants from OTC markets are weighted more heavily to the energy and minerals sector—that group of oils businesses which were listed under Rule 163 prior to the USM's inauguration. There is little to distinguish the other three categories from each other: direct entrants to the USM, direct entrants to the Official List, and transfers between the two. In other words, the industrial composition of the USM is little or no different from that of the Official List. The new market may have resulted in smaller companies being quoted, but not necessarily a greater proportion of companies in novel industrial sectors.

Profit levels and history

Another alternative measure of the relative significance of the differences between the two groups of firms is to consider profit levels reported in the year's trading prior to quotation. From Table 4.5 it is clear that relatively few (17, or 14.6%) Official List companies obtain a full listing with less than £400,000 profits. In contrast, some 58% of USM companies fall within this category, and indeed the largest number (99) in terms of frequency (31.6%) record profits of under £200,000, with only 6% of Official Listings recording profits within this band (these latter figures combining 'direct', and 'transfer' entrants to the markets).

Past profits have a significance in this market over and above their role as a proxy for firm size. One of the aspirations concerning the USM was that businesses with short or erroneous profits records, excluded from the Official List, could yet become quoted. The lowering of this entry barrier was potentially just as important as those of size, or the proportion of equity widely held. Table 4.6 shows the distribution of entrants according to the length of their profits records. One can see that almost one in five USM entrants took advantage of this particular relaxation. In most cases these entrants arrived at a quoted status either one or two years in advance of their potential qualification as Official List candidates, but there was a further substantial group, of 10 entrants, which had no trading record to report at all. Here the new USM market is seen to have effectively lowered a barrier to entry and the opportunities created for new and recently formed USM entrants are obvious.[2]

It might also be expected that USM entrants would anticipate or experience higher rates of growth of profits. It has generally been the case that the USM companies have been accorded high P:Es and capitalization rates by the stock market, and such differentials themselves suggest that expectations of profit

[2] The majority of USM entrants were well-established businesses. Ransley (1984) reported that 37% of his USM sample had been established for over 15 years, for example. The vast majority of firms in our sample had profit records in excess of 5 years.

TABLE 4.5 Entrants' Last Recorded Profit Level, by Entry Status

Count Row % Column % Total %	USM entrant	From OTC or 163[a]	OL entrant	USM transfer	Row total
Under £200th	85	14	5	2	106
	80.2	13.2	4.7	1.9	24.7
	30.1	45.2	6.1	5.9	
	19.8	3.3	1.2	0.5	
£200th–£400th	80	3	6	4	93
	86.0	3.2	6.5	4.3	21.7
	28.4	9.7	7.3	11.8	
	18.6	0.7	1.4	0.9	
£400th–£1m	91	10	30	15	146
	62.3	6.8	20.5	10.3	34.0
	32.3	32.3	36.6	44.1	
	21.2	2.3	7.0	3.5	
£1–£5m	22	4	31	11	68
	32.4	5.9	45.6	16.2	15.9
	7.8	12.9	37.8	32.4	
	5.1	0.9	7.2	2.6	
Over £5m	4	0	10	2	16
	25.0	0.0	62.5	12.5	3.7
	1.4	0.0	12.2	5.9	
	0.9	0.0	2.3	0.5	
Column total	282	31	82	34	429
	65.7	7.2	19.1	7.9	100.0
Chi square = 107.52 with 12 degrees of freedom. Significance = 0.0000. Missing = 11.					
		Average Entrant (1980 £)[b]			
Mean (£000)	537.52	452.70	2265.03	1513.64	916.56
No. of firms	282	31	75	34	422
SD	1023.03	823.22	5122.58	1900.30	2471.26
F = 11.48, significance = 0.0000; K–W chi square = 87.84, significance = 0.0000.[c]					

[a] Companies transferring from OTC markets or from quotation under Rule 163.
[b] Data for OL entrants exclude 7 privatization issues.
[c] The F test compares means parametrically, the Kruskal–Wallis (K–W) test non-parametrically.

TABLE 4.6 Years of Reported Profits, by Entry Status

Count Row % Column % Total %	USM entrant	From OTC or 163	OL entrant	USM transfer	Row total
New company	10 100.0 3.4 2.2	0 0.0 0.0 0.0	0 0.0 0.0 0.0	0 0.0 0.0 0.0	10 2.2
1-yr history	3 100.0 1.0 0.7	0 0.0 0.0 0.0	0 0.0 0.0 0.0	0 0.0 0.0 0.0	3 0.7
2-yr history	4 66.7 1.4 0.9	1 16.7 3.1 0.2	1 16.7 1.2 0.2	0 0.0 0.0 0.0	6 1.3
3-yr history	16 94.1 5.4 3.6	1 5.9 3.1 0.2	0 0.0 0.0 0.0	0 0.0 0.0 0.0	17 3.8
4-yr history	18 90.0 6.1 4.0	1 5.0 3.1 0.2	1 5.0 1.2 0.2	0 0.0 0.0 0.0	20 4.5
5 or more yrs history	244 62.7 82.7 54.8	29 7.5 90.6 6.5	80 20.6 97.6 18.0	36 9.3 100.0 8.1	389 87.4
Column total	295 66.3	32 7.2	82 18.4	36 8.1	445 100.0

17 out of 24 (70.8%) of the valid cells have expected cell frequency less than 5.0. Minimum expected cell frequency = 0.216. Chi square = 22.19 with 15 degrees of freedom. Significance = 0.1028. Missing = 0.

growth are in general higher for USM entrants than for Official List participants as a whole.

From the prospectuses one can discover whether these differences in expectations were foreshadowed by differentials in profits growth. One difficulty to be overcome is that of measuring profits growth across the samples. For consistency of measurement, available prospectus information

TABLE 4.7 Grouped Geometric Profits, by Entry Status

Count Row % Column % Total %	USM entrant	From OTC or 163	OL entrant	USM transfer	Row total
Zero or less	72	9	18	1	100
	72.0	9.0	18.0	1.0	23.7
	25.8	32.1	22.2	2.9	
	17.1	2.1	4.3	0.2	
0–20% p.a.	44	6	17	7	74
	59.5	8.1	23.0	9.5	17.5
	15.8	21.4	21.0	20.6	
	10.4	1.4	4.0	1.7	
20–50% p.a.	56	2	28	7	93
	60.2	2.2	30.1	7.5	22.0
	20.1	7.1	34.6	20.6	
	13.3	0.5	6.6	1.7	
Over 50% p.a.	107	11	18	19	155
	69.0	7.1	11.6	12.3	36.7
	38.4	39.3	22.2	55.9	
	25.4	2.6	4.3	4.5	
Column total	279	28	81	34	422
	66.1	6.6	19.2	8.1	100.0

1 out of 16 (6.3%) of the valid cells have expected cell frequency less than 5.0. Minimum expected cell frequency = 4.910. Chi square = 26.49 with 9 degrees of freedom. Significance = 0.0017. Missing = 23.

has been used to cull a measure of the annual rate of growth of cash profits reported, with the most distant as the base figure.

Table 4.7 cross-tabulates the sample by entry status and by the level of profits growth. We note, first, that substantial numbers of entrants in both the USM and the Official List arrive with a declining profits record over the last five years. The highest growth rates tend to be found among USM entrants and, from these, among firms which subsequently transferred to the Official List. Whereas only 22% of direct Official List entrants display a compound profits growth of over 50% per annum over the last five years, such rates characterize 38% of USM entrants and 56% of those transferring to the Official List.

Measures of profits growth which use past figures reflect the impact of the raw, printed cash amounts, but there must be doubts as to whether they reflect either or both of the 'true' profits growth or investors' interpretation of the information. The use of historical data for any two years may be distorted by the impact, on either year, of profits variability; thus, the growth in cash profits may be only tenuously connected to growth of profitability or dividends; or other prospectus information may label profits growth as exceptional, as growth by acquisition rather than organic growth, or as an accounting distortion. Profits records may likewise be distorted by inflation, or by the reflection of inflation through the historic cost accounting framework.

Forecast profits

Where USM entrants provided forecasts in their prospectuses (the provision of quantified forecasts is not enforced and many entrants elect to publish only their history and the directors' policy statement), these could be compared with those of contemporary Official List entrants. Comparison of forecast profits (as estimated or minimum levels of profit for the year in progress) with the last reported profits provides an alternative measure of profits growth. From Table 4.8, in which this second measure is summarized alongside the first, it is obvious that the two measures are not strongly correlated: indeed, for the 246 cases where both growth rates were calculable the Pearson's

TABLE 4.8 Average Growth Rates of Prospectus Profits Measures, by Entry Status

Count Row % Column % Total %	USM entrant	From OTC or 163	OL entrant	USM transfer	Row total
(A) Annual geometric growth of reported profits[a]					
Mean growth (% p.a.)	47.77	119.1	31.78	71.08	51.41
Count	241	26	79	34	380
SD	90.71	310.65	57.40	70.86	114.58
$F=4.32$ significance = 0.0052. K–W Chi square = 9.71, significance = 0.0212.					
(B) Growth of forecast profit over last reported profits[b]					
Mean growth (% p.a.)	151.15	−100.00	97.07	80.45	135.83
Count	168	1	56	3	228
SD	569.43	—	334.06	92.72	518.96
$F=0.23$, Significance = 0.8732. K–W Chi square = 3.29, significance = 0.3485.[c]					

[a] All entrants with 5-year prospectus profits records.
[b] All entrants providing past and forecast profits.
[c] The F test compares means parametrically, the Kruskal–Wallis (K–W) test non-parametrically.

correlation coefficient between them was −0.0113 (significance level 0.430). Whereas Table 4.8 confirms that USM entrants are, historically, companies with higher growth rates of raw, reported profits than are Official List entrants, it shows also that there is no significant distinction between these samples in the profits growth forecasted. The extremely high variability of growth forecasts in USM prospectuses may also indicate larger numbers of reorganized, recovering, or emergent growth companies. All explications highlight the increased unpredictability of the USM entrants' profits growth, a finding confirmed by Table 4.9, where the relationship between entrants' status and the variability within their profits records is observed. Here the coefficient of variation of actual against predicted, or past trend profits is measured, using the compound annual growth rate to predict profits levels for

TABLE 4.9 Variability About Trend Reported Profits, by Entry Status

Count Row % Column % Total %	USM entrant	From OTC or 163	OL entrant	USM transfer	Row total
CV under 0.5	79	3	36	14	132
	59.8	2.3	27.3	10.6	31.3
	28.3	10.7	44.4	41.2	
	18.7	0.7	8.5	3.3	
CV 0.5–1.0	83	9	16	9	117
	70.9	7.7	13.7	7.7	27.7
	29.7	32.1	19.8	26.5	
	19.7	2.1	3.8	2.1	
CV over 1.0	117	16	29	11	173
	67.6	9.2	16.8	6.4	41.0
	41.9	57.1	35.8	32.4	
	27.7	3.8	6.9	2.6	
Column total	279	28	81	34	422
	66.1	6.6	19.2	8.1	100.0

Chi square = 15.60 with 9 degrees of freedom. Significance = 0.0161. Missing = 23.

Average Variability About Trend

Mean CV	1.82	2.99	1.5	1.43	1.80
Count	279	28	81	34	422
SD of CV	2.58	3.26	2.13	2.37	2.54

$F = 2.69$ significance = 0.0462.
K–W Chi square = 4.38, significance = 0.2233.[a]

Note: CV = Coefficient of variation in profits record, around the trend compound growth profits.
[a] The F test compares means parametrically, the Kruskal–Wallis (K–W) test non-parametrically.

the interim years. USM entrants are shown clearly to have more unstable profits records than do Official List companies.

The proportion of equity issued and the significance of new money raised

It is often claimed that the USM is attractive because entrants are not constrained to show that as much as 25% of their equity is 'widely held', as for entry to the Official List (see e.g. PMM 1986*a*; Bannock and Doran 1987). This relaxation (there is no strict minimum for USM qualification, although 10% or over is the norm) is one of the important innovative features of the market. The lower is the proportion involved, the less are the difficulties both of expense and marketing (as explored in Ch. 5), and also the less are the resulting inequities among existing shareholders, through some holders selling at discounted values to new investors.[3]

Table 4.10 shows how the USM has affected the distribution of this key variable in new equity issuing. In the Official List, 93% of those entrants which needed to make a sale issued 20% or more of their equity, and 45% of share sales involved over 30% of the equity. For the USM the equivalent figures were 67% and 27%. This was clearly an economical development, especially for the smaller firm. On the other hand, Table 4.10 shows also that some USM firms did sell relatively high proportions of their equity during quotation.[4] This may simply reflect the success of the USM in encouraging entry by relatively recently formed businesses with large new money requirements, with an inevitable boost to the proportion of equity marketed. Indeed, closer examination of our population confirms this, in that companies which made issues of more than 30% of their equity were more likely to be substantial new money raisers (see Appendix Tables 1 and 2).

Fundamental to any assessment of the success of the USM is not just whether changes in formal and informal entry requirements have led to greater access for smaller, and newer, firms, but whether it has enlarged the capacity to raise new capital. Testimony to the success of the USM in raising new money for entrants is clear. While the sums involved remain well below those raised by rights and new issues on the Official List, the USM entrant is more likely to raise new money during the quotation, and the amount generated is more likely to be substantial in relation to the existing business and the issue in question (see Table 4.11 and Appendix Table 2). Table 4.11 demonstrates also that the USM issues involve an average of 44% new money, compared to 34% on the Official List. In Davis *et al.*'s (1974) study of new equity issuing during

[3] It may also be argued that the lower percentage sales provide signals of continued entrepreneurial interest which enhance USM shares' values. This is suggested also in the frequency of directors' service contracts within prospectuses, and would conform with Leland and Pyle's (1977) results linking financial intermediation with owners' retention of equity interest.

[4] Especially when it is recalled that Official List entrants included privatization issues where sale proportions are dictated by accounting peculiarities rather than by questions of efficient issuing.

TABLE 4.10 Proportion of Equity Issued by Entrants, by Entry Status (excluding Introductions)

Count Row % Column % Total %	USM entrant	From OTC or 163	OL entrant	USM transfer	Row total
Under 20%	86	0	5	1	92
	93.5	0.0	5.4	1.1	27.1
	32.7	0.0	7.0	33.3	
	25.4	0.0	1.5	0.3	
20–30%	107	2	34	1	144
	74.3	1.4	23.6	0.7	42.5
	40.7	100.0	47.9	33.3	
	31.6	0.6	10.0	0.3	
30–50%	49	0	24	0	73
	67.1	0.0	32.9	0.0	21.5
	18.6	0.0	33.8	0.0	
	14.5	0.0	7.1	0.0	
Over 50%	21	0	8	1	30
	70.0	0.0	26.7	3.3	8.8
	8.0	0.0	11.3	33.3	
	6.2	0.0	2.4	0.3	
Column total	263	2	71	3	339
	77.6	0.6	20.9	0.9	100.0

Chi square = 26.42 with 9 degrees of freedom. Significance = 0.0017. Missing = 0.

		Average entrant			
Mean(%)	27.98	22.55	33.97	32.47	29.22
Count	263	2	71	3	339
SD	18.55	0.46	16.70	31.92	18.35

$F = 2.10$, significance = 0.0995.
K–W chi square = 126.62, significance = 0.0000.[a]

[a] The F test compares means parametrically, the Kruskal–Wallis (K–W) test non-parametrically.

the late 1960s, it was noted (p. 2) that issues predominantly comprised sales of existing, 'old' shares, which is hardly surprising given the significance attached to the requirements incurred by the need for shareholders to meet death duties. Two decades later it very much matters that the primary function of the new issue market—that of raising new capital, with the implicit notion of financing new growth—has been more sharply emphasized. We should, however, remember that new money raised may also be used by firms to reduce their

TABLE 4.11 Proportion of New Money in Issues, by Proportion of Equity Being Sold

Count Row % Column % Total %	USM entrants[a]			OL entrants[b]		
	Under 30%	Over 30%	Row total	Under 30%	Over 30%	Row total
None	38 77.6 21.1 15.2	11 22.4 15.7 4.4	49 19.6	16 80.0 42.1 22.9	4 20.0 12.5 5.7	20 28.6
Under 30%	37 68.5 20.6 14.8	17 31.5 24.3 6.8	54 21.6	9 56.3 23.7 12.9	7 43.8 21.9 10.0	16 22.9
30–60%	50 83.3 27.8 20.0	10 16.7 14.3 4.0	60 24.0	10 47.6 26.3 14.3	11 52.4 34.4 15.7	21 30.0
Over 60%	55 63.2 30.6 22.0	32 36.8 45.7 12.8	87 34.8	3 23.1 7.9 4.3	10 76.9 31.3 14.3	13 18.6
Column total	180 72.0	70 28.0	250 100.0	38 54.3	32 45.7	70 100.0

Missing = 0.

[a] Chi square = 8.22 with 3 degrees of freedom, significance = 0.0416. Pearson's $R = 0.09$, Significance = 0.8230.

[b] Chi square = 10.83 with 3 degree of freedom, significance = 0.0127. Pearson's $R = 0.39$, significance = 0.0005.

present levels of indebtedness, a consideration which we probe in depth in Chapter 6.

Conclusion

The first obvious, and expected, difference between the USM and the Official List companies to emerge is that of size: USM entrants being significantly smaller, particularly in terms of their asset backing and profit records. Approximately one-half of USM share sales fall below £1m, sums which are almost never experienced in the contemporary Official List. A substantial overlap remains, however, and on size alone there would be little ground for concluding other than that the USM had differentiated the market in quotations. But the USM has attracted significant numbers of recently formed companies which would otherwise have had to delay entry to quotation for several years. Relaxation of barriers in terms of profits history affected 54 USM entrants (including transfers from OTC markets). At the same time, the relaxation of rules on the provision of quantified profits forecasts has been adopted by a substantial number of firms.

While the USM has afforded smaller firms greater access to the Stock Exchange, there is no evidence to support the belief that, in contrast with the Official List, it has particularly favoured entrants from new technologies. What does emerge, however, is the relative success of the USM in raising new money. So for smaller, newer firms seeking to raise greater elements of new capital to finance relatively high growth rates, the USM must be regarded as a major benefit.

5

The Significance of Administrative Costs

Introduction

This chapter analyses the significance of administrative expenses incurred by the sample of new entrants to the USM and Official List in the 1980s. It seeks to compare the expenses incurred by direct entry to these markets and to ascertain whether barriers to entry in the new issue markets, arising from the presence of high fixed costs incurred in obtaining a quotation, have been lowered as a result of the introduction of the USM. In consideration of the optimal policy to be adopted by firms, whether or not considering ultimate progression to full listing, an analysis is made of firms transferring from the USM to the Official List, as well as of the interactions between the method of issue adopted and various proxies for economies of scale in the issuing process. Further, this chapter tests the extent to which competition in the new issue market arising from the innovation of the USM, and the entry not only of large numbers of new companies but of new issuing houses as well, has been associated with a reduction in the real cost of issuing expenses and has thus lowered barriers to entry.

Previous research into comparative expenses of USM *vis-à-vis* Official List quotation has been based either on estimates or on relatively small groups of companies (see e.g. Touche Ross 1986; PMM 1986*a*; Bannock and Doran 1987; Newell 1985). Bradley-Jones and Hussey (1983, 1985), in their studies for Spicer and Pegler, used postal surveys of executive opinions of some entrants. They found that the majority cited the relative size of expenses as the prime reason for entering the USM rather than the Official List, but they did not examine actual costs. The present study is the first to examine actual differentials evident in a large sample of new issue market entrants, and the first to relate such variations in costs to systematic influences operating within both the USM and Official List.

The nature of administrative expenses has been well documented (Davis *et al.* 1974; Vaughan *et al.* 1977; Wilson Committee, 1979; Bannock and Doran 1987). They basically comprise a range of fees to various advisers, sponsors, underwriters, lawyers, accountants, and bankers; and the expenses of printing and advertising. Table 5.1, derived from Newell (1985), provides a typical statement of the detail involved, together with an estimate of the relative costs incurred in flotation, either upon the USM or Official List, for different methods of issue.

TABLE 5.1 Comparative Estimated Expenses for a New Entrant to the USM and Official List (£000)

	USM			Official List		
	Introduction	Placing[a]	Offer[a]	Introduction	Placing[b]	Offer[b]
Sponsor's fee	35	50	50	40	70	70
Broker's fee	10	20	20	10	25	25
Accountant's fee	15	40	40	40	40	40
Solicitor's fee	15	30	30	15	30	30
Banker's fee	—	4	12	—	4	12
Exchange fee	1.5	1.5	1.5	4	4	4
Capital duty	—	20	20	—	25	25
Underwriting	—	—	40	—	—	50
Printing	5	25	30	5	25	30
Public relations	5	10	10	5	10	10
Advertising	4	4	60	4	50	100
Total	90.5	204.5	313.5	123	283	396

Note: The table takes the upper boundary of Newell's estimates and ignores elaboration upon public offers such as Tenders or subscription offers.
[a] For a sale of shares of £2m, from a company of size £10m.
[b] For a sale of shares of £2.5m (minimum 25%).
Source: Newell (1985).

Upon entering the USM, companies disclose in their prospectuses the paid-out expenses of their quotation and of any issue, but to a varying standard. Expenses as published are not always exhaustive, but include all paid-out costs borne by the company. Table 5.2 summarizes the information on expenses available from the prospectuses of our samples, comprising 327 new entrants to the USM and 118 admissions to the Official List between November 1980 and March 1985. From this table it is clear that, for the costs borne by companies, prospectuses give a reliable and full sample of expenses data for both markets and for all methods excepting Introductions (which have the least stringent reporting regulations).[1]

I Recorded Administrative Expenses for USM and Official List New Entrants

First we analyse the incidence of actual expenses recorded for the average issuing firm. We do so by reference not only to the normal distinction between

[1] The numbers of missing or incomplete records are not significantly different between the markets, with only the groups of Introductions or transfers between the markets under-represented.

TABLE 5.2 Recorded information on issue expenses by number of companies

	Total		Estimate		Missing	
	No.	%	No.	%	No.	%
By status						
USM	214	71	68	24	13	5
Transfer to USM	5	15	11	34	16	50
Official List	82	100	—	—	—	—
Transfer to Official List	33	94	—	—	3	6
All entrants	334	75	79	18	32	7
By method						
Placing	161	75	53	25	2	1
Offer for sale	57	100	—	—	—	—
Tender	36	100	—	—	—	—
Introduction	56	50	21	19	28	25
Other methods	26	81	5	16	2	3

methods of issue but also between the status of markets used by such previously unquoted entrants and those transferring from the OTC market. Table 5.3 demonstrates that, on average, across both the USM and Official List new issue markets, the Introduction provided the cheapest access, while companies transferring from the informal Rule 163 markets by Introduction on to the USM recorded even lower costs, with an average of £38,000 in 1980 prices (£55,500 in 1985 prices[2]). By contrast, Official List new entrants by way of Introduction recorded average expenses of £90,500 in 1980 prices. Such costs support the general structure indicated by Newell's (1985) estimates.

The average costs in Table 5.3 indicate a widening of differentials as between methods compared to previous studies. Davis *et al.* (1974: 19) recorded an average cost of £80,000 (1980 prices) for 33 Offers for Sale in 1971; Vaughan *et al.* (1977) found that average costs (1980 prices) rose from £194,000 in 1967 to £250,000 in 1973. They also found that Offers for Sale were more expensive (£194,000) than Introductions (£144,000), Tenders (£106,000), and Placings (£81,000).[3]

Many of the changes over time can be attributed to size factors, as analysed below. Table 5.3 shows, however, that share sales on both the USM and Official List have become more expensive in relation to Introductions, and that the differentials in costs have widened in the 1980s. In the Official List the

[2] The levels of costs incurred are reported here in the price levels of the beginning of the sample period: costs in 1985 prices are included to facilitate comparisons with other recent studies.

[3] All figures are averages over 1966–74 converted to 1980 prices; from Vaughan *et al.* (1977: 61, 136).

TABLE 5.3 Average Real Issue/Quotation Expenses (£000)

Mean No. of times SD	Placing	Offer for Sale	Tender	Introduction	All methods
1980 prices					
USM	90.91	235.11	244.63	72.14	106.59
	209	22	9	23	263
	44.58	198.46	111.25	127.09	93.87
Transfer to USM	—	—	—	38.13	38.13
				17	17
				49.15	49.15
Official List[a]	175.62	716.40	627.93	90.54	542.68
	10	37	26	11	84
	68.98	1,054.42	631.99	116.41	814.70
Transfer to Official List	127.59	217.51	—	46.13	58.60
	1	2		31	34
	0	51.22		51.83	65.90
All entrants	94.93	526.47	529.36	57.72	191.61
	220	61	35	82	398
	49.00	858.75	570.52	88.71	422.41
1985 prices (means only)					
USM	132.27	368.28	355.94	104.96	155.09
Transfer to USM	—	—	—	55.48	55.48
Official[a] List	255.53	1,042.36	913.64	131.74	789.60
Transfer to Official List	185.64	316.48	—	78.53	95.17
All entrants	138.12	766.01	770.22	88.17	279.17

[a] Including the seven privatization issues.
Chi square = 355.25 with 9 degrees of freedom. Significance = 0.0000.

typical Placing is now twice as expensive as an Introduction. In the USM, however, the relaxation of entry requirements has kept the cost of Placings down to levels comparable to those for Introductions: a powerful factor in favour of entry to this market.

Table 5.3 shows very clearly that the Placing, used by over 200 USM entrants, was on average hardly any more expensive than entry through an Introduction; and it displayed considerable cost savings over any other share sale for the purpose of joining the Official List. In 1980 prices, USM Placings cost, on average, £90,000; whereas the average Placing on to the Official List incurred expenses of £175,600. If put in 1985 prices, this disparity is more marked than that, for example, suggested by Bannock and Doran (1987). It indicates that the cost of selling shares, at the time of quotation, has been made much smaller by the innovation of the USM and by the encouragement of the extensive use of the Placing method of issue. Many Placings, indeed, incur expenses which are lower than the average for Introductions, a finding not suggested in previous research.

The influence of scale on administrative costs

Beyond the fundamental differences arising from the method of issue adopted, we now consider the influence of variations in the size of firm or issue involved in relation to the method of issue adopted. A great deal of the variations within Table 5.3 can be explained by the scale of sale involved. One way of controlling for the effects of firm or issue size upon the expenses involved is to consider percentage or proportionate costs as distinct from cash totals. Two measures are examined here: costs as a percentage of the issue size or value of the shares sold; and costs as a proportion of the entrant's equity. Tables 5.4 and 5.5 indicate how proportionate costs were related to issue method and to market entry status over this period.

Issue costs as a percentage of issue size should decrease as size increases, since substantial costs of quotation and sale preparation are fixed. Table 5.4, therefore, compensates for the relatively greater size of Official List issues over USM ones, as well as of Offers for Sale and Tenders over Placings. Davis *et al.* (1974: 19) found that the percentage cost of Offers for Sale varied between 7% and 11%, and this seems to be largely unchanged. At the foot of Table 5.4 we include comparable data from other historical studies; on this basis, average costs would seem to be higher now than in the 1960s and 1970s and particularly so for Placings.

What is also significant here is not the expected factor of an inter-method differential, but the differential between the markets. Offers for Sale and by Tender are cheaper in absolute terms for USM entrants than for Official List entrants, but Table 5.4 shows that this merely offsets the potential disadvantage of using such methods in relatively small-scale issues. Average flotation costs are maintained at around 6.5% of issue for Tenders and at around 8.5% for Offers for Sale. These averages are very little different from those observed in the 1960s and 1970s; but when we turn to Placings, Table 5.4 confirms the major cost disadvantage of the Placing as a means of entry to the Official List. Being confined to a small scale, the percentage flotation costs for Official List entrants by Placing averages 16.1% of the issue, which represents a much higher barrier than in the past. On the USM by contrast, even where still smaller issues by smaller firms are the norm, average percentage costs for Placings have been reduced to 12.3% of the issue. This strongly supports the view that a major reason for the success of the USM has been that it has

TABLE 5.4 Administrative Expenses as Percentage of Gross Size of Issue

Mean No. of firms SD	Placing	Offer for Sale	Tender	Other[a]	All methods
USM	12.30 209 14.04	8.57 22 5.33	6.54 9 2.06	10.44 26 8.80	11.62 266 12.91
Transfer to USM	0.00 0 0.00	0.00 0 0.00	0.00 0 0.00	9.09 2 0.99	9.09 2 0.99
Official List	16.11 10 8.00	7.71 37 6.42	6.31 26 3.13	8.33 3 3.08	8.36 76 6.38
Transfer to Official List	7.86 1 0.00	2.14 2 0.02	0.00 0 0.00	7.42 1 0.00	4.89 4 3.18
All entrants	12.45 220 13.80	7.84 61 6.00	6.37 35 2.87	10.06 32 7.99	10.81 348 11.76
M, H & N[b]	8.6	9.6	6.4	n/g	n/g
V, G. & B[c]	10.9	5.8	5.3	n/g	n/g

Chi square = 177.94 with 9 degrees of freedom. Significance = 0.0000.

[a] Includes costs of quotation by offers by subscription, or combinations of reorganization, sale, and Introduction.

[b] 1959–63 (Vaughan *et al.* 1977: 137).

[c] 1966/7–1973/4 (ibid.).

brought the costs of small share issues back down to levels at which entrants are willing to enter the market. It suggests also that the Stock Exchange's relaxation of size limits on Placings (as of 1987 up from £3m to £15m), may be influential in bringing percentage costs down again and thus in encouraging more direct entry at the Official List level.[4]

Since all shareholders should benefit from quotation of their company, for shareholders the best measure of the cost of quotation may be the proportion of the value of the equity which is spent on gaining entry. Here economies of scale are crucial, since the earlier entrance of rapidly growing businesses must mean entrance at a substantially smaller size. It is here that entry costs for the Official List were argued to be inhibiting entry. The loss to shareholders from

[4] It will, however, tend to squeeze out the numbers of Offers for Sale to the public; a factor which may destabilize demand for such increasingly rare occurrences as well as reinforcing brokers' influence over initial share registers. Fig. 2.1 shows that, following relaxation of the Placings size limit, the Official List has attracted more entrants, which might otherwise have joined the USM.

TABLE 5.5 Administrative Expenses as Percentage of Market Capitalization

Mean No. of Firms SD	Placing	Offer for Sale	Tender	Intro-duction	Other[a]	All methods
USM	2.49	2.27	1.35	1.94	2.71	2.42
	208	22	9	21	28	288
	21.2	1.98	0.79	2.31	1.99	2.08
Transfer to	0.00	0.00	0.00	0.59	1.72	0.72
USM	0	0	0	16	2	18
	0.00	0.00	0.00	0.46	0.11	0.57
Official List	4.14	2.23	1.78	3.07	2.83	2.45
	10	36	25	11	3	85
	2.67	2.28	0.99	3.87	1.47	2.37
Transfer to	0.96	0.89	0.00	0.38	0.47	0.43
Official List	1	2	0	30	2	35
	0.00	0.70	0.00	0.58	0.10	0.57
All entrants	2.56	2.20	1.67	1.22	2.54	2.19
	219	60	34	78	35	426
	2.16	2.13	0.95	2.12	1.89	2.12

Chi square = 357.98 with 12 degrees of freedom. Significance = 0.0000.

[a] Includes costs of quotation by offers by subscription, or combinations of reorganization, sale, and Introduction.

entry costs outweighed considerations of the likely gain in capitalization: Table 5.5 summarizes the position. Overall, entry to a secondary market expends 2.2% of the firm's equity market value. The economies of the USM, however, have effectively enabled entrants to secondary markets to enter with the same proportionate costs as are incurred on the Official List; and this is so even for Placings, whereas Placings onto the Official List can be and on average are an expensive means to secondary quotation. Table 5.5 again highlights the crucial advantage of the USM for small firms making a Placing or Introduction.

Our previous research (Davis *et al.* 1974) examined the influence of scale economies in administrative expenses. Table 5.6 extends our analysis of this factor. We do so by considering only USM Placings (to eliminate the effect of method), and we consider the influence both of issue size and firm size. Table 5.6*A* demonstrates the very great economies of scale in relation to issue size, reflecting the high element of fixed cost in a USM Placing. Table 5.6*B* shows that size of firm is of less weight in percentage issue costs, although there is still a link, through the ability of larger entrants to make larger issues. The third section, 5.6*C*, establishes the cost to shareholders in general. Only for extremely small entrants, with capitalization of under £2.5m at 1980 prices, does the cost of quotation reach the 4% which has been seen to be normal for the much larger entrants to the Official List.

TABLE 5.6 Relative Significance of Administrative Expenses
(A) As a Percentage of Issue Capitalization, by Size of Issue (Placings only)

	Under £200,000	£200–400,000	£400,000–1m	£1m–5m	Over £5m	Total
Mean	63.20	19.46	12.44	7.91	1.30	12.59
No. of firms	5	33	76	93	3	20
SD	67.91	9.77	4.45	4.19	1.02	13.80

$F=34.97$, significance 0.0000.
K–W Chi square = 93.55, significance = 0.0000

(B) As a Percentage of Issue Capitalization, by Size of Firm (Market Capitalization), (Placings Only)

	Under £2.5m	£2.5–7.5m	£7.5–15m	£15m	Total
Mean	18.09	12.00	8.32	11.50	12.49
No. of firms	49	109	48	4	210
SD	24.93	8.17	6.28	6.31	14.08

$F=4.22$, significance 0.0064.
K–W Chi square = 32.62, significance = 0.0000.

(C) As a Proportion of Entrant Capitalization by Size of Firm (Market Capitalization), (Placings Only)

	Under £2.5m	£2.5–7.5m	£7.5–15m	£15m	Total
Mean	4.71	2.34	1.09	0.52	2.57
No. of firms	49	109	48	4	210
SD	2.94	1.47	0.49	0.50	2.20

$F=36.73$, significance 0.0000.
K–W Chi square = 106.05, significance = 0.0000.[a]

[a] The F test compares means parametrically, the Kruskal–Wallis (K–W) test non-parametrically.

II The Cost of Transfer

One of the more important considerations for the prospective new issue is whether total market costs of obtaining a 'full' quotation may be influenced by the decision to proceed to the USM first by Introduction, then subsequently to transfer to the Official List by Introduction. Where companies used an Introduction to transfer from the USM to full listing, we can see from Table 5.3 that further expenses averaging £46,000 in 1980 prices (£78,500 at 1985 prices) were incurred. Thus the cost advantage of the USM route is not such that a quotation via Introduction onto the USM followed by a later Introduction to the Official List would necessarily or normally be cheaper than a delayed direct entry to the Official List.

Closer examination of the equities which transfer from USM to the Official List shows such a double Introduction route to have been a little-used procedure: of the 41 transfers, only nine accomplished their Official List entry by such indirect means. For the other 32 firms a sale of shares was necessary, at either USM or Official List entry, in order to meet the requirements of widely held shareholding. One-half of the 41 adopted the sequence of an initial USM Placing followed by an Introduction to the Official List, with some combination of share sale involved in the remaining 11. The 'normality' of this sale-plus-Introduction routine again highlights the USM's important role in making it possible to establish a quotation, albeit at a 'junior' level, during the process of securing a sufficiently wide base of shareholders for eventual full listing.

For 27 transferring companies, prospectus data on expenses are available at both USM and Official List stages. Table 5.7 shows the typical expenses (averages, again in 1980 prices), for these companies, broken down by the combination of methods adopted. This table shows that the 'average' and 'typical' transferring firm arrived at the Official List by the Placing–Introduc-

TABLE 5.7 Combined Costs of Entry for 27 Companies Both Entering the USM and Transferring to the Official List

Route to Official List	No. in sample	£000 (1980) average combined costs[a]
Introduction–Introduction	9	71.00
		3
		17.43
Placing–Introduction	21	108.00
		15
		74.73
Other combination	11	321.67
		9
		151.63
Total	41	175.52
		27
		135.01

Note: Fifteen companies where prospectus data on expenses were missing at *either* USM entrance *or* at transfer to the Official List were excluded from the calculations.

[a] Figures are mean, no. of firms, standard deviation.

tion route, and for a total administrative cost of £108,000: hardly a significant difference from the average £90,500 for the Official List Introduction, and with the advantages both of earlier quotation and a sale of shares. The USM has proved itself an effective and efficient route to later quotation on the Official List, representing a clear reduction of entry barriers.

In introducing this chapter the question was raised as to whether the innovation of the new market and the increased competition of sponsoring/issuing brokers were lowering entrants' costs. Press comment on research into USM administrative expenses by Touche Ross and Co. has indicated that USM costs are increasing, and are rising at a faster rate than inflation (Kellaway 1986). We investigated this by means of multiple regression analysis, to test for association between costs of issue and the time of entry. Again, only USM Placings were used, and stepwise regression was conducted on two designs. First, we regressed issue, firm capitalization, the proportion of new money, the proportion of equity in issue, and the time of entry[5] on issue costs as a percentage of issue size. Second, we regressed those variables on issue costs as a percentage of the company's market capitalization.

Table 5.8 summarizes the results of these tests, showing that there is no evidence of any time trends in these data. The USM Placing has become neither more nor less expensive over time: changes in real costs can be attributed only to changes in entrant size and the proportions of equity involved in the issue. With other methods, of course, sample sizes are still too low to investigate time trends in a multiple regression context, but there is no evidence of consistent positive signs on time variables in such samples either.

Conclusion

The typical firm transferring from the USM to the Official List over the period reviewed did so by a Placing followed by an Introduction, for a total cost relatively little more than that incurred by direct entry to the Official List by means of an Introduction; with the difference that the former carried with it the benefits of earlier quotation and a sale of shares. Barriers to entry for prospective newly quoted firms have been decidedly reduced, with percentage costs for obtaining a Placing on the USM being significantly lower than for the Official List, even after allowing for the effects of firm or issue size. This research confirms the known influence of the method of issue upon relative costs but highlights the major cost disadvantage of the Placing for direct entry to the Official List. The existence of the USM has restored costs of quotation to the levels seen during the last boom in new entry during 1967 to 1973, but

[5] These variables were selected as those which are hypothetically intrinsically significant and also found to be statistically related to variation in expenses. Extensive investigation of other potential links failed to support any hypotheses linking other variables to issue expenses (see also Buckland and Davis 1987).

TABLE 5.8 Regression Analysis on Costs of USM Placing, 1980–1985

	Expenses/issue size (%)		Expenses/entrant size (%)	
	Stepwise	Forced entry	Stepwise	Forced entry
Constant	22.36 (2.48)	25.38 (3.46)	1.35 (0.32)	1.26 (0.43)
Proportion of equity issued (fraction)	−21.38 (5.89)	−22.47 (5.86)	6.11 (0.68)	6.12 (0.70)
Proportion of new money in the issue (fraction)	out of limits	—	0.0071 (0.0033)	0.0071 (0.0036)
Entrant size (£000)	−0.00076 (0.0002)	−0.00076 (0.0002)	−0.00015 (0.000025)	−0.00015 (0.000025)
Issue size (£000)	out of limits	—	out of limits	0.0000082 (0.000030)
Months since Nov. 1980	out of limits	−0.077 (0.06)	out of limits	0.0021 (0.0074)
Adjusted R^2	0.079	0.082	0.456	0.451
F	9.686	7.175	56.847	33.819
Significance	0.0001	0.0001	0.0000	0.0000

Note: Figures are estimated beta and (standard error of beta).

costs for entry to the Official List are now substantially higher than historical levels. We have shown that USM entry costs have been stable over time, and that there is no evidence that increased competition for such flotations by issuing houses has reduced costs of entry, nor that USM costs are escalating towards Official List levels. The existence of scale economies in the new issue market has been re-examined, and found to exhibit a classic size effect in relation to the size of issue involved. Again, in terms of the cost of progression to the Official List, it seems clear that as far as administrative expenses alone are concerned, smaller firms would still benefit by deferring entry until able to take advantage of the economies of scale available to Placings on the USM, and then to proceed to the Official List by way of Introduction. The innovation of the USM has undeniably helped the entry of smaller firms to quotation, but has not altered the fact of significant economies of scale in the issuing process; it is these, in effect, which constitute the supposed gap in the capital market investigated in turn by the Macmillan, Radcliffe, and Bolton Committees.

6

Debt Management by Companies entering the Unlisted Securities Market

Introduction

Without quotation on secondary markets, an equity's value is uncertain and its liquidity is restricted. As a result, equity capital costs are relatively high and available volumes are low. Without access to equity funding, the growing firm will be over reliant upon debt, particularly short-term debt, with its restrictive burdens of interest and repayment schedules. Debt providers, in their turn, will be reluctant to lend where the firm is unable to extend its equity base, where there may be other significant creditors exhausting corporate security, and where the gearing of the firm is such as to threaten its liquidity and solvency.

This constraint upon small, growing firms was articulated by Gupta (1969) and is the penalty of barriers to entry to secondary equities markets. Lenders will face significant agency costs in advancing funds to the unquoted business, and the premiums demanded by lenders for the default risk will be higher than for an equivalent quoted business. Equity investment in unquoted firms will be inhibited by the uncertainties and costs of attaining sufficient size, stability, or repute to overcome entry barriers. Firms which are discouraged from that change in status will not be able to expand as quickly as is feasible. Investors will be deprived of opportunities to invest and will do so instead in firms which are already mature, or which are exploiting the existence of barriers by the acquisition of smaller firms caught in the financial trap.

These problems constituted the original 'Macmillan gap' of the 1930s (Macmillan 1931), defined by reference to the unavailability of long-term loans and subsequently pursued in the UK by the Radcliffe (1959), Bolton (1971), and Wilson (1980) committees. Firms' independent growth is restricted, and while this matters for all firms it is of more consequence for the relatively small, high growth firms which are prime candidates for entry to the USM. The most important small firm, represented by the high technology, high growth enterprise, suffers virtually by definition from a capital constraint.

In this chapter the financial behaviour of new entrants to equity markets is studied to identify whether such firms are characterized by accumulated financing pressures, and whether they utilize their access to secondary markets to revise their financial structure. In Section I the literature on quotation and new issues is used to derive hypotheses about entrants' behaviour; in Sections II and III the evidence of new entrants from November 1980 to March 1985 is considered; in Section IV conclusions are drawn as to the behaviour of companies, the financing norms of businesses, and the operation of markets.

I Financial Structure, Firm Size, and Quotation

The issue of the financing gap is intimately bound together with that of smallness: the small firm can only gain an independent financial standing and credit-worthiness by growing to quoted status, but growth capital is scarce and expensive because of that lack of status. In the research conducted for the Wilson Committee at the end of the 1970s it was observed that 'small' and 'intermediate' size firms (of up to £4m total assets in 1975) were characterized by higher ratios of bank borrowing and of current liabilities in general than was the typical large firm (Wilson 1979: para. 2.1). This disadvantage (as the Wilson Committee (1980: para. 2.3) concluded, it cannot be properly called discrimination) constitutes a barrier to small firm growth. During the 1970s it appeared to be a major barrier to the growth of the small independent British business.

The decision concerning a change to quoted status is bound together also with the firm's choice of a target or appropriate financial policy and financial structure. Particularly if such a structural imbalance is itself a trigger for entry to the secondary market, the firm and its owners will be influenced in the manner of that entry by the accumulated structural problems within the business. The contemporary finance literature offers a choice of paradigms in this area. For 30 years, the agenda for the debate over financial structure has been dominated by Modigliani and Miller's (1958) irrelevance hypothesis, suggesting that in equilibrium the financial structure of the firm has no impact upon shareholders' wealth. Challenging that hypothesis are the proponents of 'frictional' theories of firm leverage, who argue that some 'optimal' gearing level exists, determined by the exploitation of corporate tax shelters or by bankruptcy costs (see e.g. Baxter 1967).

This inconclusive debate has been revitalized in recent years by the analysis of disequilibrium and behavioural models of financial structure, notably those based upon the asymmetries of information possessed by 'insiders' (managers, or existing owners of businesses), in contrast to that available to 'outsider' investors and lenders. When it is recognized that such asymmetries of access to as well as quality of information and expectations exist, then the nature of the contractual, agency relationship between manager and investor becomes of vital interest (see, e.g. Grossman and Hart 1982; Blazenko 1987). The firm's capital structure becomes one element of the public information upon the confidential activity and the uncertain prospects of the business. Moreover, managers choosing a particular financial structure for the business may be guided not by first-best wealth maximizing principles on the lines of Modigliani and Miller's arguments, but along second-best principles within which the level of corporate gearing is regarded as one element of a package of signals from manager–insiders to investor–outsiders (see e.g. Leland and Pyle 1977; John 1987; Franke 1987).

Firms' adoption of target debt ratios

In such a transactions cost, agency relationship, and signalling view of the firm, the debt behaviour of new entrants to equity markets becomes of great importance. Theoretically, the choice of debt ratio acquires a role in signalling management's confidence and expectations to the less well informed outside providers of finance. Empirically, the debt ratios taken up by firms have been related to their size, industry, riskiness, and asset composition (see for the UK e.g. Brealey *et al.* 1976, Briscoe and Hawke 1976). The key UK study (Marsh 1982) analysed the issuing behaviour of firms and showed that, when raising new funds, firms appear to be oriented to target levels of the debt: equity ratio, with these targets related to size, bankruptcy risk, and the firms' asset composition (Marsh 1982: 121). His evidence is less equivocal than earlier, similar studies on US data, notably that of Taub (1975), whose sophisticated econometric techniques failed to produce economically or statistically significant results (Taub 1975: 415).

The targets of firms may be neither optimal (*pace* Modigliani and Miller), nor second-best signalling equilibria. An alternative explanation may be found in managerial theories of the firm (see, in the context of new quotation, Ray and Hutchinson 1983). Firms with common economic characteristics may nevertheless have different business strategies, cultures, and goals. Such differences, in particular managerial attitudes to risk, may well explain variations in the level of financial risk which firms are willing to accept. So, for example, previous research into management policies towards risk management in the foreign currency area has suggested that there may not be a financial 'norm', due to the coexistence of groups of firms with distinct behavioural characteristics (Collier and Davis 1985).

Such behaviour is arguably quite likely in firms whose management structures and policies are undergoing significant evolution as part of their decision to go public. Entrants, perhaps particularly USM entrants, undergo a transformation from entrepreneurial towards managerial control. The application of contingency theory to such an interpretation is relevant: previous research has suggested that financial control systems within the organization respond to the specific situation (Anthony and Dearden 1980; Dermer 1977). The structural form and process which such systems assume depend upon other, contingent variables suited to the goals and strategies of the particular firm. The 'objective' elements (analysed here by a secondary data survey methodology) which make up the structural form and process of a financial control system interact with the norms of individuals and groups working within the firm's cultural and goal system (Ansari 1977; Ray and Hutchinson 1983: 76 ff).

Within this methodological approach we cannot attend directly to the potential for distinctions of culture within and between entrants. Instead we make the conventional assumption that firms' managers are bound by agency relationships to adopt common wealth-maximizing criteria. In this chapter the entry of firms to secondary markets will be studied to determine whether they display any such regression upon 'target' levels of gearing, or whether the financial structure of such firms, at a critical point in their development, is unaffected by the influences posited in the literature. If it is accepted that incentive signalling and information asymmetries will make a firm's financial structure important even in quoted status, then debt behaviour at the time of quotation becomes of great interest. If there are, as Marsh (1982) suggests, target levels of debt, then a 'Macmillan gap' and entry barriers in equity markets will be revealed in the leverage of entrants and in their behaviour following entry. Marsh's study of quoted companies' issues suggests that new entrants who make new money issues will display regression towards their target debt levels. Those targets will, in turn, be characterized by association with the size, industry, and other features of the business.

The significance of the USM for small firms' financial structures

Hutchinson *et al.* (1988) have argued that the financial structures of rapidly-growing small businesses are significantly different, more extended and illiquid than those of slower-growing firms. On the basis of their research, which also makes use of a (small[1]) sample of USM entrants, they suggest that the 'growth small firms' entering the USM are characterized by 'their high gearing and low liquidity which are indicative of the financial stress of growth' (Hutchinson *et al.* 1988: 17). The evidence of our much larger sample can throw more light upon this hypothesis. In particular we can examine whether firms, particularly small firms, which have entered the USM, did so to correct imbalances in their financial structure built up during their period of unquoted growth.

It is, of course, known from previous studies of new equity issue markets that entrants' financial structures are one common trigger for entry. Davis *et al.* (1974) and Vaughan *et al.* (1977) showed that to be true for entrants to the UK Official List. Small-scale studies of USM entrants have identified it as a continuing concern (see e.g. Bradley-Jones and Hussey 1985). Apart from the re-examination of that broad question, however, we seek here to address more complex aspects of the quotation decision and its aftermath. Even if a gap or deficiency in financial structure forms the motive for quotation, it is by no

[1] This sample is confined to 31 USM entrants in the manufacturing sector, with a control sample of unquoted manufacturing firms.

means clear that this will be simply associated with correction of an overreliance upon debt financing. It is, indeed, just as possible that the unquoted firm has been prevented from gaining access to debt (and hence has become restrictively undergeared) as prevented from expanding its equity base. Here we investigate the nature of the imbalance in entrants' financial structures and the relationship between this and other features of the firms. Having established the characteristics of entrants' financing difficulties, one can then proceed to consider whether the quotation is aimed at providing a solution by closing the gap between actual and desired structure.

Prospectus declarations and firms' debt behaviour

This chapter also considers how entrants actually behave, by reference both to their opening debt positions and also to their prospectus declaration at entry. Here we are addressing two issues. The first is whether entrants' financial 'problems' are in fact alleviated by their access to secondary, quoted equity markets, for we should not presume that quotation resolves any such problems. Accordingly the debt behaviour of entrants after quotation was compared with their opening positions and their prospectus declarations, exposing contradictions and analysing their relationship to the firms and to the markets which those firms are joining. The second recognizes that, on entry, firms may have incentives to specify financial structures and intentions as part of a package of information or signals to the imperfectly informed investing public. Since newly quoted businesses are firmly in a position where their managers and their existing (unquoted) owners possess asymmetrically good quality information about the firm's prospects, entrants may use signals such as their intended dividend policy (Miller and Rock 1985), the size of retained equity holdings (Leland and Pyle 1977), managers' service contracts and aggressive (expansionary, highly geared) intentions.[2]

In analysing the financial structure of firms it is necessary to be clear as to the measurement of gearing. In the ideal, one would wish to relate the market values of various financing assets to each other: that is the basis of the debt:equity gearing ratio of the finance literature. In terms of new equity issues, however, there are substantial drawbacks to that measure. It is unobservable in the issue prospectus, prior to any objective market evaluation of the traded equity. Also this summary measure may not capture significant shifts in or patterns of the various elements within the category of debt. Thus, one may be interested in the hypothesis that unquoted businesses are pressured into burdens of relatively short-term debt rather than institutional term-lending; or quotation might be hypothesized to permit significant restructuring within unchanged global totals of debt.

[2] In a signalling context, some suboptimal debt ratio may be selected by informed managers to inform insecurely informed outsiders about the level of managers' confidence in earnings prospects (see e.g. Blazenko 1987).

There are also active debates about the place and measurement of working capital within financial structure: questions concerning the inclusion of all trade debt, or the netting off of the firm's working capital position, before measuring debt in relation to net assets employed (or, indeed, in relation to shareholders' funds). There is no universally correct approach to measurement of the debt ratio. Here the levels of and movements in various short-term and long-term components of corporate debt are explored; and we relate them to the image of the typical 'small' firm and the typical 'large' firm constructed by previous research and by the longstanding presentation in *Business Monitor MA3* (DTI annually).

In our overall measure of entrants' gearing, financial structure is proxied by calculation of the ratio of total company indebtedness to the book value of capital employed. We chose this in preference to measures calculated using only long-term debt, or only short-term debt, since those disaggregated measures are both structurally related to company size, and because the term structure of debt is likely to change systematically over a period of new quotation. Book values are adopted in line with the consideration that, at the time of first quotation, market values of financing assets are unobservable; and that book value measures are closer to the information conveyed in company accounts and used by managers (Marsh 1982: 131). This gearing ratio was recalculated for intervals of 12, 24, and 36 months after quotation commenced, to identify movements in financial structure subsequent to quotation.[3]

Other major variables employed in this part of our analysis consisted of, first, the industrial classification of the entrant, as discussed in Chapter 4. Firm size was proxied by the total book value of assets at the time of issue (avoiding the biases inherent in alternatives such as turnover, net assets, capitalization, employees, or value added.[4] The scale of the issue was measured by the proportion of equity being marketed (if any share sale was taking place). The level of risk of the firm and of the issue was measured by the variability of its past earnings as recorded in the prospectus profits history, by the proportion of 'new' money raised by the business during the sale, and by the market-related estimators of the equity's beta and specific risk, as generated by the London Business School following quotation. Company profitability was measured retrospectively, in the reported profit and yields of the prospectus, and also prospectively, by any forecast profits and yields to which the prospectus commits the firm. The entrant's P:E ratio was measured at the issue price when it was given in a prospectus: for Introductions, of course, this information was not available, and prospectuses rarely offer any forecast of yields upon which a P:E could be constructed.

[3] Movements over 12 months are reported in this analysis, since the data is incomplete for the full 36-month period over the whole sample; the results based upon the 24- and 36-month tests are structurally the same, however.

[4] Relationships with alternative size measures have been analysed, but are not reported here in detail.

II The Evidence on Debt Levels, Motives for Entry and Debt Behaviour

The financial structures of entrants are summarized in Table 6.1, with an accompanying comparison of contemporary sectoral structure from the statistics in *Business Monitor MA3*. There is little if any evidence here that newly quoted firms are in general over borrowed or financially stretched. Average gearing ratios are in line with the levels for large UK companies in this period; when compared with the small and intermediate size firms, entrants show lower average debt ratios and less reliance on creditor or short-term bank finance.

Differences between categories of entrant are somewhat more important. While Table 6.1 shows USM and Official List entrants to be very similar in their average financial structure, those firms transferring between quoted markets are typically lower geared, particularly in respect of their trade credit position. This may reflect an industry bias, with a relatively large proportion of low debt oils and minerals businesses being introduced to the USM in 1980/1 and then later transferring to the Official List. It may, on the other hand, reflect unquoted entrants' desire to lower their gearing by share sales at entry.

Grouping prospectus debt levels by the method of issue confirmed the influence of gearing on the sale of shares. There were significant differences between Introductions and all other new entrants (42.57% compared with 63.45% for total debt; 18.66% compared with 27.89% for creditors and accruals). Again, this must be viewed in the context of the numbers of oils and minerals businesses using the Introduction route to their quotation.

The clearest evidence of entrants' purpose in using entry to make adjustments to their financial structures is contained in prospectus motives for entry and in their opening gearing positions. Table 6.2 summarizes the relationship between gearing levels at entry and the motive given for joining the exchange. Here firms were categorized as to whether they expressly set out in their prospectus that their motives included that of repaying outstanding corporate borrowings. It can be seen that roughly one in six new entrants cited debt repayment as one motive for entry, which constitutes some initial, crude evidence that quotations are being effected in order to aid in the correction of overextended corporate borrowing. This proportion is very little different as between the two markets of the (old) Official List and the (new) USM.

The gearing measures confirm that, on average, entrants which express their intent to repay borrowings are very significantly more highly geared upon entry than are other entrants. Where companies cite debt repayment as a motive, average gearing is some 10% of capital employed higher than otherwise. This differential is confined to the USM, however: the gearing of Official List entrants is indistinguishable when related to repayment motive, whereas the USM firms citing this reason for quotation display an average

TABLE 6.1 Financial Structure, by Market Status; and UK Sectoral Financial Structure, 1980–1985

(A) New Equity Market Entrants, 1980–Mar. 1985

	USM entrant	From OTC or 163	OL entrant	USM transfer	Row total	F ratio	K–W chi square
Total debt	56.43	34.54	56.43	47.88	54.17	12.78**	29.23**
	293	32	80	34	439		
	21.12	22.39	15.76	18.54	20.96		
Long-term debt	6.89	7.51	5.97	6.60	6.75	0.16	0.38
	294	32	78	33	437		
	13.20	13.10	9.94	9.58	12.44		
Overdrafts	8.90	7.52	9.05	4.72	8.51	1.77	5.96
	281	23	75	33	412		
	10.85	7.34	9.87	7.58	10.29		
Creditors, accruals	26.94	16.00	26.77	21.35	25.76	4.83**	14.72**
	284	27	76	33	420		
	16.63	12.33	15.27	13.87	15.95		
Debt:equity at market price	0.50	0.65	0.64	0.43	0.53	0.32	9.82*
	292	32	79	33	436		
	1.57	1.05	1.03	0.67	1.40		

(B) Sectoral[a] Financial Ratios, Average Percentage, 1980–1985[b]

	Small and medium companies	Large companies
Total debt	65.44	56.97
Long-term bank debt	1.60	5.40
Short-term bank debt	16.22	11.44
Creditors, accruals	41.66	26.64

Notes: Raw figures are, respectively, mean (percentages of total assets, except debt:equity ratio in *A*); no. of firms; standard deviation. Notes to significance tests as Table 4.1.

[a] 'Small' is under £100,000 total assets, 'large' over £4.16m.

[b] 1980–2 for small and medium category, not separately reported after 1982.

Source for B: Business monitor MA3: Company Finance, annually, HMSO.

TABLE 6.2 Mean Gearing Level (Borrowing as Percentage of Total Assets), by Entry Status and Declared Repayment Motive

Mean (%) No. of firms SD	Yes	No	Row total
USM entrant	63.87 51 17.09	54.86 242 21.58	56.43 293 21.12
From OTC or 163	—	34.54 32 22.39	34.54 32 22.39
OL entrant	56.75 16 14.19	56.36 64 16.24	56.44 80 15.76
USM transfer	—	47.88 34 18.54	47.88 34 18.54
Column total	62.17 67 16.62	52.73 372 21.35	54.17 439 20.96

1 out of 8 (12.5%) of the valid cells has expected cell frequency less than 5; minimum expected frequency = 4.890; chi square = 14.65 with 3 degrees of freedom, significance = 0.002.

debt: asset ratio of almost 64%. The prime sources of this differential are found, as would be expected, in the sharply higher prospectus levels of both long- and short-term bank debt carried by these USM businesses. In the USM firms predicting repayment of loans financed an average of 10.68% of assets by long-term debt, compared to 6.26% elsewhere. The average bank overdraft figures were 13.14% and 7.96%, respectively. Turning to the data on the reduction of gearing following entry, it is found that, as anticipated, the entrants which highlight debt repayment motives do on average reduce their gearing levels more. Mean values of debt reduction are 18.03% over the first 12 months for such entrants; significantly higher, at better than 1%, than the 6.90% gearing reduction for the complete sample. In both markets, the repayment motive is followed by large falls in average gearing: in the USM, the difference in means is 18.45% (repayment signalled) against 7.61% overall, in the Official List 16.76% against 10.41%.

If we examine the gearing levels of entrants in more detail it is clear that there is some considerable variation in the levels of borrowing. This variability is more marked for USM firms than for Official List entrants. Table 6.1

showed that the spread of gearing levels within prospectuses was wide, particularly in the USM and it was, in the case of high gearing levels, closely related to the explicit motivation for entry. There was also a strikingly high variability in the movement in gearing ratios, particularly, again, for the USM firms. Indeed, when we examined the behaviour of entrants which cited repayment of loans as a motive for entry, considerable anomalies were uncovered. Of the 51 USM firms which gave repayment as a motive for entry, 10 proceeded to increase their gearing ratios after entry; 13 actually increased the absolute levels of their formal borrowing over the first year of quotation. The contrast between this group of contradictory motive and behaviour and those entrants with consistent repayment intent is very clear: firms in the first group show an average increase in gearing of +6% over the year, while the latter display an average fall of −22%.[5]

Table 6.3 shows the extent to which this group is anomalous in its behaviour. While predicting repayment of debts, these 10 USM entrants recorded levels of gearing indistinguishable from the average, as opposed to the relatively high levels within the group which displayed consistent behaviour. In the period subsequent to entry, the 10 entrants increased their average gearing, to levels which were significantly higher after one year than those of the other firms. The 10 firms actually substantially increased their borrowing levels, despite their express contrary intent.

The proposition that entrants are being propelled into quoted status by the need to correct financial structure imbalance is supported by a consideration of entrants' raising of new equity capital at the time of quotation: the 'new money' raised within the issue.[6] Examining the new money content of USM issues, there is ample evidence of a greater recourse to the markets for increased equity. The average issue on the USM included 44% new money, significantly higher than the 34% for the contemporaneous Official List, and in contrast to the historical pattern where new issues were predominantly composed of 'old', existing shares (Davis *et al.* 1974: 45). These links between the market's quotation and money-raising characteristics lead further into the ways by which the USM may have changed firms' ability to reform their

[5] This contradiction of motive by behaviour does not occur in the Official List sample. The asymmetry strongly suggests that the prospectus motive is being used for purposes other than informing investors about intent: perhaps to signal to investors about interpretation. When market-based measures of gearing are considered rather than asset-based ones, this group of contradictory entrants were shown to have significantly higher debt:equity ratios; those ratios were becoming yet higher in the first year of quotation, and the value of the firms were significantly lower as a multiple of the assets' book values. These entrants were not any more prone to failure or takeover than other USM firms, however.

[6] For 24% of entrants, entry is made by an 'Introduction', with no sale even of existing shares. Introductions are most frequently used where entrants change trading location from OTC markets to USM, or from USM to Official List. This may confirm a restructuring link, with 'seasoned' entrants less prone to corrective issue activity than 'unseasoned' new entrants. Or, it may simply be that the method is perceived to have cost advantages over share sales (see Ch. 5).

TABLE 6.3 Gearing, Repayment Motive, and Entrant Behaviour

	USM				Official List			
	Opening gearing	Next gearing	Difference in gearing	Change in borrowing[a]	Opening gearing	Next gearing	Difference in gearing	Change in borrowing
Inconsistent	51.77	57.99	6.22	577.70				
	10	10	10	10	—	—	—	—
	15.30	16.80	6.90	897.48				
Consistent	67.17	42.40	−4.77	−302.18	56.75	39.99	−16.76	1181.41
	39	39	39	34	16	16	16	15
	16.61	18.97	23.45	1663.42	14.19	12.48	13.48	11449.19
No repay motive	52.54	47.89	−4.62	475.00	53.42	48.06	−5.35	1586.89
	276	253	253	235	98	97	94	90
	22.53	19.24	20.85	2301.37	17.45	18.15	16.19	17077.04
Column total	54.27	47.52	−6.86	383.94	53.89	46.92	−7.01	1528.96
	325	302	302	279	114	113	110	105
	22.20	19.14	22.06	2208.73	17.02	17.64	16.28	16347.18
F ratio	7.81**	2.94	17.69**	1.89	0.53	2.92	7.09**	0.01
K–W chi square	16.87**	5.07	44.91**	15.00**	0.40	4.10*	9.11**	3.58

Notes: Figures are mean (percentages, except change in borrowing, which is £000); no. of firms; standard deviation. Notes to significance tests as Table 4.1.
[a] Change in total bank borrowing from issue to plus 12 months.

financial structure. Both the Wilson Committee and the Stock Exchange saw it as a solution for entrants to improve their access to new equity: the opposite pole of the financing gap from the debt-raising capacity. Table 6.4 indicates the extent to which firms with high levels of gearing at quotation were associated with corrective, new money issues. For the 184 firms where issues included over 30% new money, 82 (44.6%) had gearing levels above 65%; of the 66 firms where no new money was raised during an introductory share sale, 51 (77.3%) had gearing levels below 65%.

The size relationships

There should be significant associations between entrants' size and their gearing if the hypotheses of financing gaps and of gap closure at entry are to have any validity. Table 6.5 examines how the dimensions of entrants' financing were linked to their prospectus total assets. Recognizing that the size distributions of the USM and Official List samples overlap, the table separates entrants accordingly. It shows how size was associated with gearing at entry, and how size may be linked to the firms' behaviour following entry, proxied here by the difference between debt:asset ratios at prospectus and after 12 months of quotation. There is some evidence, though not strong evidence, that

TABLE 6.4 USM and Official List Companies by Percentage of New Money Raised and Level of Opening Gearing (Excluding Introduction)

Count Row % Column % Total %	Under 35%	35–50%	50–65%	Over 65%	Row total
None	12	14	25	15	66
	18.2	21.2	37.9	22.7	20.6
	30.8	23.7	24.0	12.7	
	3.8	4.4	7.8	4.7	
Under 30%	6	15	28	21	70
	8.6	21.4	40.0	30.0	21.9
	15.4	25.4	26.9	17.8	
	1.9	4.7	8.8	6.6	
Over 30%	21	30	51	82	184
	11.4	16.3	27.7	44.6	57.5
	53.8	50.8	49.0	69.5	
	6.6	9.4	15.9	25.6	
Column total	39 12.2	59 18.4	104 32.5	118 36.9	320 100

Chi square = 14.38 with 6 degrees of freedom. Significance = 0.0257. Missing = 19.

TABLE 6.5 Entrant Financial Structure, by Total Assets

	Under £2.5m	£2.5– £7.5m	£7.5– £15m	Over £15m	Row total	*F* ratio	K–W chi square
USM							
Total	58.16	51.57	48.63	55.81	54.41	2.92*	6.56*
	146	133	31	14	324		
	22.53	20.30	25.86	18.46	21.83		
Next gearing	45.13	49.36	47.37	58.62	47.66	2.59	8.67*
	137	125	26	13	301		
	18.60	18.96	22.32	15.44	19.13		
Change in gearing	−12.45	−2.34	−3.54	1.17	−6.89	5.69**	17.36**
	137	125	26	13	301		
	25.77	17.71	16.79	13.52	21.59		
Creditors, accruals	27.50	26.50	19.50	21.71	26.07	2.28	8.64*
	139	128	30	13	310		
	15.98	16.90	18.10	11.50	16.43		
Long-term debt	6.51	6.53	8.95	11.32	6.98	0.88	5.11
	146	133	31	15	325		
	14.89	10.64	12.63	17.01	13.20		
Debt:equity after 12 months	0.33	0.79	1.15	1.19	0.63	8.21**	44.57**
	134	122	26	13	295		
	0.38	1.32	1.55	1.20	1.07		
Official List							
Total debt	59.56	55.08	51.66	52.35	53.89	0.71	1.80
	11	41	23	39	114		
	14.29	16.69	19.16	16.89	17.08		
Next gearing	49.12	49.69	44.39	44.79	46.92	0.73	2.16
	10	42	22	39	113		
	16.75	14.39	22.42	18.21	17.70		
Change in gearing	−12.12	−5.63	−6.62	−7.52	−7.01	0.40	1.68
	9	41	22	38	110		
	15.21	17.23	12.35	17.72	16.41		
Creditors, accruals	29.14	29.93	22.58	20.13	25.13	3.38*	7.48
	11	40	22	36	109		
	13.51	16.83	14.48	11.85	15.01		
Long-term debt	3.61	4.04	7.25	8.61	6.16	1.79	10.45*
	11	41	22	37	111		
	5.66	9.14	10.49	10.64	9.69		
Debt:equity after 12 months	0.24	0.59	0.45	0.78	0.60	1.39	8.93*
	9	41	21	38	109		
	0.17	1.04	0.37	0.86	0.84		

Note: Figures are mean (percentages of total assets, except B:S ratio); no. of firms; standard deviation. Notes to significance tests as Table 4.1.

creditors and accruals ratios were linked to size; and some evidence that the smallest entrants in the samples, firms with total assets of under £250,000 in the prospectus, started with relatively high gearing and proceeded to reduce it more sharply. Overall, however, Table 6.5 suggests that there were no simple links from entrant size to financial structure, but that the typical entrant made substantial reductions in overall debt: asset ratios after gaining quotation.

We note, however, that the picture was less straightforward when alternative measures of gearing were introduced. If one considers that managers, shareholders, and lenders use the equity capitalization of a quoted firm, rather than the written-down historic cost of net tangible assets, as a measure of asset backing, then measures of gearing based on market values are relevant. Table 6.5 shows the smallest USM entrants to have had debt averaging 58.16% of total assets, or a debt: book equity ratio of 139%. The average debt: equity ratio at the equity issue price, however, was a mere 28%, and this was very significantly smaller than the overall averages of 52% for all USM entrants, 58% for all Official List entrants. This strong size differential persisted in both markets: smaller entrants were unambiguously lower geared than larger entrants when gearing was measured by market values.[7]

This evidence of direct links between size, financing positions, and financing behaviour is equivocal. Entrants in general were not as highly geared as the contemporary sectoral averages; and on average much less financially extended than the small and medium-sized firms in the *Business Monitor* samples. In both markets the smallest size category of entrant displayed higher debt levels, particularly of trade and other creditors, than did other firms in the samples. These smallest firms also made the biggest reductions in their debt: asset ratios, so that by 12 months after entry, gearing ratios of USM firms were indistinguishable when related to size, while in the Official List the largest entrants showed the higher gearing ratios. Quotation also affords entrants the additional signal of debt security by way of equity capitalization, as opposed to the book values of net assets. Here the smaller firms displayed significantly lower debt: equity ratios than their larger fellows.

Prima facie, therefore, the evidence of means classifications points to entrants having distorted financial structures at the time of their entry to the market. To determine whether this is independent of the other characteristics of these samples—their size, risk, industry and/or yield differentials, for example—we now consider whether these firms could be expected to display such widely differing gearing ratios. Beyond this we proceed to discuss whether entrants' subsequent debt behaviour is consistent with the hypothesis that financing 'gaps' are being closed.

[7] Debt: equity ratios at market values lie around 60% in both markets, but larger USM firms display relatively high ratios, reflecting the size bias in the premium of market over book values in the USM. Differences in means are significant in both markets (by the Kruskal–Wallis chi square test, $p < 0.05$ in both years for the Official List, $p < 0.01$ for both years in the USM). Differences in the change in debt: equity ratios are not significant in either market, however.

Bivariate relationships with gearing

In Marsh's analysis of issuing behaviour, target financial structures were associated with company size, risk, and asset composition (Marsh 1982: 121). In Hutchinson *et al.* (1988) also, firm size and firm growth rates were found to affect financial structure, with newly quoted firms displaying both higher growth rates and higher debt ratios than did a matched sample of unquoted businesses. Here we proceed to test whether debt positions and debt behaviour are significantly associated with the variables variously hypothesized in the literature. It is recognized that several of the measures are correlated with each other as well as potentially related to firms' debt. It is also to be expected that variables may be related in a non-linear manner. Even if the underlying characteristics were linearly related, the chosen proxies may not be. From a comparison of parametric (Pearson's product–moment correlation) and non-parametric (Spearman's and Kendall's rank or associative) statistics it is possible to test the superiority of various log-linear, exponential, or hyperbolic associations between variables at the bivariate level. This produces transforms of the basic variables which more precisely mirror the variability in entrants' characteristics; it is these transforms that are used in the analyses reported here.

Many of these variables show statistically strong associations with the measures of entrants' gearing and with the changes made to their financial structures. The correlation matrices for the raw variables in each market are reported in Appendix Table 3. As well as revealing the strength of correlation with financial structures, this table also details the strong relationships between individual variables. There were significant links between financial structure variables and size proxies, risk and growth proxies, between gearing and issue composition. Changes in gearing following first quotation were solidly linked to the levels of opening gearing.

These links of outturn behaviour to initial gearing positions are perfectly consistent with the hypotheses of gap closure and of target structures for entrants. However, many of the bivariate links are weak, even in the non-parametric approach, and many of the associations between non-financial variables are as strong or stronger than those between them and the gearing measures, bringing dangers of multicollinearity in any multivariate analysis. In extending our analysis to a multivariate one and to allow application of statistical techniques which presume independence of variables (such as multiple discriminant analysis), it is valuable to employ a set of proxies for the data characteristics which is freed from any multicollinearity.

Many measures are alternative proxies for the underlying characteristic about which one is hypothesizing. Thus, firm growth is proxied by the P:E ratio, by past profits growth and/or by forecast growth; none of these is either a perfect or a complete measure of the underlying rate of anticipated growth of equity value. Similarly, risk is measured retrospectively by systematic (beta) risk and by the specific risk of equity returns, but it is also proxied by profits and price variability, and even by industry class.

The underlying and independent characteristics within the sample are explored by the use of principal component analysis. The data are fitted to a model extracting principal components, with a subsequent varimax orthogonal rotation of the factor matrix to enhance individual factor loadings of the principal components, while preserving the independence of the components.[8]

Table 6.6 shows the results of factorizing the complete sample, with the first four principal components, the amount of variability explained for each variable (communality) and for the data set as a whole (% variation explained). Fifty-one per cent of the variability in the raw variables is explained by these four independent principal components, with forecast yields, firm size, risk measures, and the proxies for issuing process emerging as the prime distinguishing features of variability within the data. Part *B* of Table 6.6 shows the factor loadings, or strength of relationship between the principal component scores and the raw variables, after rotation of the factor matrix.

In developing the strength of any systematic influences upon financial structure, these principal component scores for the entrants will be used to test hypotheses freed of multicollinearity. The correlation of the principal components with financial structure variables is reported in Table 6.7. The size component in the data remained extremely weak; and it was contradictory between the samples, being slight and positive in the Official List, slight and negative in the USM. In the USM there is some evidence of the emergence of a size effect: with longer duration of quotation, larger firms show higher gearing and are raising it significantly. Given the opposite association in the Official List, however, this contrary result carries little weight.

It can be seen from the bivariate tests in Table 6.7 that gearing reductions subsequent to entry to secondary markets were very strongly associated with the level of opening gearing reported in the prospectus. The correlation coefficient is estimated to be -0.62 for the USM entrants, -0.44 for the Official List. This test presupposes, of course, that any 'target' gearing level is the same for all entrants. We note that the associations with later gearing and with market based measures were different between the markets (see also Appendix Table 3). To clarify this, and to test the other hypotheses developed above, we now turn to multivariate tests of the relationships in this data.

[8] Selection is conventionally controlled by setting a critical eigenvalue, normally 1. This produces seven principal components in this data. We take a more conservative approach, applying the scree test and accepting only eigenvalues which plot on the 'rock face' of the scree plot, ignoring those on the lower 'scree' slope. This gives the four substantive components. The collinearity of components is tested by oblique rotation of the factor matrix. Such tests confirm that the four factors identified are independent.

TABLE 6.6 Principal Components Analysis, Combined Markets Sample

(A) Communality (Percentage Variation explained) and Factor Statistics

	Communality	Factor	Eigen value	% variation explained	Cumulative % variation explained
Total assets	0.87	1	2.73	18.2	18.2
Equity capitalization	0.83				
Issue size	0.62	2	1.99	13.2	31.4
Proportion new money	0.40				
Proportion equity issued	0.74	3	1.65	11.0	42.4
Beta risk	0.44				
Specific risk	0.58	4	1.25	8.3	50.7
Profits variability	0.13				
Profits growth	0.27				
Value: assets premium	0.70				
Subscription ratio	0.07				
Discount on entry	0.15				
Forecast yield	0.65				
Forecast dividend cover	0.46				
P:E ratio	0.72				

(B) Rotated Factor Matrix: Orthogonal Varimax Rotation, Showing Factor Loadings (correlation of components with raw variables) Ordered by the Size of Coefficient

	Factor 1	Factor 2	Factor 3	Factor 4
Prop. equity issued	*0.84*	−0.03	−0.01	0.17
Forecast yield	*0.75*	−0.02	−0.27	−0.06
P:E ratio	*0.74*	0.15	0.35	−0.15
Forecast Cover	*0.58*	0.17	0.23	−0.19
Equity capitalization	−0.01	*0.89*	0.17	−0.03
Total assets	−0.08	*0.84*	−0.28	−0.28
Issue size	0.26	*0.74*	−0.07	0.08
Value: asset premium	−0.10	−0.01	*0.82*	0.15
Profits growth	0.04	−0.09	*0.47*	0.18
Prop. new money	−0.10	−0.00	*−0.45*	0.42
Subscription ratio	0.09	−0.02	*0.19*	−0.14
Specific risk	−0.28	−0.08	0.11	*0.70*
Beta risk	0.08	0.27	0.22	*0.56*
Discount on entry	0.08	−0.06	−0.07	*0.37*
Profits variability	−0.05	−0.06	0.04	*0.34*

Note: Factors in B are as follows: 1, Yields; 2, Size; 3, Issue Process; 4, Risk.

TABLE 6.7 Correlation Coefficients: Gearing Measures and Principal Component Scores

	Yields	Size	Issue process	Risk	1st year gearing	3rd year gearing	Change in gearing	B:S ratio
Combined samples								
Opening	0.29**	0.05	0.16**	0.07	0.46**	0.09	−0.59**	0.04
1st year	0.21**	0.01	0.04	−0.16**	—	0.26**	0.45**	0.32**
3rd year	−0.01	−0.03	0.06	0.05	—	—	0.15**	0.12*
Change	−0.11*	−0.02	−0.12	−0.23**	—	—	—	0.24**
B:S	−0.15**	0.04	−0.26**	−0.05	—	—	—	—
USM sample								
Opening	0.32**	−0.05	0.16**	0.02	0.44**	0.04	−0.62**	0.03
1st year	0.22**	0.11	−0.07	−0.22**	—	0.21**	0.44**	0.32**
3rd year	−0.05	0.15*	0.06	−0.02	—	—	0.14*	0.10
Change	−0.13*	0.12*	−0.23**	−0.21**	—	—	—	0.25**
B:S	−0.15**	−0.01	−0.31**	0.05	—	—	—	—
Official List sample								
Opening	0.34**	0.02	0.11	0.24**	0.57**	0.47**	−0.44**	0.09
1st year	0.16*	−0.10	−0.08	0.07	—	0.68**	0.49**	0.31**
3rd year	0.12	−0.11	−0.04	0.05	—	—	0.26**	0.32**
Change	−0.21*	−0.15	−0.20*	−0.16*	—	—	—	0.18*
B:S	−0.20*	−0.04	0.09	−0.13	—	—	—	—

Note: Figures are Pearson's product–moment correlation coefficients. Coefficients significant at better than 5% are marked*; better than 1% marked**.

III Multivariate Classification: Firms' Movement towards Target Debt Ratios

Having found evidence of the use of entry as a closure of some financing 'gap', we proceed to investigate the determinants of these financial structure adjustments. Firstly, we deal with the hypothesis advanced by Marsh and others that firms have target gearing or debt structures, and that therefore the behaviour of entrants during entry and afterwards will be with a view to some movement towards such targets (Marsh 1982; Taub 1975; Ray and Hutchinson 1983).

Correlation coefficients have already shown that post-quotation adjustments of financial structure are closely related to the level of gearing that entrants record when they are about to enter the markets. In the USM a coefficient of −0.62 weakens to +0.14 when the adjustment was correlated with gearing three years post-quotation; for the Official List the corresponding coefficients were −0.44 and +0.26. This would indeed indicate that the adjustment is away from the opening level and less closely tied to some subsequent target. We can, however, more firmly determine the source and direction of any link through multivariate analysis; and we can also judge whether the gearing levels to which entrants move were 'target' levels in the Marsh sense of being related to firm characteristics.

Firstly, by use of multiple regression analysis we can test whether the size of gearing adjustments is related to prospectus information in general, to returns, or risk data; and particularly whether there are any significant influences upon the gearing adjustment other than that of the opening gearing level. Regression analysis can also be employed to test whether there are systematic multivariate associations between entrants' (opening/target) financial structures and observable characteristics of their businesses. When entrants' change in gearing was regressed on industrial sector, yields, riskiness, size, and opening gearing it was clear that the level of opening gearing was most powerful in explaining the variation in later gearing adjustments. The results in Table 6.8 show this variable contributed 35% to the explanation of variation in gearing changes for USM entrants in stepwise designs. The USM entrants exhibited a significant size effect, consistent with the gap closure hypothesis and also with that of small firms' difficulties. The sign on total assets is positive and significant, and in this multivariate setting shows that the smallest firms make lower reductions in their gearing. It is already evident from earlier classifications that the smallest firms had relatively high gearing on entry, so that this result implies that their subsequent reduction in gearing was less than that of larger, but otherwise similar new entrants.

The mechanisms of issue—new money, subscription levels (here the proxy for 'acceptance' of the issue), and issue size have the anticipated negative signs, but the level of opening gearing is the overwhelming influence. Testing for collinearity through the alternative design with principal component scores as independent variables is also supportive of this. The issue process and entrant size were significant, but dominated by the opening gearing level. Indeed, the USM was as important for enabling the energy and minerals sector entrants to adjust their gearing levels downwards (by over 5% of total assets in this multivariate context) as it was for small firms. Contrast with the Official List shows gearing adjustments less closely tied to the opening gearing position, and influenced to a greater extent by conventional risk and yield measures. In this market, however, the explanatory power of models was sharply reduced, and no strong forces determining gearing changes are uncovered.

Explicit movement away from an unquoted financial structure on becoming quoted begs the question of whether entrants are moving to some rational target. By regressing the outturn post-quotation gearing levels of entrants on their business characteristics, we can gain a first impression of the determinants of their chosen financial structure when quoted.[9] This is reported in Table 6.9. The ability to explain variation in quoted companies' gearing levels is very restricted. With designs addressing the asset based debt: total assets ratio, the first models of Table 6.8, with gearing after 12 months of quotation as the dependent variable, show a continuing size effect in the USM firms. The smallest entrants still had relatively high debt: total assets ratios (indeed, since the previous analysis identified them as decreasing this ratio less, that is to be expected). Risk measures (beta and specific risk) are also significant, but overall only 21.5% of variation in gearing is explained. Once again, the Official List contrast suggests the absence of any size effect in firms joining the first-tier exchange: but here still less of the gearing ratio can be explained, with an R^2 of only 13.9%.

Accepting the loss of degrees of freedom with the unavailability of full data on the later years of this sample, we can examine the influence of size on gearing after three full years of quotation. Neither in the USM nor in the Official List does regression analysis account for any substantial variation in financial structure. There remain weak associations with size in the USM (still positive, but adding only 1% to the R^2), and with profits growth (again positive) in the Official List. While accepting that there may be significant divergence in the independent variables over the period, these regressions support those on the 12 month data and suggest that the target debt: asset structures of entrants are not linked to conventional sector, risk yield, or size characteristics. In other words, it appears that entrants were using quotation

[9] The possibility that entrants' opening gearing levels were systematically related to their characteristics is investigated in the models reported in Appendix Table 4. In the USM some variability is associated with entrants' prospective yields and profits variability, but the R^2 is only 19%. The most significant variable is that identifying the oils and minerals industry, with its low debt ratio. For Official List entrants, only profits growth and forecast yield are selected in stepwise designs, with an R^2 of only 10%. The hypothesis that entrants' size is a crucial factor when unquoted is rejected for both samples.

TABLE 6.8 Regression Analyses, Gearing Adjustment Regressed on Industry Sectors and Transformed Variables (Dependent variable: change in gearing from prospectus to entry plus one year)

	USM					Official List				
	Step	Change in R^2	t	Significant t	Beta	Step	Change in R^2	t	Significant t	Beta
Stepwise[a]										
Opening gearing	1	0.35	13.82	0.000**	0.53	1	0.19	−4.16	0.000**	−0.35
Total assets	2	0.05	6.29	0.000**	0.26					
Energy, minerals	3	0.05	−5.57	0.000**	−0.24	5	0.03	−2.20	0.030*	−0.18
New money	4	0.02	−4.67	0.000**	−0.19					
Subscription	5	0.02	−3.77	0.000**	−0.15					
Issue size	6	0.02	−3.75	0.000**	−0.16					
Profits variability						2	0.04	−2.33	0.021*	−0.17
Proportion issued						3	0.03	−3.42	0.001**	−0.34
Forcast yield						4	0.04	2.20	0.030*	0.21
Forced entry[b]										
Opening gearing			−14.24	0.000**	−0.59			−4.22	0.000**	−0.37
Total assets			6.88	0.000**	20.19			−0.90	0.371	−4.16
Equity capitalization			−3.45	0.001**	−10.70			0.35	0.730	1.37
Issue size			−3.93	0.000**	−0.22			0.18	0.860	0.00
Proportion new money			−4.22	0.000**	−13.91			−1.67	0.098	−10.45

Proportion equity issued	1.95	0.052	1.14	−2.91	0.005**	−1.60
Beta risk	3.10	0.002**	19.08	0.05	0.963	0.57
Specific risk	−2.62	0.009**	−0.15	−0.29	0.774	−0.03
Profits variability	1.35	0.178	0.36	−2.26	0.026*	−2.80
Profits growth	−0.40	0.687	−0.79	1.78	0.078	5.97
Value:assets premium	3.00	0.003**	16.42	−1.06	0.294	−11.28
Subscription ratio	−4.02	0.000**	−13.16	−0.92	0.361	−3.69
Discount on equity	1.97	0.050*	0.02	−0.47	0.640	−0.03
Forecast yield	1.44	0.152	0.54	2.46	0.016*	1.37
Forecast dividend cover	−0.06	0.952	−0.03	0.68	0.500	0.43
P:E ratio	0.64	0.523	4.13	1.17	0.246	5.55
Time from Nov. 1980	0.15	0.152	0.01	0.57	0.570	0.05
Industry sector dummies[c]						
Management services	2.87	0.005**	5.28	0.13	0.897	0.39
Energy and minerals	−2.53	0.012*	−9.24	−0.96	0.338	−5.35
Consistent motive dummy[d]	1.27	0.205	6.07			

Note: Coefficients significant at better than 5% are marked *; better than 1% are marked **.

[a] For USM, $R^2=51.0\%$; $F=55.54$; significance = 0.000**. For Official List, $R^2=32.7\%$; $F=10.89$; significance = 0.000**.

[b] For USM, $R^2=57.0\%$; $F=20.30$; significance = 0.000**. For Official List, $R^2=39.4\%$; $F=3.35$; significance = 0.000**.

[c] Leaving all other industries as the reference sector.

[d] 1 if repay motive not followed; no inconsistent cases in Official List.

TABLE 6.9 Regression Analyses, Target Gearing, Regressed on Industry Sectors and Transformed Variables (stepwise designs)

	USM					Official List				
	Step	Change in R^2	t	Significant t	Beta	Step	Change in R^2	t	Significant t	Beta
Debt: total assets after 12 months[a]										
Energy/minerals	1	0.08	−6.10	0.000**	−21.78	1	0.07	−2.27	0.025*	−12.90
Total assets	2	0.02	5.82	0.000**	11.26					
Beta risk	3	0.02	3.95	0.000**	26.78					
Specific risk	4	0.01	−2.98	0.003**	−0.18					
Profits growth						2	0.04	2.81	0.006**	10.49
Forecast yield						3	0.03	2.50	0.014*	1.32
P:E ratio						4	0.03	1.99	0.049*	10.52
Debt: total assets 3years after first quotation[b]										
Discount	1	0.02	2.54	0.011*	0.06					
Total assets	2	0.01	1.98	0.049*	7.15					
Profits growth						1	0.03	1.76	0.081	5.47
Debt: equity capitalization ratio after 12 months[c]										
Equity premium[d]	1	0.21	−8.17	0.000**	−1.59	1	0.27	−6.97	0.000**	−1.47
Equity capitalization	2	0.01	−2.33	0.021*	−0.28	3	0.04	−2.78	0.006**	−0.28
Profits growth						2	0.07	3.55	0.001**	0.52

[a] For USM, $R^2 = 22.7\%$; $F = 18.82$; significance = 0.000**. For Official List, $R^2 = 16.8\%$; $F = 5.72$; significance = 0.000**. *Forced entry design:* for USM, $R^2 = 25.9\%$; $F = 7.24$; significance = 0.000**. For Official List, $R^2 = 21.4\%$; $F = 2.01$; significance = 0.024*.

[b] For USM, $R^2 = 2.9\%$; $F = 4.78$; significance = 0.009**. For Official List, $R^2 = 2.6\%$; $F = 3.10$; significance = 0.081. *Forced entry design:* for USM, $R^2 = 4.9\%$; $F = 1.07$; significance = 0.387. For Official List, $R^2 = 13.6\%$; $F = 1.16$; significance = 0.319.

[c] For USM, $R^2 = 22.1\%$; $F = 46.06$; significance = 0.000**. For Official List, $R^2 = 38.2\%$; $F = 23.45$, significance = 0.000**. *Forced entry design:* for USM, $R^2 = 24.3\%$; $F = 6.67$; significance = 0.000**. For Official List, $R^2 = 41.3\%$; $F = 5.17$, significance = 0.000**.

to move away from an undesired financial structure, but that there was no observable pattern to the financial structures to which they moved.

Once quoted, it may be that new entrants shift attention from the backwards-looking balance sheets to the market values agreed by markets. We have noted earlier that the smaller firms (by book assets measures) attract relatively high market evaluations of their equities, with high share price: asset backing ratios. Therefore, even though one finds debt: total assets ratios regressing on an almost uniform level around some arbitrary 50% target, with little discernible variability explained by risk, sector, or size, it is possible that there are rational targets underlying the choice of the debt: equity ratio. This should, if the finance literature and the influence of efficient markets is to be believed, assume prime importance as the key measure of financial structure and indebtedness.

Accordingly we regressed the risk, sector, yield, and size variables upon the market-generated debt: equity ratio as well as on the debt: total assets ratio. The results for 12 months after quotation are reported in the third section of Table 6.9. We note that in the USM the level of overall explanation (R^2) is much the same as that achieved with the assets-based measure: 21.7% compared with 21.5%. The key difference, however, lies in the analysis' selection of significant variables. Most of the variation explained is accounted for by the market premium of equity value over net assets, and this has a strong, negative regression coefficient. Thus USM-quoted firms with low asset backing for their market value have relatively low debt: equity ratios. The other significant association is with equity capitalization itself, and again this has a negative sign to the coefficient: smaller firms have higher debt: equity ratios than do large ones with the same share price: net assets per share ratios.

These results are strongly supportive of the hypothesis that asset composition, leading to differentials in available security for borrowing, is crucial in gearing decisions. They are also strongly supportive of the hypothesis that smaller USM firms have higher gearing ratios than larger but otherwise equivalent businesses. The contrast with results of the same regression design applied to Official List entrants support this further. In the Official List, market value based models explain more of the variation in financial structure ($R^2 = 36.5\%$ one year after entry), and again the price: net assets ratio is the crucial determinant of observed variability. The crude size effect is even stronger than in the USM, with the debt: equity ratios of larger entrants significantly lower than those of smaller ones.

There is, therefore, much evidence to suggest that newly quoted firms were adopting some common, conventional debt: assets ratio, around the 50% level, and that the fact of quotation assisted them in achieving this. There is a size effect consistent with the hypothesis that small firms face difficulties which are simply due to smallness, but the 'target' ratios do not appear to have any basis in the conventional axes of risk, sector, or yields of firms.

Multiple discriminant analysis

It is, of course, possible that regression analysis, treating financial structure and changes to financial structure as continuous variables, may not uncover underlying significant factors influencing the direction of entrants' change. Multiple discriminant analysis can be used as an additional check, where gearing adjustment is treated as a dichotomous variable—gearing either rises or falls—and the other dimensions of variability between entrants are used to test whether a function can be generated which discriminates between the two poles of behaviour.[10]

We explore the samples by the inclusion of raw scores on the variables identified as potentially influential: firm size, risk, industry class, yields; and also use the principal components identified in the data. The use of principal components scores enhances analysis by adherence to orthogonality in 'independent' variables. The results, summarized in Appendix Table 6, confirm and reinforce the conclusions reached from our earlier analyses of the data. A knowledge of the entrant's opening gearing level is of use in discriminating as to whether the firm will be reducing or increasing its gearing following its quotation on the exchanges, both for the USM and for the Official List. The incorporation of the data studied here improves markedly upon random selection, but the performance of the function is almost wholly dependent upon the level of opening gearing within the prospectus: once that is known, there is little advantage or improvement gained by incorporation of other information.

IV Summary and Conclusions

Two areas of dispute within the literature are illuminated by the data analysed here. First, there is the proposition that firms entering a secondary equity market may be doing so to conclude a phase of development during which they have been inhibited in their choice of financial structure by entry barriers, credit shortages, or lack of security for lenders. In that hypothesis, one would expect to find entrants displaying inappropriate structures, altering them in systematic ways, and moving, following entry, towards some target financial structure appropriate to their circumstances. Second, there is the area of debate surrounding the characteristics of an 'appropriate' financial structure for the firm, whether large or small, growing or not, quoted or not. The choice here is between Modigliani and Miller's position that the specific structure is immaterial, the position of adherents of frictional theories of structure, and

[10] Multiple discriminant analysis preserves a multivariate approach but allows for discrete, nominal variation in the dependent variable: in this case dichotomous, up or down. It can be developed into a predictive tool for analysts (assuming that a discriminant function splits the sample better than random selection); here it is employed simply to test for the existence and power of any function (see e.g. Hedderson 1987: ch. 10).

that of the emergent literature upon agency and signalling bases for gearing level choice.

The gearing behaviour of entrants

The gearing levels, creditor and bank borrowing ratios exhibited by new entrants to equity markets between 1980 and 1985 were not higher than one would expect. The averages were substantially below those for the sectoral average and much lower than the ratios for the small and medium firm sectors in the UK. This casts grave doubt upon theories that firms seeking quotation are financially stretched, or are specifically inhibited by overborrowing. In the USM there was much variation in debt ratios, both relatively high and relatively low. The evidence is that around one-sixth of USM entrants entered the market wishing to reduce borrowing, and there were indeed substantial reductions in debt: asset ratios shortly after quotation was gained. The direction and size of changes in entrants' financial structures after entry was investigated by means comparisons, correlation analysis, multiple regression analysis, and multiple discriminant analysis. Correlation analysis revealed links between debt levels and entrants' behaviour and characteristics: weakening of links with past profitability and accounting measures of returns risk, strengthening of links to market-based risk measures.

Gearing changes in the USM firms were related to firm size, and this has been confirmed by the later multivariate analysis. The impact of firm size has been shown to be small in relation to the firms' shift towards some conventional target level of gearing: a level not itself connected to conventional risk, sector, or yield measures. The smallest firms came to the markets with the highest debt ratios, and they made lower reductions in the debt ratio than did larger but similar businesses. Any financing 'gap' would appear to be still present, in that the small quoted firms do not immediately move to the debt: assets levels adopted by others.

The financing norms of business

Implicit in any notion of a 'distortion' of the debt ratio of the pre-quotation business is the belief that there are optimal or target levels of gearing which the firm would prefer and which would benefit the shareholder through a lower average cost of capital for the business. The literature suggests that there may be 'target' levels of the debt ratio (as in Marsh's 1982 review): clearly, a rational destination is a prerequisite for finding rational, systematic debt behaviour in entrants. We find that USM firms did appear to be working towards target ratios. However, we have found little evidence to support hypotheses linking gearing to firm size, industry, riskiness, yields or other factors. Newly quoted firms' behaviour and levels of gearing reveal no patterns of targets for the gearing ratio. We do, however, find that firms were moving towards something which they saw as a target, by their choice of the method of entry and the raising of new money. That the destination is largely obscure would suggest that the selection and pursuit of a debt ratio by firms, which forms such an important aspect of their entry to quoted status, is an informational or signalling medium as much as an optimization process. Or, as was outlined in Section II, it may be that these firms' managers exercise wide discretion in selecting some financial structure which is appropriate to their own culture and their attitudes towards risk, control, and earnings.

The operation of markets

The conclusions and practical implications to be drawn from this analysis concern advisers' treatment of entrants, the regulation of entrants' prospectus disclosure and, of course, entrants' use of the USM and Official List. The particular financial structure adopted by firms which become quoted does not appear to be of much significance and is likely to be an accident of the past access of the firm to financing sources, not a product of good or poor past management. Hence entrants should be encouraged to use quotation as an opening for restructuring their finances, when the costs of doing so can be shared with the costs of quotation. On the other hand, it would be difficult to justify any particular structure more rational than that with which a firm happens to arrive initially. Both entrants and advisers should concentrate upon access as opposed to detailed structure. The choice of target and the stance of the entrant towards structure is more likely to be indicative of managers' expression of confidence in the future earnings for imperfectly informed shareholders than any conscious maximization policy.

There are cases in the early years of the USM where entrants have forecast some repayment of borrowings and have subsequently increased the firm's gearing after quotation. It is unclear whether 'low' or 'high' debt ratios correspond to 'good' or 'bad' information. The composition of assets and the resulting level of debt security is a crucial consideration here. Regression analysis has pinpointed that the market's view of gearing, the debt:equity capitalization ratio, is closely connected to net asset valuation. There is a significant size component, and it has a negative sign, indicating that small firms operate with significantly lower debt:equity ratios than their larger peers. The UK banking system is known to operate with relatively conservative attitudes towards debt security and small firms are at a continuing disadvantage, even when they have become quoted and possess the objective, market valuation of their net assets.

7

The Pricing of New Issues on the USM

Introduction

The extent to which the pricing of new issues is associated with systematic discounting can itself serve as a significant barrier to entry to prospective entrants, as we have considered in theory in Chapters 2 and 3. It is very much a question of public concern, therefore, whether, and in what way, this continues to affect firms joining the USM. In Section I we examine the general evidence on discounts and seek to relate these with specific firm and issue characteristics. The methodology adopted in this section is bivariate analysis, relating the level of discount to the quality of prospectus information offered, firm size, or issue method. We continue this approach in Section II, taking in such 'market'-based influences as the method of issue and the specific adviser employed. In Section III we undertake a multivariate analysis of the pricing of new issues, seeking to interpret the potential interrelationship between individual variables. In the Addendum to this chapter we provide information on the implications of stock market volatility and levels of subscription for the reception of issues on the USM and the Official List.

Analysing discounts: competing models

The earliest models of discounting developed analysis of equity prices in terms of single-equation equity valuation models, inferring value and price from fundamental variables such as yields, financial structure, and asset backing (cf. Henderson 1950; Merrett *et al.* 1964). The approach is fatally undermined by the deficiencies of single-equation valuation models (see e.g. Keenan 1970), and also flawed in the incapacity of such models to deal with a cross-sectional sampling framework addressing observations across long periods of time. In addition to variation in the levels of fundamentals, estimation procedures necessarily include the impact of changes in the reference levels of opportunity costs, market shifts, and altered economic climate.

Consequently, estimation procedures have decisively shifted to ones which relate pricing to issue characteristics, both in terms of prospectus forecasts to investors and in terms of the issuer's broader relation to equity markets. This approach was followed in Davis *et al.* (1974), in Vaughan *et al.* (1977), in Buckland *et al.* (1981), and it will be followed here. Essentially, this approach hypothesizes that the 'correct' level of discount will be influenced by information provided within the prospectus and by the circumstances of market buoyancy at the time of quotation. Inefficiencies in issue pricing (the channelling efficiency of the market) will be reflected in the over-accentuation or under-accentuation of proper signals (as e.g. biasing the issue prices of issues from relatively small businesses downwards), and in the misapprehension of investors' reactions to market shifts and sentiment. Further, it has been demonstrated that measurement of inefficiency in price-setting will be biased by the recursive nature of the generation of discounts: by offering too generous a discount, issuers excite excessive demand and artificially inflate the market's expectations (see Buckland *et al.* 1981 for an analysis of such effects).

I The Evidence on USM Pricing

This chapter is primarily concerned to explore the pricing mechanisms through the influences above, and also to compare contemporary experience with the evidence of the market's past operation. This leads away from an alternative, formalized examination of discounts as a reflection of option pricing, after the manner by which Dimson (1979) analyses new issue pricing. The models here do, however, address the links between discounts and the option elements of issuing by looking directly at the reflection of returns risk measures within discounts.

Table 7.1 shows that the discounts encountered by USM entrants show a marked and significant difference to those in either contemporary or historical Official List experience. The overall average is double that experienced over 1965–71, and 10% higher than for contemporary entrants to full listing. In addition, discounts on the USM have fluctuated more widely than on the Official List. The pattern of discounting has fundamentally altered. While the average for tendered issues lies close to that for Official List Tenders, Offers for Sale have been accompanied by lower price adjustments, and Placings—the dominant USM method of issue—have averaged a startling 27.92% increase in value from offer price to market closing after one month's dealing. In this section we examine whether the influences on the size of USM discounts are compatible with hypotheses linking them to entrant and issue characteristics, or whether these discounts are explicable only in terms of the market's inefficiency at pricing new entrants' equity correctly.

The significance of the information content of prospectuses

The first hypothesis to be considered is that discounting would be affected by the level of information provision during issuing: the more secure and complete is the prospectus information base, the less critical is the resolution of uncertainty during issuing and, therefore, the lower might be the discount on value necessary to move shares into the hands of new owners.

To comply with Stock Exchange rules, entrants to listing must provide records of profits and forecasts of earnings and dividends. Issues may be

TABLE 7.1 Average Recorded Discounts, by Method of Issue and by Market Status

Mean (%) No. of firms SD	Av. Nov. 1980–Mar. 1985[a]			Apr. 1965– Mar. 1971[b]
	USM entrant	OL entrant	Row total	
Placing	27.92 205 52.01	8.46 9 14.92	27.10 214 51.13	17.48 36 17.94
Offer for Sale	5.59 21 19.46	21.74 35 28.22	15.68 56 26.31	13.80 67 16.07
Tender	12.13 10 28.12	10.36 23 16.74	10.90 33 20.39	4.62 31 11.87
Other	32.08 25 61.74	8.43 3 13.82	29.55 28 58.80	4.75 2 2.68
Column total	25.92 261 50.78	15.72 70 23.46	23.76 331 46.52	12.54 136 16.34

[a] Chi square = 142.73 with 3 degrees of freedom. Significance = 0.0000. Missing = 3.
[b] Period of stable markets. $F=4.12$ for 3 degrees of freedom. Significance = 0.0050. Davis *et al.* (1974: 48).

differentiated by the quality of such provision of historical records and forecasts. One might reasonably expect that if discounts are related to uncertainty resolution, then they would be bigger for those issues where managers decline or are unable to make detailed forecasts, or where profits histories are short or absent altogether.

Tables 7.2*A* and *B* suggest that there may indeed be some influence from information factors. Table 7.2*A*, showing average measured discounts according to the length of entrants' profit histories, declares discounts to be higher for recently formed businesses, with particularly variable discounting on the wholly new ventures. On the other hand, sample sizes here were so small that no statistical inference can be drawn. Slightly more USM entrants were characterized by imprecision in the profits information given (as opposed simply to company formation). Table 7.2*B* shows that the discounts measured for entrants which provided exact histories were lower and less variable than those which provided estimated, incomplete, unclear, or missing records. It would seem that issue prices of these latter entrants were systematically lower than for entrants providing full information.

Table 7.3 addresses the differences in discounts measured where profits forecasts were absent from prospectuses or in some way unclear. Here it is possible to compare USM with Official List entrants, and in both cases higher

TABLE 7.2 Average Recorded Discounts for USM Entrants

(A) By Years of Company Formation

	New company	2 years	3 years	4 years	5 or more years	Row total
Mean (%)	44.05	13.84	30.43	37.14	25.69	26.67
No. of firms	3	3	12	15	220	253
SD	120.22	21.61	48.12	33.98	51.79	51.27

$F=0.32$ with 4 degrees of freedom. Significance = 0.8629. Missing = 10.

(B) By Information on Past Profits

	Exact	Estimate	Incomplete/ unclear	Missing	Row total
Mean (%)	22.91	32.80	101.01	−3.08	25.92
No. of firms	218	24	10	9	261
SD	35.43	52.38	171.63	17.90	50.78

$F=9.55$ with 3 degrees of freedom. Significance = 0.0000. Missing = 2.

average discounts were associated with missing or otherwise inexact forecasts. We must conclude that discounts were lower and much less variable for issues where a firm forecast of the next dividend and earnings was provided within the prospectus. The premium offered was substantially lower, particularly for USM entrants.

Market discount and firm and issue characteristics

The next hypothesis to be examined is that discounts on issue price are related to operating or financing characteristics of the entrant, and, in particular, to those characteristics which were seen in Chapter 4 to differ for USM and Official List companies, (and indeed at least in part, reflect the argument for the USM). This is addressed initially through correlation analysis of the key variables reported in prospectuses (see Table 7.4).

Table 7.4 confirms that the USM, like new equity issue markets of the past, produces discounts which are strongly correlated with levels of quantitative information provided in the prospectus. There is some evidence (at this level of simple correlation) that discounts may be inversely related to the size of the firm, the issue, and past profits. It remains to be seen whether this is merely a reflection of the differentials in issue method for the small USM issues, but size effects were found in previous studies of new equity issue markets (Davis *et al.* 1974: 45); and the contrast of the USM relationship with the absence of size effects in the contemporary Official List requires further examination.

The USM also displayed higher discounts on issues where relatively low

TABLE 7.3 Average Recorded Discounts for USM and Official List Entrants, by Accuracy of Profits Forecast and Market Status

Mean (%) No. of firms SD	USM entrant	OL entrant	Row total
Exact	16.52 15 33.28	10.58 5 13.26	15.03 20 29.33
Estimate	17.21 19 33.10		17.21 19 33.10
Minimum	25.22 120 33.81	15.08 46 21.89	22.41 166 31.23
Recent basis	30.38 11 51.57	24.13 1 0.00	29.86 12 49.20
Unclear	−2.58 2 4.96	7.37 1 0.00	0.74 3 6.73
Missing	30.16 94 70.80	18.96 17 30.86	28.44 111 66.27
Column total	25.92 261 50.78	15.72 70 23.46	23.76 331 46.52

5 out of 12 (41.7%) of the valid cells have expected cell frequency less than 5.0. Minimum expected cell frequency = 0.634. Chi square = 13.27 with 5 degrees of freedom. Significance = 0.0209.

proportions of the equity are involved. Not only is this phenomenon unrelated to new money proportions, but it is stronger than that estimated for the Official List, where discounts do not vary significantly in relation to the proportion of the equity issued.[1] Since the lowering of the proportion issued is central to the USM's development, it is necessary to ascertain whether this association reflects merely the method of issue and advisers' underpricing of such offerings, or whether it signifies penalties attached to pricing relatively small issues as well as relatively small entrants.

[1] This is, however, disturbed by the outliers of privatization issues, with very high proportions of equity involved in the initial issues.

TABLE 7.4 Correlations with Recorded Discount, for USM and Official List Samples

	USM	Official List	Combined
Prospectus data			
Real total assets	−0.0976 (262)*	−0.0520 (73)	−0.1105 (335)*
Real size of issue	−0.1931 (261)**	0.1300 (73)	−0.1435 (334)**
Real profits level	−0.0701 (253)	0.0969 (73)	−0.0688 (326)
Real expenses of issue	−0.1926 (251)**	0.0773 (73)	−0.1523 (324)**
Proportion equity issued	−0.1741 (263)**	−0.0577 (72)	−0.1662 (335)**
Proportion new money	−0.0619 (249)	−0.0402 (72)	−0.0334 (321)
Debt ratio	0.0920 (261)*	−0.0788 (71)	0.0631 (332)
Past profits growth	0.1631 (250)**	0.1313 (68)	0.1661 (318)**
Past profits variability	0.0585 (209)	−0.0525 (68)	0.0337 (277)
Forecast profits growth	0.0759 (161)	0.0539 (54)	0.0701 (215)
Forecast dividend yield	−0.1660 (219)**	−0.1449 (66)	−0.1615 (285)**
Forecast dividend cover	0.2238 (167)**	0.1034 (66)	0.1885 (233)**
Forecast P:E	0.0020 (193)	0.1038 (66)	0.0304 (259)
Asset composition[a]	0.0096 (253)	0.3531 (70)**	0.0754 (323)*
Market data			
Real market capitalization	−0.1906 (263**)	0.3162 (72)**	0.1565 (335)**
Debt:assets after 3 years	−0.0269 (149)	−0.1870 (54)*	−0.0588 (203)
Change in debt ratio over 3 years	−0.0636 (147)	−0.0589 (53)	−0.0624 (200)
Beta risk	0.0433 (261)	0.0061 (72)	0.0318 (333)
Specific risk	0.0267 (260)	−0.1169 (72)	0.0025 (332)
1st-year returns	0.0481 (261)	0.0532 (71)	0.0495 (332)
1st year debt:equity ratio	−0.2454 (242)**	−0.2397 (70)*	−0.2499 (312)**
Subscription ratio	0.4981 (30)**	0.3221 (48)*	0.3914 (78)**

Note: Figures are Spearman's rank correlation coefficient (valid pairs of observations); * denotes statistically significantly different from 0 at better than 10%, ** at better than 1%.

[a] As footnote 2, p. 97.

USM discounts would appear to have been more strongly associated with levels of forecast yield than are those for the Official List. Reinforcing the earlier evidence that more precise forecasting was accompanied by lower discounting, the USM would appear to have placed a premium upon the size of dividend yield being promised. In the share issues on the Official List, on the other hand, yield and earnings forecasts were unrelated to discounts. The strong associations for the USM were with issue size (negative), the proportion of equity issued (negative), forecast yield (negative), and past profits growth (positive). In the Official List the sign on issue size is positive, and the relationships with yield and past profits growth are no longer statistically significant, although remaining positive. In contrast the variable proxying asset composition[2] achieves a high, significant positive correlation for Official List entrants but not for the USM.

Turning to Table 7.4*B*, it is clear that the anticipation or expectation of financing policy had no impact upon discounts. Just as the gearing measures of the prospectus were uncorrelated with recorded discounts, so discounts failed to foreshadow any debt reduction. Nor do discounts relate to the beta, or systematic risk of the entrants. Neither the USM coefficient of 0.0433 nor the Official List counterpart of 0.0061 is statistically significant, and it would appear that issue prices efficiently reflected the eventual risk class of the equity within an efficient market.

The data shows only weak links between discount and annual returns for the USM sample. The experience of positive USM discounts, in other words, is not a reliable guide to returns on the new equity. The relationship between subscription levels and recorded discount was also less strong in USM markets. Given that USM aftermarkets are thinner and less liquid than those of the Official List, this is a completely counter-intuitive finding,[3] supporting the hypothesis that the discounts observed in the USM are related to issues' riskiness and uncertainty resolution, rather than simply to advisers' errors, reinforced by instability in applicants' behaviour and the aftermarkets. The capitalization of entrants is found to be related to discount with a strong positive sign.

The effect of firm size

To the correlation analysis above we can add the evidence from tests of analysis of variance and means classification. Size influences in USM discounts are evidenced in Tables 7.5 and 7.6, where average discounts are classified first by issue size and second by the capitalization of the business. The smaller USM issues reveal very high levels of introductory discount to

[2] Measured by the sum of corporate debt and equity capitalization, divided by total book assets.

[3] In a thin aftermarket, one would expect the signal of oversubscription to drive prices upwards, thus increasing recorded discounts.

TABLE 7.5 Average Recorded Discount, by Issue Size and Market Status

Mean (%) No. of firms SD	USM entrant	OL entrant	Row total
Under £200th	113.75 8 191.15		113.75 8 191.15
£200–£400th	40.69 36 45.94	−4.05 1 0.00	39.48 37 45.89
£400th–£1 million	23.99 82 39.91	5.42 4 19.43	23.13 86 39.32
£1 million–£5 million	19.05 122 31.82	14.55 34 25.36	18.07 156 30.51
Over £5 million	7.69 11 30.07	18.98 31 21.93	16.02 42 24.44
Column total	26.06 259 50.94	15.72 70 23.46	23.86 329 46.63

1 out of 10 (25.0%) of the valid cells has expected cell frequency of less than 5.0. Minimum expected cell frequency = 1.702. Chi square = 93.20 with 4 degrees of freedom. Significance = 0.0000. Missing = 5.

applicants, while those issues of equivalent size to Official List entrants recorded discounts consistent with the 'senior' market levels. Similarly in Table 7.7, relating discounts to the proportion of the equity involved in the issue, it would seem that it was at levels below 20%, in the range not addressed by Official List issues, that higher (and more variable) discounts occurred for USM entrants.

Table 7.8 shows the extent of the association of risk measures with discount levels. USM issues have been, on the whole, of much greater specific risk than were Official List issues; and average discounts were significantly higher, with variability appreciably greater, when specific risk was also high. The systematic risk profiles of the samples were very similar, however; and Table 7.8*B* confirms that beta risk was unconnected to discount.

To summarize, prospectus information is related to recorded USM discounts in several ways. Better quality of information is associated with

TABLE 7.6 Average Recorded Discount, by Firm Size (Equity Capitalization) and Market Status

Mean (%) No. of firms SD	USM entrant	OL entrant	Row total
Under £2.5 million	11.28	−3.31	10.09
	56	5	61
	29.45	4.71	28.51
£2.5–£7.5 million	31.94	11.48	30.84
	124	7	131
	62.78	14.57	61.32
£7.5–£15 million	29.72	6.74	23.45
	56	21	77
	37.80	11.54	34.28
Over £15 million	20.32	24.19	22.63
	25	37	62
	41.43	27.72	33.65
Column total	25.92	15.72	23.76
	261	70	331
	50.78	23.46	46.52

Chi square = 82.68 with 3 degree of freedom. Significance = 0.0000. Missing = 3.

lower discounts, and the levels of information provided have significant links. It is possible that USM discounts are larger for small issues by small firms, but otherwise issue prices appear to reflect the subsequent market view of new money, financial policy, and risks. Otherwise, issues offering relatively high dividend yields may be sold at lower discounts in the USM. On the Official List there are no clear size relationships to mirror the historical evidence of discrimination against the issues of small firms; but it is possible that issuers and their advisers undervalue the market's reactions to profits growth and intangible assets and have been overcautious in relation to the extent to which the markets price down issues of high fractions of firms' equity. The regression analysis of Section III will examine this more clearly.

II The Influence of Issue Methods on Discount Variability

Before turning to a multivariate analysis of pricing, it is necessary to address the extent to which methods of issue determine pricing and hence discounts for USM issues. Table 7.1 showed the extent to which discounts varied between issuing methods. Such disparities, both contemporary and historical, are

TABLE 7.7 Average Recorded Discount, by Proportion Equity in Issue and Market Status

Mean (%) No. of firms SD	USM entrant	OL entrant	Row total
<20%	34.30	17.74	33.56
	85	4	89
	71.69	12.03	70.16
20–30%	24.77	16.54	22.79
	107	34	141
	33.31	26.84	31.97
30–50%	21.86	14.98	19.60
	49	24	73
	44.40	21.95	38.45
>50%	6.37	13.44	8.39
	20	8	28
	24.99	19.17	23.35
Column total	25.92	15.72	23.76
	261	70	331
	50.78	23.46	46.52

Chi square = 22.49 with 3 degrees of freedom. Significance = 0.0001. Missing = 3.

difficult to account for logically or consistently. Official List discounts on Offers for Sale and Tenders appear to have virtually doubled from their norms of a decade earlier, while the accuracy of advisers' pricing of new issues has been markedly worse than before, and dramatically worse for USM securities. This may, of course, be due to the vagaries of this new market: but the reference group of Tender issues suggests that discounts need not be very substantially higher on the USM than on the Official List.

In the bivariate analysis of the last section, two key potential factors have been uncovered which may account for the disparities and size of USM discounts. It may be that the market requires higher levels of incentive to issue and quote shares of the very small proportions of small businesses handled by the USM; and it may be that the issues of very high specific risk, seen only in the USM, have to be accorded high discounts. In Section III we shall examine these points in more detail.

Before doing so, however, we consider the phenomenon of the greater variability in USM discounts. The increased spread of discounts available in the USM has produced a large sample of issues where the market price represents a fall from the issue price paid. As Table 7.9 demonstrates, USM

TABLE 7.8 Average Recorded Discount, by Specific Risk, Systematic (beta) risk, and Market Status

Mean (%) No. of firms SD	USM entrant	OL entrant	Row total
Specific risk			
<30%	18.73	17.39	18.31
	101	46	147
	29.22	22.11	27.13
30–45%	26.98	7.04	24.38
	100	15	115
	36.30	11.41	34.72
>45%	36.93	16.63	34.43
	57	8	65
	88.55	39.17	84.11
Column total	25.95	15.05	23.65
	258	69	327
	50.95	22.94	46.65
Chi square = 16.68 with 2 degrees of freedom. Significance = 0.0002. Missing = 3.			
Systematic (beta) risk			
<0.85	21.52	20.45	21.31
	45	11	56
	27.88	25.40	27.19
0.85–1	29.83	14.03	26.71
	134	33	167
	64.21	21.52	58.58
>1	21.34	14.01	19.60
	80	25	105
	32.29	24.28	30.62
Column total	25.76	15.05	23.54
	259	69	328
	50.94	22.94	46.65
Chi square = 0.72 with 2 degrees of freedom. Significance = 0.6993. Missing = 6.			

investors have been relatively twice as likely to encounter sharp falls of over 10% (or, indeed, rises of over 50%) than have Official List investors.[4] Within the USM, of course, the dominance of Placings ensures that initial investors bear the risks of such negative discounts: there is no intervening underwriting

[4] These averages and higher variability would not be anticipated in the context of the long, bull market conditions (see Buckland *et al.* 1981), where out-turn discounts are historically found to be lower.

TABLE 7.9 Level of Discount, by Market Status

Count Row % Column % Total %	USM entrant	OL entrant	Row total
Down over 10%	22 88.0 8.4 6.6	3 12.0 4.3 0.9	25 7.6
Down less than 10%	52 75.4 19.9 15.7	17 24.6 24.3 5.1	69 20.8
Up less than 10%	44 74.6 16.9 13.3	15 25.4 21.4 4.5	59 17.8
Up 10–50%	94 76.4 36.0 28.4	29 23.6 41.4 8.8	123 37.2
Up over 50%	49 89.1 18.8 14.8	6 10.9 8.6 1.8	55 16.6
Column total	261 78.9	70 21.1	331 100.0

Chi square = 6.30 with 4 degrees of freedom. Significance = 0.1780.

mechanism, nor the security of provision of a signal that the issue is underwritten.

Since the Placing method is unique in that applicants also serve as issue underwriters, it can be argued that this variability in itself justifies an increase in average discount in order to compensate the applicants for the increased probability of facing a short-term loss on their newly acquired shares. This would very conveniently account for the peculiarity of the much higher discounts on USM Placings *vis-à-vis* other methods,[5] although superficially it

[5] Excepting that the increased incidence of negative discounts within the USM is occasioned by the adverse performance of (underwritten) Offers for Sale, rather than of Placings; 22.5% (46) of USM Placings experienced negative discounts, compared to 47.6% (10) of USM Offers for Sale.

would appear to be an inefficient mechanism for buying underwriting as typical underwriters' fees on larger Offers for Sale are less than 2%. From the point of view of the researcher, it is also unfortunate that the allocation process, the demand for issues, and the behaviour of aftermarkets are so difficult to observe within the close management of the Placing.

Two indirect tests of any such link between discounts and issue-underwriting can be made. We can link the issues' 'success' (measured by subscription or, in the case of Placings, by initial discount and price variability in the aftermarket) to future activity, hypothesizing that entrants' anticipated issues, acquisitions, or existence would be threatened by adverse performance of the issuing process. Or we can relate issuing outcomes to brokers/issuers, here hypothesizing that more active brokers, offering more issuing opportunities to their clients, will be 'charged' lower implicit undewriting fees. Thus if brokers' clients have access to a large pool of Placings, they will have lower exposure to risk of loss through discount variability on individual issues.

The essential difficulties of conducting such an indirect test are that large numbers of firms are involved in Placings (between November 1980 and July 1986 there were 82 brokers and 120 sponsors involved in USM issuing), and that it is hard to draw inferences (see Buckland and Yeomans 1977). In this sample there were several firms which were relatively highly active, and in Table 7.10 we show the discounting experience for the five most active brokers. From this table it would appear that, first, differences between specific brokers can be and have been significant. Restricting comparison to the five active firms, the average discounts on their Placings were significantly different at better than the 0.5% level.

Second, however, it also would appear that the discounts for the active firms, as a group, were no different from those of less active or less intensive issuing brokers. The statistical test here decisively rejects the hypothesis that average discounts for the five most active brokers were different from the average for the others, all of which made under five Placings during the period

TABLE 7.10 Average Recorded Discounts, by Issuing Broker (USM placings only)

	Broker 1	Broker 2	Broker 3	Broker 4	Broker 5	Other brokers	All brokers
Mean (%)	5.26	46.45	34.46	26.32	11.50	28.61	27.92
No. of firms	16	15	11	6	5	152	205
SD	25.33	34.37	31.35	25.99	21.99	57.27	52.01

Missing = 1.
Between Brokers 1–5, $F=4.356$ with 4 degrees of freedom. Significance = 0.0044.
Between 1–5 as a group and others, $F=0.102$ with 1 degree of freedom. Significance = 0.7495.
Between 1–5 separately and others, $F=1.133$ with 5 degrees of freedom. Significance = 0.3440.

in question. Active brokers did not, therefore, appear either to offer superior pricing performance or to develop a clientele of 'underwriting' purchasers.

In terms of the first indirect test, on the hypothesis that adverse experience would threaten the entrants' survival or their ability to deliver on prospectus promises, we can compare the survival rates of issues where discounts and/or applications are observable. With discounts, there are differences in the means for USM survivors (+31.89%) as compared to failed, suspended, or acquired USM entrants (+19.97%); but these are not statistically significantly different for these samples,[6] with considerable overlap of distributions. The evidence of applications ratios is more supportive of the hypothesis: the mean logarithm of the ratio is 0.90 for USM survivors, −0.47 for USM failures, withdrawals, and acquired entrants; significantly different at a level of 0.0058 for the F-ratio of 9.1558. We note that this is observable only for the restricted numbers of public sales (Offers for Sale and by Tender) in the USM; and there is no such significant differential in subscription ratios within contemporaneous Official List entrants. This suggests that adverse experience with a public sale in the USM has very often been followed by early withdrawal from the market.

There is some, very slight, support for the hypothesis from an examination of the discounts and subscription ratios of entrants who fail to make any acquisitions heralded in their prospectus; again, stronger for USM entrants than in the Official List, but never statistically significant. In line with the greater variability of discounting itself, it would appear that USM entrants' equities were more susceptible to destabilization by the market's reception, but that such pressures were not the dominant factors in entrants' future success or failure.

III Regression Analysis of USM Pricing

In this section we use multivariate analysis to examine the linkages between firm, issue, and market variables to probe the extent of significant interrelationships. So we shall be concerned, for example, with the relationship between discount levels, firm size, method of issue, and quality of prospectus information offered. The linkages are complex, and we shall need to account for various subordinate influences involved, reserving publication for the major and significant results.

The design of this analysis is crucial, particularly in that there are distinct subsamples within the data which can lead to biased results if inappropriately handled. As elsewhere in this chapter, entrants transferring from another quoted status have been excluded, along with Introductions, where there is no discount to be observed. Additionally, however, there are distinctions as

[6] The F-ratio carries a significance level of only 0.3710. In the Official List, the difference in means of +18.26% and +7.08% respectively carries an F-ratio significant at 0.1866. For comparison with rates of failure and takeover in the past, see Buckland (1982).

between the other methods of issue. Firstly, it is reasonable to suppose that Offers by Tender will exhibit relationships different from issues by other methods, since both the issue and the market price are influenced by investors' express preferences. It is also reasonable to suppose that different adviser-influenced methods may be characterized by different factors: the role of subscription levels for Offers for Sale; the absence of underwriters' signalling of riskiness for a Placing; the uncertainties of post-rights values when a complex rights-plus-introduction method is adopted.

It must be anticipated, also, that discounts may behave differently in the USM than in the more tightly controlled Official List. If the differences between General Undertaking and Listing Agreement are themselves significant, one might hope to find some shift of emphasis as regards significant signals in the two markets.

Such differences render the application of regression analysis to pooled samples problematic. The samples may be characterized by differing constant terms and/or by different coefficients or functional forms of key variables. In investigating the multivariate links to discount, therefore, we have worked from the simple and partial correlation analysis to multiple regression designs tested on both disaggregated and aggregated samples. Where contrasts between subsamples are called for, we report the tests of hypotheses applied to pooled samples, using dummy variables to test both for intercept and slope variations across the samples.

Does size still matter?

We are able to provide conclusive tests of the price:pressure hypothesis in the USM and in the contemporary Official List markets. In brief, there is no evidence of any price:pressure effect on issues' discounts, and there is no support for the hypothesis that larger issues required, or received, higher introductory discounts at their flotation. Indeed, far from confirming any positive association, multiple regression analysis confirms the alternative hypothesis—that in the USM, the smallest issues were marketed at the highest discounts. In Table 7.11, reproducing the results for the regression model on USM discounts which performs best statistically, both issue size and its square root are significant independent variables, and the sign of the square root of issue size is significantly negative.

These size effects survive any alternative model structure for the USM and suggest that size is not standing in for any other variable.[7] The effects echo the findings for the 1960s Official List, viz. that smaller issues, by smaller firms, attracted disproportionately high levels of discount (Davis *et al.* 1974: 42–6). It is instructive to note here that, as in the 1960s, size did not affect discount measured on Offers by Tender. The evidence (not reported in detail) is hardly

[7] This particular non-linear formulation performs statistically slightly superior to that (size, logarithm of size) utilized in ch. 6.

TABLE 7.11 Regression Analysis: USM Issues (dependent variable: discount)

Independent variable	Order of entry[a]	Coefficient	t	Sig (t)	95% confidence interval	
					Low	High
Constant		25.52	2.113	0.034*	1.737	49.31
Placings dummy	4	17.08	2.522	0.012*	3.745	30.42
Precise profits history	2	−14.80	−1.994	0.047*	−29.41	−0.1836
Definite forecast	—	−9.392	−1.055	0.292	−26.92	8.138
Energy sector	3	−32.60	−2.105	0.036*	−63.09	−2.101
Communications/ leisure sector	—	12.23	1.324	0.181	−5.714	30.17
Issue size	5	0.00267	1.895	0.059	−0.1051 E3	0.00545
Root issue size	1	−0.6135	−2.721	0.007**	−1.058	−0.1694
Specific risk	6	0.4321	2.426	0.016*	0.08140	0.7827
Forecast yield	—	−103.0	−1.587	0.1136	−230.7	24.76

$R^2 = 0.1147$. $F = 3.727$. Significance = 0.0002.**

[a] Stepwise with entry limit of Sig (t) = 0.08.

strong, since the sample of Tenders, even if combined with Official List Tenders, is very small. However, there is no support from these tendered issues that discounts need be bigger for relatively small issues.

It is of course true that the smallest issues in the sample would not, conventionally, be regarded as capable of being tendered; and it may still be true that advisers reduced the issue price of the smallet issues to compensate clients and initial applicants for the illiquidity of 'economic' blocks of shares in the small issues. What is clear is that the size effect on discounts is over and above any association with other proxies for risk and uncertainty resolution in the issue.

Table 7.11 highlights other rejected hypotheses. Discounts do not appear to have been affected by issues' exposure to market fluctuations prior to dealing.[8] (This variable failed to reach any significant level and it did not do so within any other regression design.) This suggests that the shorter 'exposure' times of Placings did not advantage entrants, since advisers appeared to be able to protect entrants and applicants against such vagaries.

Among the standard proxies for business riskiness, it is clear that entrants' debt ratios influenced neither advisers nor investors. Rather, discounts were significantly related to the level of specific risk (not, of course, known in that measure to the adviser or the investor at the time). There appears to be no single prospectus or issue variable, nor any combination of such variables, that stand in for the post hoc specific risk measures. It was, on the other hand, related to discount in addition to such pseudo-proxies as size and yield.

The information content of prospectuses

Table 7.11 confirms that the issue prices of entrants with imprecise records and forecasts, particularly the former, were significantly marked down: a reflection of the view of discounting as the penalty for uncertainty resolution. It also confirms that the Placing method led to significantly higher discounting than Offers for Sale or Tenders: once again, this is an association over and above the significant size, risk, and information effects.

We note, of course, that even the best fit from the regression designs explains only a very small part of the variation in discounts on the USM. Apart from the energy sector, where USM issue prices would seem to have been peculiarly optimistic in the past, there were no strong sectoral effects, no associations with the fashionable 'people-business' sectors in management services or with the electronics sector boom of the early 1980s. One must remember, however, that USM issues were overwhelmingly Placings, where one not only faces advisers' intervention in discounting, but where also any disequilibrium in demand is unobservable.

8 Further illustrated in the Addendum to this chapter.

Regression analyses of methods of issue

In applying regression analysis to samples of issues made by diverse methods, attention must be paid to the potential complexities of interaction between methods, advisers, pricing, and demand. Alternative regression designs have been tested to search for evidence of other systematic factors.

We have distinguished between methods of issue on the USM by the use of additive dummies. Multiplicative interactions have been explored, as have non-linearities, but no significant departures from the pooled model exemplified in Table 7.11 were uncovered. In disaggregated samples, the numbers of Offers for Sale and Tenders inhibit regression analysis by their relatively small sample sizes. However, they do allow inspection of the interaction between subscription and discounting and we have made use of them in this way.[9]

It is possible to explain considerably more of the discounts variation in Offers for Sale than in either the USM as a whole or for Tenders as a whole. While the closest single association was with the applications ratio itself, one should not directly include the applications ratio within Offers for Sale regressions, since both variables result from the same independent-root influence: that of shifting the issue price away from the price at which the issue can be floated. Table 7.12 displays the strength of the links between prospectus variables and Offer for Sale discounts. It would appear from these investigations that advisers' attentiveness to and caution about profits records and forecasts are the source of contemporary discounting of these issues. There were no strong disparities between the USM and Official List markets (tests for significant differences in slope between USM and Official List subsamples were also inconclusive); and although past profits growth was the single most influential variable, it seems to have been standing in for a group of other, independently powerful factors: profits variability, yield forecasts, entrants' specific risk, and the proportion of new money. With these variables one can explain almost 60% of the variation in discounts on Offers for Sale.

As we have moved away from the USM sample, it is apparent that discounts are related to different variables and that there is more statistical regularity in the samples. If one examines the Official List entrants as a group, this shift is sharply highlighted. It is not possible to find any significant size or riskiness relationships here; instead the Official List entrant's discounts are characterized by their association with yields growth and profits variability.

[9] It is clear that the discount on Tenders is not at all affected by subscription levels (measured at the striking price). For fixed-price Offers for Sale, in contrast, it does appear that recorded discounts and subscription levels are codetermined by pricing behaviour: Discounts are very substantially higher when subscription ratios are high, producing an R^2 of 26%). Results of alternative regression designs are summarized in the addendum to this Chapter and in Appendix Tables 11 to 13.

TABLE 7.12 Regression Analysis: Issues by Offer for Sale (dependent variable: discount)

Independent variable	Order of entry[a]	Coefficient	t	Sig (t)	95% confidence interval	
					Low	High
Constant	—	63.12	5.516	0.000**	40.17	86.22
Official List dummy	—	1.598	0.287	0.775	−9.59	12.79
Profits growth	1(6)	0.04471	1.490	0.1426	−0.01559	0.1050
Profits variability	5	0.6372	1.869	0.068*	−0.04794	1.322
Forecast yield	4	−3.847	−3.173	0.003**	−6.283	−1.410
Proportion new money	3	−0.2706	−3.363	0.002**	−0.4323	−0.1089
Specific risk	2	−0.8014	−4.929	0.000**	−1.128	−0.4747

$R^2 = 0.5925$. $F = 11.817$. Significance = 0.0000**.

[a] Stepwise with entry limit of Sig (t) = 0.08. ( ) indicates variable removed at step indicated.

V Conclusions: USM Pricing, 1980–1985

Putting prices on unquoted equities is a skilled but inexact science; and no one should be surprised that the most important factor in recorded discounts is an inexplicable error variation. In the USM in particular, quoted markets have been opened up to hitherto unimagined entrants: firms with relatively explosive profits growth, relatively small amounts of marketed equity, relatively sparse information. During the first five years of USM operation there would appear to have been a shift in new entrant pricing, reinforcing the presumed 'conventions' of the Official List—past growth signals, yields, and variability—joining an emphasis on size, security of information, and specific risk. Although we cannot find confirmation through the Tenders sample that these are reasonable factors (in the sense that USM investors treat them as important), they cannot be rejected on that basis. Issues made by the tendering process could conceivably be argued to be sufficiently different of themselves that it would not be legitimate to argue from them as to 'valid' or 'invalid' influences on discounts.

It is also quite clear that any discriminatory influences on USM discounts are minor and in particular are small in relation to the general uncertainty over pricing. The initial price 'performance' of a USM entrant is a poor guide to even first-year returns, and they are set apart from Official List entrants by their levels of specific risk as much as by any other criterion.

The Placing as a method of issue involves significantly higher discounting for USM entrants: it is the single most important reason why USM discounts have been, on average, higher than those in the Official List and it imposes costs upon vendor shareholders in the USM which may well be avoidable by either a change of issue method or a change of timing. This crucial trade-off will be examined in Chapter 9, in the light of our analysis bringing together the deadweight cost of market entry and the wealth transfers from issue discounting.

Addendum

Lags in issuing and vulnerability

From the nature of the issuing process, it is apparent that pricing is vulnerable to the period between price-fixing and first dealing. Shifts in investor attitudes during this period could potentially invalidate a 'correct' price and may precipitate the offering of discounts as a defence. For two-thirds of the issues there is a lag of five to ten days between pricing and dealing, but the crucial determinant is that of issue method. For Placings, the average lag is 7.86 days; virtually all entrants experience a lag within the period of ten days, and only one in ten Placings involve any longer exposure. For an Offer for Sale, on the other hand, the typical period of exposure to shifting markets is 14.05 days, nearly three dealing weeks.[10] Some very long delays, several months in fact,

[10] The lag has apparently changed little for Placings (the average over 1965–71 was 8.53 days); for Offers for Sale it has increased from the 11.99 days during that period (Davis *et al.* 1974: 23–4).

have been experienced in the USM, but these have been confined to the hybrid, complex issues early in the market's history, when recently reconstructed businesses were brought to the market.

On the whole, the period of exposure for USM issues has been no different, allowing for variation in issue methods, from in the Official List.[11] Given that Placings have been used more widely, however, the exposure to change does imply that the USM issues have been, on the whole, subject to less dramatic market changes than are issues on the full market. If the industrial index of equity prices moves by more than 2% between pricing and dealing, the shift may be classed as 'fast'. Since prices were, broadly, rising throughout this period there are many more 'up fast' cases than 'down fast' cases. Nonetheless, Offers for Sale were over twice as exposed to sharp downward index movements than were Placings (40.0% for fixed-price Offers for Sale, 28.6% for Tenders, as opposed to 14.1% for Placings). Since exposure periods were similar, this was true also for the Official List entrants; this is the clearest justification for the contemporary move towards a greater use of the Placing for these markets.

Market demand and industry effects

The impact of market-wide movements has always been found influential in explaining the levels of discount (Merrett *et al.* 1964: ch. 7; Davis *et al.* 1974: 46–7). Earlier in this chapter it was noted that subscription levels can also have an impact. We tested whether subscription levels in the USM were significantly different from those in the contemporary Official List. The measure is appropriate only for Offers for Sale, and the data confirmed that, with both markets exhibiting buoyant subscription levels, there was no statistically significantly different applications behaviour between them (Appendix Table 7). Offers by Tender are, naturally, characterized by lower and less variable subscription ratios than are fixed-price offers.

It might be hypothesized that industry effects would influence pricing or issue reception, but the data show the paucity of industry influences in pricing. In both markets any significance was occasioned by the impact of method of issue, rather than by industrial sector (Appendix Tables 8, 9).

Alternative regression designs

The 'best-fit' designs reported in the body of the chapter were accompanied by regression testing of alternative hypotheses, such as the links of pricing to information provision, to wider stock market factors, to company structure and motive, and to market reception. Appendix Tables 10 onward illustrate the rejection or inconclusive nature of these hypotheses. Table 10 details designs for the pooled sample of USM issues, with uniformly low R^2, little relationship with company structure or motive, and the emergence of quality of information, issue method, and size as the only significant characteristics. Table 11 addresses designs for pooled samples of the three methods of share sales, confirming the peculiar role of issue size in Placings and the strength of interaction with issue subscription (applications ratios) in Offers for Sale. Table 12 explores the reference group of Tenders further and demonstrates the absence of hypothesized links to risk, yield, and company structure.

[11] For Official List Placings, 7.11 days; Offers for Sale, 12.97 days. Offers by Tender averaged 13.80 for the USM, 13.42 in the Official List.

8

Secondary Markets: Alternatives and Parallels

Introduction

In this chapter we undertake an overall review of the experience of other unlisted securities markets with which the development of the USM may be compared. We examine the origin of regulated second-tier markets in France and unregulated second-tier markets in the UK in the form of the OTC as but two examples of several which have occurred in different countries, including Japan, Germany, and the United States. Indeed, there are observers who feel that the US OTC market is a more appropriate model than the USM for small firm securities. But in other respects it is more beneficial for us to contrast the USM with one continental version, and, of course, with the British OTC, which while materially different from that of the US nevertheless drew from that experience to serve as a significant catalyst for the introduction of the concept in the UK.

The similarities between the London Stock Exchange's USM and the French Second Marché are many and compelling. The markets arose in parallel and in response to the declining attractions of costly official markets during the 1970s. There are also prominent differences, however. These can both drive the new markets apart – as, for example, in the French emphasis on regionalization of exchange activity—or they can cross-fertilize the procedures and operation of secondary share trading. This chapter compares and contrasts the new markets of France and the UK, drawing out the lessons of experience for both and highlighting the evolving features which will differentiate them in the future. In Section I we concentrate upon the development of the French Second Marché, while in Section II we examine aspects behind the growth of the UK OTC, concluding with a short evaluation of the potential significance of the Stock Exchange Third Market.

I The Evolution of Second-tier Markets in France

By regulating the information produced by companies, exchanges are considered to give security to prospective traders, lowering their costs and increasing the volume of trading and the value of equities. The quid pro quo for regulation is cost and exclusion: costs borne by traders and by companies wishing to join the club of traded equities; and exclusion of companies regarded as incapable of compliance with the exchange's rules. As a result, only a very few companies achieve the status of 'quoted' businesses. On the French bourses about 1,100 different equities can routinely be bought and sold, compared with 2,500 on the London Stock Exchange.

In both Britain and France, the secular problem of exchanges during the 1970s was that of attracting prospective new quoted companies. We have already considered in Chapter 2 how in the latter half of the 1970s the supply of new entrants to the London Stock Exchange dried up almost completely. The new, growing businesses in this period were unable to gain entry to the secondary markets. Entrepreneurs in energy, in electronics, in robotics, both in emergent industries and in rebuilt firms, could not enter the regulated exchanges. They were either prohibited by the terms of the exchanges' rules, or were inhibited by the costs of entry and the costs of trading. In France, the absence of new entrants to markets was heightened by the processes of nationalization under the Socialist administration: the capitalization, members, and turnover on the bourses declined as large and active *actions* were withdrawn into the public sector. In the UK the shortage of companies was joined by a long-term shift in share ownership, which further handicapped smaller firms in the market. Over several decades, the ownership of UK-quoted shares has become increasingly concentrated in the very large, managed funds of pension funds and insurance companies. As the number of individual holders declines, the liquidity of secondary markets becomes more problematic and the attractions of membership diminish. In Paris, the Cote Officiel, also chronically short of new entrants, was joined by the Second Marché in June 1983, gaining 50 entrants in its first 20 months and expanding to 127 by December 1985. The rush of entrants to this market, as with the USM, clearly demonstrates the extent to which businesses were previously inhibited from obtaining quotations. The number of entrants in both countries outstripped those gaining first quotation on the official markets. Investors, too, proved to be eager to take up the new securities. In 1983/4, in particular, new issues in second-tier markets were massively oversubscribed and the prices of new shares rose sharply.

In France as in the UK, the crucial feature of the new exchanges has been to lower the regulatory barriers to entry and to reduce the costs levied upon companies when quotations were granted. The innovation of the Second Marché prompted a relaxation in regulatory requirements, in a form similar to that which facilitated the growth of the USM in the UK. Second-tier disclosure requirements on the Second Marché are less stringent, although still tightly controlled by the issue departments. Firms with shorter histories are admitted, and reporting requirements are relaxed. Most importantly, the minimum proportion of equity (in France *actions*) to be held in public hands is dropped from 25% to a much less onerous 10%.

This last alteration is the most important of the regulatory changes in both the UK and France. For the owners of companies, it permits them to retain greater levels of control and to hold back sales of their equity until markets adjust wholly to the proofs of the firm's growth. For brokers and sponsors of the issue, it lessens the pressures of searching for great numbers of immediate purchasers and assures them that existing owners remain committed to the business' success. Not least, of course, it lessens the costs of selling the shares, particularly in relation to the value of the company as a whole. Flotation costs of 10% on an issue of minimum size in the UK Official List represent 2.5% of the company's worth: the same costs in the minimum second-tier issue involve only 1%. In return, second-tier markets are inherently less liquid and more risky than the more tightly-regulated official ones. This thinness of trading is seen as the most serious continuing problem of the USM, in that with less equity in public hands there are fewer willing buyers and sellers to make a market. In Paris, the problem has been recognized in the institution of the Syndicat de Liquidité, charged with ensuring a market in shares over the first 12 months of quotation. This significant difference between the two markets will be analysed further below.

Costs of entering second-tier markets in France

We have already considered at length that, next to shifts in regulatory entry barriers, the major attraction of second-tier entry is its cheapness relative to official markets. By economizing on advertising and advice, firms should be able to gain access to secondary markets without having to meet the escalating costs of joining the Official List or the Cote Officiel. From Chapter 5 we know that the cost of joining the Official List by means of an Offer for Sale averaged £716,000 in 1980 prices for the period 1980–5, and in Paris the Commission d'Operation de Bourse (COB) puts the minimum costs at FF 1m (Coutty *et al.* 1984: 42), with large issues costing up to FF 5m. Such costs represent a substantial investment.

The impact of second-tier markets upon accession costs can be examined through the costs recorded by firms upon entry. In the context of the Second Marché the COB anticipated that issue costs would be as little as one-tenth of those for the Cote Officiel (Coutty *et al.*: loc. cit). In the event, costs in 1983 and 1984 varied from as little as FF 87,500 to FF 2.3m, with an average of FF 836,000. In Table 8.1 the total costs are related to the size of issue, as measured by equity capitalization. Costs are nearly always below 1% of capitalization and when related to the issue size at quotation are below 5% for over 60% of entrants, with all but one of the others being firms of under FF 200m equity capitalization (COB 1985*a*: para. 8).

These issue costs are indeed relatively low and would justify moves to quotation on the Second Marché even for quite marginal falls in the resultant capital costs and irrespective of increased access to higher volumes of capital

TABLE 8.1 Issue Costs and Size of Firm

Grouped issue costs (FF 000)	Grouped firm size (FF 000)				
	Below 300	300–750	750–1,000	Over 1,000	Total
Below 100	2	4	2	1	9
100–250	—	4	3	1	8
250–500	1	—	1	—	2
500–1,000	—	1	—	3	4
Over 1,000	—	—	—	2	2
All	3	9	6	7	25

Source: Adapted from COB 1985*a*.
Note: Average cost FF 836,000.

investment. This does, however, reflect the lower costs of issuing in general in French markets. Legal costs are very low for Second Marché entrants (below FF 30,000); and 70% of entrants face bills of below FF 0.5m for the preparation and publication of the necessary accounts, contracts, and documentation (COB 1985*a*). Bourse fees are very considerably reduced. In Britain, issuing costs in both Official List and the USM are higher than for the French counterparts.

Regionalization of secondary markets in the UK and France

The sharpest distinction between the objectives of the two markets—USM and Second Marché—is to be found in their relationship to regional activity in equity trading. In the UK and Ireland the regulated markets have, since 1973, been formally combined in the London Stock Exchange, with the consequent disappearance of the provincial trading floors in Belfast, Bristol, Leeds, Liverpool, Newcastle, and Manchester. The (London) Stock Exchange now encompasses the activity of all of these, and the Irish exchange in Dublin is also integrated in the London structure. Prior to this amalgamation of trading, there were some equities traded solely on the provincial trading floors, albeit relatively inactively. These were fairly small businesses which would have found it expensive to inform the wider national and largely disinterested investing community. As communications became cheaper, the rationale for specialized, regional markets became weaker, and the logic of centralization was strengthened. At present, it is not possible to distinguish 'provincial' business from 'London' business: all quotations are on a unified exchange, and all business is recorded as being transacted in London.

Such centralization depends upon the elimination of any significant regional asymmetries in the information presented and in the set of investors addressed by markets. If any asymmetries exist, then a market which neglects the regionally specialized investor, or regionally specialized information, will fail to attract all potential traders. There will be some investors who would trade at an equity's price, but only if they possessed specialized information which cannot be economically provided at national level. There will be elements of information which have content for a regionally specialized group of investors but which are devoid of meaning at a national level.

In centralizing the Official List in 1973, the London Stock Exchange implicitly took the view that the marginal benefits of accessing regional pools of investors and generating regional information were less than the costs of fragmenting the trading floor and of losing economies of scale in producing nationally codified information. Equities which previously chose to be quoted only on regional floors now had to choose between joining the integrated national floor or leaving the official market altogether. In choosing the former, shareholders might retain the chance to trade at a cost of a less liquid, more unstable, and less valuable quotation. For the latter, they would forego any of the valuable advantages of quotation, perhaps until their business was capable of being sustained on a national as opposed to a regional exchange.

Without doubt similar pressures were to be found in France, where annual trading of *actions* on the 'Officiel' regional exchanges of Bordeaux, Lille, Lyon, Marseille, Nancy, and Nantes had fallen to some FF 1.25b by 1984. This compares to over FF 67b trade in *actions françaises* on the Paris Bourse (COB 1985*b*: 139, 37). In both countries, the second-tier market has been seen as a route to revitalization of trading in regionally specialized businesses, but in France it is also seen as a route to revitalization of the regional exchanges themselves.

In other words, the USM in Britain encourages the regional firm and investor by making it less costly to access national and integrated securities trading. Firms which are disadvantaged by the absence of regionally specialized trading floors are tempted into quotation by reducing the costs attached to gaining a (still suboptimal) national quotation. In France, where the regional floors had, just, survived the pressures to centralize generated by the improvement in communications during the 1970s, the Second Marché has been made available both nationally and regionally.

In Britain, therefore, USM trading is done in London. Although some of the most active advisers have regional bases (as with Birmingham-based brokers Smith, Keen, Cutler; Stock Beech in Bristol; or the very active Birmingham USM department of accountants Peat, Marwick, McLintock), the typical sponsors, brokers, advisers, and traders are located in the City of London. The USM has had little or no apparent impact upon the regional nature of business during its first five years of growth, although with a turnover of £1.75b in 1985 it represented 1.6% of equities business on the Stock Exchange. In France, in contrast, the Second Marché has had a very strong regional aspect, even in its early stages. Ernst (1984: 166 ff.) suggested that less than half of early Second Marché quotations were centred in Paris (44%), compared to 11.5% in the Lyon Bourse, for example. In the first month of the Second Marché two quotations were established in Lyon, out of the nine issues in total; and of the 50 quotations gained by the end of March 1984, 17 were in the regional exchanges (Coutty *et al.* 1984). At the end of 1985 there were 80 *actions française* on the Paris Second Marché, 47 on regional exchanges' Second Marchés (COB 1986). Table 8.2 shows both the importance of Second Marché entrants in general and their dominance in the French regional exchanges.

The contribution of the Second Marché to the regeneration of regional exchange trading is yet more revealing. During 1985, 21 of 56 Second Marché entrants entered regional exchanges. Although the regions accounted for only 3.3% of the total turnover in *actions française* in France during 1985, 13.13% of Second Marché business was done in the regions (and this figure had dropped from 23.6% in 1984). As Tables 8.3 and 8.4 demonstrate, there is a very strong regional dimension to the French version of second-tier markets. In total, only 4% of bourse equity capitalization is quoted regionally; only 3.0–3.5% of trading in *actions* is carried out on regional exchanges. There were no entrants to the regional Cote Officiel Lists in 1983 or 1984, save only one transfer from the Second Marché. However, one-quarter of regional bourse capitalization is now in Second Marché actions, compared with only 8% in Paris. Around 40% of all regional business in *actions* is business in the Second Marché, compared with only 7% in Paris. The growth of the Lyon Bourse is particularly striking: from 42 *actions* (37 Cote Officiel) in 1983 to 59 (still 37 Cote Officiel) in 1985. Lyon Bourse capitalization and turnover have similarly flourished.

It would seem, therefore, that the introduction of the second-tier market in France has had a prime effect on regenerating regionally based equity trading. This is particularly evident in Lyon and in Lille, where activity in Second Marché equities has outstripped that in the regionally based Cote Officiel securities (COB 1985*b*: 139). This is a feature absent in the British market, since the unification of trading floors in London has precluded specific, provincial trading. The only relevant comparison from the London exchange is that of a relatively small number of quotations of businesses in Eire: even here there were only two instances out of the total 347 where quotation was made solely on the Dublin exchange floor.

Liquidity management in second-tier markets

By reducing the security and the quality of information given to investors and by allowing the quotation of much smaller blocks of equities, the second-tier markets are inherently less liquid than are the official exchanges. Fewer trades are made, and in smaller bargains, so that the twin problems of illiquidity arise: quoted prices may be outmoded, and isolated trades may be possible

TABLE 8.2 Numbers of Actions Françaises Quoted in France, 1984 and 1985

	1984 total		1984 entrants		1985 total		1985 entrants	
	Cote Officiel	Second Marché	Cote Officiel	Second Marché	Cote Officiel	Second Marché	Cote Officiel	Second Marché
Paris	504	46	4[a]	20[b]	489	80	3[c]	35[b]
Bordeaux	24	1	—	—	23	3	—	2
Lille	24	5	—	3	22	6	—	1
Lyon	38	8	1[d]	4	37	22	—	14
Marseilles	30	2	—	2	27	3	—	1
Nancy	37	6	—	2	35	7	—	1
Nantes	9	4	—	1	9	6	—	2
Sub total, regions	162	26	1[d]	12	153	47	—	21
Total France	666	72	5[e]	32[b]	642	127	3[c]	56[b]

[a] 1 from Second Marché; also 6 overseas entrants.
[b] Also 1 overseas entrant.
[c] Also 12 overseas entrants.
[d] From Second Marché.
[e] 2 from Second Marché; also 6 overseas entrants.
Source: COB (1985*b*, 1986).

TABLE 8.3 Turnover in Actions Françaises on French Bourses, 1984–1985

	1984		1985			
	Total (FF bn)	% in Second Marché	Total (FF bn)	% change from 1984	% in Second Marché	% change in Second Marché from 1984
Paris	70,446	4.62	142,003.3	101.50	7.16	212.36
Bordeaux	106.4	1.06	312.8	194.00	16.82	4,554.87
Lille	230.8	68.80	444	92.40	40.92	14.42
Lyon	1,315.8	54.33	3,067.3	133.11	34.55	48.23
Marseilles	181.5	17.91	315.2	73.66	13.10	27.08
Nancy	281.6	21.02	562.4	99.71	26.39	150.68
Nantes	148.9	27.07	138.2	−7.19	39.07	34.00
Sub total regions	2,264.4	44.42	4,839.9	113.74	31.77	52.87
Total France	72,730.4	5.86	146,843.2	101.90	7.97	174.72
Percentage regional	3.11	23.6[a]	3.30	3.48[b]	13.13[a]	7.14[b]

[a] Percentage of Second Marché turnover recorded in regional exchanges.
[b] Percentage of increased turnover accounted for by regional exchanges.
Source: COB (1985*b*, 1986).

TABLE 8.4 Capitalization of Actions Françãises on French Bourses 1984–1985

	1984		1985			
	Total (FF bn)	% in Second Marché	Total (FF bn)	% change from 1984	% in Second Marché	% change in Second Marché from 1984
Paris	413,852.5	4.84	649,610.9	56.97	7.94	157.60
Bordeaux	1,312.1	3.62	1,844.6	40.58	10.29	299.79
Lille	2,948.0	24.64	2,983.9	1.22	18.40	−24.45
Lyon	7,866.5	18.63	12,995.9	65.21	32.70	189.98
Marseilles	1,720.7	3.58	1,963.1	14.13	10.17	224.19
Nancy	2,940.2	14.21	4,789.0	62.88	20.69	137.09
Nantes	855.0	21.18	1,120.7	31.08	27.23	68.67
Sub total, regions	17,642.5	16.44	25,697.1	45.65	25.23	123.58
Total France	431,495.0	5.31	675,308.0	56.50	11.63	153.29
Percentage regional	4.19	12.65[a]	3.81	3.30[b]	11.17[a]	10.20[b]

[a] Percentage of Second Marché.
[b] Percentage increased capitalization accounted for by regional bourses.
Source: COB (1985*b*, 1986).

only by relatively large shifts in price or by large spreads in quotations. The two national exchanges have developed sharply different approaches to this problem. In the USM, trades are regulated in the same manner as are Official List trades. Market-makers can deal for other principals and, after the deregulation of 1986, on their own account.

In the early years of the USM, these arrangements were accompanied by a relative weakening of liquidity in the market. During the 1980s the Official List saw a marked and steady growth of trading volume and steady improvement in the average liquidity of stocks. The crucial measure of bargains per company per trading day has advanced from under 10 in 1981 to over 16 in 1986. In the USM, by contrast, the growth in trading volume is wholly accounted for by the expansion of entrants: average stock liquidity on the USM peaked in 1983 and remained at around five bargains per company per day.[1]

In part this reflects the departure of many USM 'successes' for the Official List. However, it signifies that the average USM entrant can expect to experience thin trading, with the attendant instability of price, degradation of information value, and erosion of the benefits of quotation. The perils of early illiquidity have heavily influenced UK sponsors in their preference for the Placing method of issue on the USM. Whilst it is cheap, a Placing sacrifices some of the initial receipts from shares issued in return for an assured initial spread of ownership. It forms the UK brokers' mechanism of managing the early months of the quotation by their knowledge of the clients with whom shares have initially been placed.

The deregulation of trading in 1986 may well alleviate some of these problems, now that market-makers can take positions in USM stocks on their own account. In France, however, the Bourse took action to control the problems of illiquidity by formalizing the positions which could be taken by market-makers. Facing a market which is, in general, more illiquid than the London Exchange, the Bourse allowed the sponsors of Second Marché issues to form a 'Syndicat de Liquidité, with powers and a contractual obligation to intervene to stabilize the market in an equity for a period of 12 months after issue. This syndicate of banks, broker, and broker's clients aims to prevent the thinness of early secondary markets from damaging the longer-term success of the quotation. The syndicate would appear to have a prominent part to play in the success of a less regulated market, although specific research in this area would be useful. The only UK counterpart of such arrangements is that of the work of licensed dealers in the OTC market, but their unregulated role as principals in 'thin' stock has not been universally encouraging.

With deregulation and single-capacity status for UK brokers, the potential for innovation of this nature is opened up and the French experience will be

[1] Prior to and disregarding the hiatus in market liquidity associated with the falling market of autumn 1987.

most valuable. Studies of the French system of liquidity management should be encouraged. In return, the French market might be enhanced by study of USM pricing. Twenty Second Marché issues in Paris during 1984 showed an average price increase of 57% from offer to dealings; the 35 Paris entrants during 1985 showed an average increase of 45%. These transfers of wealth from existing to new shareholders were an additional cost of entry which offset France's underlying cost advantage over the London markets. As Chapter 7 showed, USM discounts in the UK are lower and more widely distributed. It is far from clear that discounts on the French scale are needed to ensure smooth marketing of equities. Although the utopia of efficient markets with zero discounts is approached only by secondary issues (see e.g. Bhagat *et al.* 1985), new equities should not need over 10% to assure success and high levels lead only to disrupted and destabilized after markets (see Buckland 1987; and Buckland *et al.* 1981, for examples of the UK experience).

Comparison of the USM and the Second Marché

The two second-tier markets discussed here are very similar in conception and objective. The USM is larger in terms of the number of quoted equities, capitalization, and the money raised for USM businesses by rights issues and acquisitions. The Second Marché is, however, more significant in terms of its proportionate growth in its first two years, and it has had the particular role of injecting new equity trading into France's regional exchanges, which has not happened in the UK. This might suggest that there will be room for further changes in the UK markets as a result of the deregulation of securities trading and with the introduction of cheap, decentralized, automated trading. The French experience suggests that in the UK there will again be scope for businesses to be quoted away from the capital's internationalized exchange, and it should be practicable for such markets to be created within a deregulated environment.

The French evidence is particularly strong here, since in the Second Marché firms are able to choose between a regional quotation and a national one. Given that choice, French second-tier entrants have made the Second Marché the dominant source of new entrants to regional markets, and they have skewed their entries away from the national Bourse towards the regional ones. British USM entrants are prevented from making those choices, but it is probable that there are some which would have preferred a regional trading floor to the integrated London one, and there may be potential USM entrants who have been inhibited from entry because the regional option was not available.

The common experience of the two new markets is that a lowering of entry costs and a relaxation of qualification barriers to entry have resulted in a very rapid growth in the number of new entrants. The rapid growth of the two markets, and the sustained popularity of the USM in particular, strongly suggests that the regulatory framework of the official markets has become too stringent, too costly, and overprotective of investors. In the UK the entrants to the USM and the Official List are in the main drawn from a continuum of size, sector, and profitability. While there are a group of USM entrants which could not qualify as entrants to the Official List, the majority choose USM quotation in preference to the attainable, but more highly regulated market. This must suggest that the costs of attaining that higher level of regulation are not, for many businesses, justified by the benefits.

The Second Marché may also have lessons for the USM in terms of its initial management of quoted securities. Much of the mystique of advice on quotation arises from the twin problems of share valuation and of thinness of share trading. The French experience of early liquidity management within thin markets may well be helpful in developing the practice of market-makers' intervention in the UK in future.

II The Growth of the OTC

In Chapter 2 we considered the relevance of both the UK OTC and its American antecedent for influencing the introduction by the Stock Exchange of the USM. In this chapter, we continue our comparative review by exploring aspects of UK OTC performance in more detail. In doing so we shall be concerned to identify features which have contributed to the continued growth of this market, and which may reflect upon the attractiveness of the USM. The decision by the Stock Exchange in 1987 to introduce its own third-tier market (the Third Market) serves to emphasize the value of examining the present operation of the OTC in its own right. With the introduction of the USM it had been felt that the original low-cost attractions of old '163(2)' (now '535(2)') companies (by which Stock Exchange members could, with the approval of the Stock Exchange's quotation department, match transactions in unquoted UK companies) would diminish as companies sought transfer to the USM. In fact, a number of companies trading under this rule have shown no inclination to move, with approximately 250 securities traded in 1985 over a 6-month period (Tait 1986). The biggest change in this market has been the result of OTC expansion, with about 15% of these companies being OTC companies where Stock Exchange members have applied to do matched bargains. The overlap of OTC expansion with 'genuine 535(2) business' has significance for the subsequent development of the Stock Exchange's own third-tier market.

An important factor in stimulating the growth of the OTC market in the UK was the establishment of the Business Expansion Scheme in 1982 (Knowlman *et al.* 1985). The introduction of this scheme enabled individual tax payers to claim tax relief on investments in companies subject to a number of restrictions of which the most relevant in this context is that the shares could not be listed on a Stock Exchange and had to be held for five years. Companies quoted on the USM are considered by the Inland Revenue to be listed, whereas OTC companies are not formally regarded as quoted. There was some logic in this, for in many respects the fact of OTC quotation represents an illusion, by virtue of the inevitably restricted market in OTC shares: not least because any secondary purchases of the equity in the market place are not eligible for the tax benefits enjoyed by BES participants.[2]

In Table 8.5 we provide a detailed summary, derived from data prepared for Peat Marwick's OTC survey, of principal features of OTC performance. It breaks down the number of new entrants to this market by industry, separately distinguishing those accorded BES status. It distinguishes the various methods of issue adopted, the mean size of issue, and mean market capitalizations of companies joining the OTC. Values for market capitalization, of course, are inevitably affected by the narrowness of the markets in such securities, whereby prices recorded for a small percentage of shares may not adequately reflect some more objective or realistic valuation.

From Table 8.5 it is apparent that the mean market capitalization of OTC entrants, some £2.5m, is substantially less than that indicated in Table 4.1 for USM entrants (£7.3m). This impression is reinforced when we contrast Table 8.6 with Table 4.1. Of 294 USM entrants, 224 had market capitalizations on entry in excess of £2.5m; two-thirds of OTC entrants, in contrast, recorded capitalization beneath this level.

Here we must bear in mind that values for market capitalization at quotation are dependent upon the volume of shares traded and market price, which, especially, for small transactions, may be quite unrepresentative of the firm's total market value. Effective total market capitalizations may be much less than that represented in this table. While this is true to an extent for USM companies also, it is likely to have a particular significance for OTC companies. When, subsequently, we consider Tables 8.9 and 8.10, we shall note that less than one-third of all OTC companies issued more than 50% of their equity at quotation, so that the valuation of 'minority' proportions of relatively small lines of stock is inevitably tentative. The substantive point, however, is that OTC companies' 'prospective' market capitalizations, even on this optimistic basis, were much smaller than those of USM entrants.

We should expect that the size of OTC new entrants, as with USM new entrants, would indicate corresponding economies of scale in administrative expenses incurred. In Tables 8.7 and 8.8 we report mean percentage costs of issue by the grouped size of issue for Placings and Offers for Sale. While it would be tempting to compare absolute percentage costs for these issues with corresponding issues on the USM, the validity of so doing must be constrained by, *inter alia*, the obvious difference between the two markets in expenses as a

[2] Hence although BES investors may observe a 'price' at which trades might be carried out, they would be inhibited in doing so by the consequential loss of considerable tax reliefs.

TABLE 8.5 OTC Companies by Industrial Sector: Summary Characteristics

Industrial sector	No. of Firms	Firms with BES	Method of issue			Mean market capitalization on quotation (£m)	Mean size of issue (excluding Introductions) (£m)	Mean market capitalization post entry (Sept '86) (£m)
			Offers for Sale	Placing	Introductions			
Beer, wines, and spirits	7	3	3	3	1	2.2	0.638	8.4
Building, timber, roads	9	4	5	4		4.5	2.1	9.6
Chemicals and plastics	3	1	1	2		6.05	1.1	1.2
Drapery and stores	8	4	5	3		5.0	0.86	2.4
Electricals	26	11	11	10	5	3.4	1.2	3.0
Engineering	14	7	9	5		2.6	0.94	3.0
Food and groceries	1	1	1			0.5	0.55	1.3
Hotels and caterers	7	4	6	1		2.0	0.4	13.3
Industrials (misc.)	28	15	13	13	2	1.7	0.646	2.5
Leisure	32	13	15	13	4	2.6	0.97	2.5
Motors, aircraft	7	6	4	1	2	1.6	0.47	11.8
Newspapers, publishers	8	6	4	4		1.3	0.865	1.3
Paper, printing, and advertising	1	0	1			2.8	0.371	2.8
Property	16	7	8	3	5	2.4	1.64	1.9
Trusts, finance, land	22	0	9	8	5	2.4	1.24	2.75
Oil and gas	6	1	3	2	1	4.1	1.77	0.7
Miscellaneous	18	7	10	4	4	1.8	0.72	2.8
All sectors	212	90	108	76	29	2.5	1	3.45

Source: Adapted from PMM (1986*b*).

TABLE 8.6 Market Capitalization of OTC Companies at Quotation, by Industry and Grouped Market capitalization (excluding Introductions)

	Building	Electricals	Engineering	Misc. industry	Leisure	Property	Finance	Misc.	Row total
Under £2.5m	4	17	8	20	17	8	10	14	98
£2.5–7.5m	4	4	6	5	10	4	7	2	42
£7.5–15m				1	1	1	1		4
Over £15m	1	2							3
Column total	9	23	14	26	28	13	18	16	147

Source: Adapted from PMM (1986*b*).

TABLE 8.7 OTC Administrative Cost, by Grouped Size of Issue for Placings

Grouped size of issue (£000)	No. of firms	Mean cost (£000)	Mean size of issue (£000)	Cost of issue (%)
Under–200	7	33	152	21.7
201–400	25	53	305	17.4
401–600	12	76	483	15.7
601–800	8	82	705	11.6
801–1,000	5	124	943	13.2
1,001–2,000	4	130	1,405	9.3
2,001–3,000	7	161	2,341	6.9
Over 3,000	3	250	5,066	4.9

Source: Extracted from data prepared for PMM (1986*b*).

result of different entry requirements. What is more meaningful, however, is the evidence of similar economies of scale in the issuing process. Companies with very small issues (for example, below £0.4m) clearly incurred substantially higher costs than those raising over £3m, in which latter category can be found examples such as Apricot Computers plc.[3]

When we consider the distribution of issue size for OTC companies, however, we can see that for Placings, almost exactly 50% of the 76 companies represented in Table 8.9 made issues of less than £0.4m, and only 15 companies placed sums in excess of £1m. When Offers for Sale by OTC companies are examined (Table 8.10), it appears that the proportion of companies issuing amounts in excess of £1m was significantly greater, at around 40% of the total, than the corresponding value for OTC Placings. This is to be expected, in that this method of issue would have particular appeal for smaller offerings. Taking both methods of issue together, however, it remains true that well over half the OTC companies made issues of less than £1m.

The differences in the size characteristics of USM and Official List new entrants may be further examined by reference to mean profit levels before quotation. From Table 4.5 we know that mean profits for USM entrants were £0.54m (Table 4.5*B*) and that, out of 282 direct entrants to the USM, 197 (70%) recorded profits greater than £200,000 prior to quotation (Table 4.5*A*). For 170 OTC new entrants, on the other hand, we can see from Table 8.11 that nearly two-thirds either recorded losses or did not have eligible profits in the run-up to quotation. Of those 60 which did record profits, again two-thirds (38) fell within the smallest profit category of £0–200,000. It is here that we find

[3] Appendix Tables 13*A* and *B* show information on expenses relative to entrant capitalization, analogous to that produced for USM and Second Marché entrants.

TABLE 8.8 OTC Administrative Expenses, by Grouped Size of Issue for Offers for Sale

Grouped size of issue (£000)	No. of firms	Mean cost (£000)	Mean size of issue (£000)	Cost of issue (%)
Under–200	6	39	152	25.7
201–400	16	52	327	15.9
401–600	15	75	490	15.3
601–800	6	111	682	16.3
801–1,000	8	160	889	18.0
1,001–2,000	21	212	1,335	15.9
2,001–3,000	11	282	2,408	11.7
Over 3,000	7	325	6,970	4.7

Source: Extracted from data prepared for PMM (1986*b*).

TABLE 8.9 Mean Size of Issue (£000) and Number of Firms, by Percentage of Equity Issued, for OTC Placings

Equity issued	Under 200	201–400	400–1,000	1,001–5,000	Over 5,000
Under 25%	131 (8)	315 (12)	582 (3)	2,068 (3)	—
25–50%	200 (1)	287 (11)	604 (14)	2,353 (4)	—
51–75%	—	350 (3)	726 (2)	2,111 (4)	—
76–100%	—	300 (2)	636 (3)	1,659 (4)	—

Note: Figures in parentheses are number of firms (for a total of 76).

TABLE 8.10 Mean Size of Issue (£000) and Number of Firms, by Percentage of Equity Issued, for OTC Offers for Sale

Equity issued	Under 200	201–400	400–1,000	1,001–5,000	Over 5,000
Under 25%	140 (5)	296 (5)	659 (6)	1,557 (5)	—
25–50%	156 (4)	341 (13)	641 (15)	1,688 (18)	—
51–75%	—	341 (4)	590 (9)	1,948 (5)	—
76–100%	—	300 (1)	750 (2)	2,910 (11)	9,238 (4)

Note: Figures in parentheses are number of firms (for a total of 108).

TABLE 8.11 . OTC Pre-tax Profit Levels before Quotation, by Principal Industries

	Building	Electricals	Engineering	Misc. industry	Leisure	Property	Finance	Misc.	Row total
Losses/n.a.	6	19	10	18	18	12	12	15	110
Under £200,000	1	2	2	7	11	4	5	6	38
£200–400,000	—	1	—	1	1	—	5	1	9
£400–1m	1	2	1	2	2	—	—	—	8
Over £1m	—	2	1	2	—	—	—	—	5
Column total	8	26	14	30	32	6	22	22	170

Source: Adapted from PMM (1986*b*).

the essential difference between the USM and the OTC. Not only are OTC companies much smaller on average, but the nature of their profits histories indicates a much greater risk potential for investors. As a very rough approximation we can compare mean market capitalization values at quotation with corresponding values post-quotation. From Table 8.5, we can see that while for OTC companies as a whole mean market capitalizations have increased from a mean of £2.5m on quotation to £3.45m post-quotation, there is considerable variation around the mean. Partly this reflects the fact that in some cases issues were not fully subscribed at quotation.

We can note further that while 90 (42%) of OTC companies had BES status, 24 such companies were listed as having their quotations suspended or cancelled, or being in the hands of the receiver, out of a total of 36 listed in this category. For companies traded under the Stock Exchange's Rule 535(2) (previously 163(2)), it appears that the Exchange maintains only minimal checks (see e.g. Tait 1986). While companies' accounts are open for inspection by the exchange's quotations department, and while all offers to the public must, following the 1948 Companies Act, contain an accountant's report, in other respects the investor is not so well served. Interim accounts are unlikely to be available, and the submission of annual accounts may be delayed. Further, the quotations department can at any time withhold its dealing permission, while some of the '535(2)' companies have themselves the right to restrict transactions in their own shares.

The risk in the OTC market, represented in these very approximate illustrations, is that of relatively very new and small-scale enterprises. The fact that the market is concerned with relatively small companies, coupled with the reduced minimum requirement on proportions of equity to be made available, means that such modest volumes of stock are available as to render the concept of liquidity, if not meaningless, a very unlikely attribute of most OTC securities. The dependence on matching transactions means that a seller has to wait for a prospective buyer and vice versa. Similarly for those companies trading under Rule 535(2), matching means that, in the past, jobbers could not officially quote two-way prices (i.e. buying and selling).

Further, for OTC companies, as distinct from Rule 535(2) companies, transactions were dependent on in-house rules made by dealers, which lacked consistency across the market (Tait 1986). So, for example, some OTC sponsors required less regulation than the Stock Exchange did, with a less onerous general undertaking to be signed by the directors, which inevitably provided a lower level of protection for investors. Within this market we can distinguish two separate groups of OTC market-makers which sought to regulate their own members. The first, designated the Over-the-Counter market, was regulated by the National Association of Security Dealers and Investment Managers (NASDIM) and was recognized by the Department of Trade and Industry, which licensed its members as securities dealers. Only two of NASDIM's 640 members were active on the OTC. The larger of the two, Granville and Co., conducted a matched bargain market for 30 companies (often family-controlled), with an aggregate market capitalization of over £200m. The second group, OTC Trading, was regulated by the British Institute of Dealers in Securities (BIDS) and the Department of Trade and Industry, and has only four OTC market-makers. The largest of these over this period was Harvard Securities, which either singly or with others made a market in the securities of about 60 OTC companies.

The problem of OTC liquidity was compounded by the extent of competition between market-makers in this market. Table 8.12 summarizes, as of May 1985, the structure of the OTC market by market-makers, the number of securities in which they make a market, and the number of companies. The table distinguishes between those securities quoted on a dealing price and those quoted 'basis': that is, the price for the shares which would be quoted if any stock were available.[5] It provides a rank order both by number of securities and by number of companies for each market-maker, and further distinguishes securities by the number of market-makers in the security.

From Table 8.12 we find that for the UK OTC market, 68% of the companies were dealt in by only one market maker. In comparison the US OTC market has typically seven to eight market-makers for each NASDAQ security, with an average of 17.1 market-makers in each NASDAQ national market security at the end of 1982 (NASDAQ, 1986). Clearly, differences of this nature in the competitive structure of markets are likely to have implications for the liquidity of British OTC securities.

The USM and the Third Market

The decision by the Stock Exchange to introduce the Third Market as its own third-tier market can be regarded as a natural competitive response. Unlike the USM and Official List, shares of BES companies can be traded on the Third Market, but, as with similar shares traded on the OTC, restriction of the qualifying period of tax eligibility to five years will have a corresponding impact upon liquidity. Indeed, marketability of Third Market shares is perceived as a problem in its initial stages, with only about two market-makers in every stock and no minimum percentage of equity required to be in public hands (Alexander 1987).

In this sense, the Third Market may be little different from the OTC, except in one fundamentally important element. Investors in the Stock Exchange's Third Market do at least enjoy the advantage of a proper regulatory framework and the full protection of the Stock Exchange's compensation fund, which recompenses investors in the event of failure by a member firm.

[4] In other words, of the total 221 OTC companies at May 1985, there are 68 companies whose quoted 'price' does not necessarily correspond to any potential for dealing at that price.

TABLE 8.12 Ranking of OTC Market-makers by Number of Securities Traded

Rank	Name of market-maker	No. of securities[a]	No. of companies[a]
1	Harvard Securities	59	50
2	Prior Harwin Securities	21 + (8)	19 + (8)
3	Chartwell Securities	16 + (2)	14 + (2)
4	Afcor Investments	15 + (13)	15 + (13)
5	Hill Woolgar	9 + (2)	8 + (2)
5	UTC Securities Management	9 + (5)	7 + (5)
	Ravendale	6	6
	NK Cosgrove & Co.	8 + (2)	8 + (2)
	General and Overseas	6	6
	Schroder Asia Securities	2	1
	Baynard Securities	13	12
	Singer & Friedlander	2	1
	Security Exchange	1	1
	Procroft	2	2
	Fox Milton & Co.	1	1
	Peter Gawagan	1	1
	Cleveland Securities	1	1
	Guidehouse	7	6
	Granville	31	26
New	Ulster Venture Capital	1	1
New	Clarke Farquharson	2	2
New	Montano Securities	1	1
		172 + (74)	153 + (68)

Securities, by Number of Market-makers in the Security

One market-maker[b]	Two market-makers	Three market-makers	Four market-makers	Five market-makers	Total
106	35	11	2	3	157

[a] Traded at OTC dealing prices; number traded at OTC basis prices are given in parentheses.
[b] Granville and Co. account for 31 of these.
Source: USM/OTC Review (May 1985).

The fact that the Stock Exchange's quotations department does not vet Third Market companies before flotation (unlike Official List and USM companies) but leaves this to the sponsoring firm (which must itself be a member of the Stock Exchange) means that trading on this market incorporates a greater element of risk than trading on the two 'official' exchanges. Indeed, it has been argued 'that the Stock Exchange's unique contribution to company listing lies in its long developed expertise in prospectuses and periodic reporting. If these resources are not to be brought to bear on the Third Market the Exchange's case for exclusivity is weak' (*Financial Times* 1986). But further protection may be derived from the 1987 Financial Services Act, whereby broker–dealers in the Third Market are required to show that any investment in such securities will be a suitable investment for the client on whose behalf it is purchased. From the standpoint of the issuing company, the attraction is that, in the first instance, BES eligibiity may be retained, together with a greater element of informality in the listing rules. In contrast to the five years and three years of audited accounts required for Official List and USM listing, companies seeking to enter the Third Market need only produce one year's accounts, and even this may be waived for new start-ups able to demonstrate planned as distinct from realized profits.

While the Third Market does serve to widen the financing options available to small companies and affords a better framework for regulation than that available to OTC securities, the fundamental problem remains that of ensuring adequate liquidity of the shares concerned. Given that dealings in USM stocks amount to less than 2% of the turnover in UK listed securities, we can hardly expect the problem of thinness of trading not to be a feature of the Third Market as well, and problems readily apparent in bull markets are likely to be far more serious in recession. By contrast, the US OTC market can depend upon an extensive regional dealer network, comprising over 5,000 member firms, in which investors can trade through a computerized communications systems—a factor which contributes to greater market equilibrium.

Conclusion

In this chapter we have considered two different secondary market models with which to assess the relative performance of the USM. The first of these draws upon the experience of the Second Marché, whose foundation derives from the precedent set by the USM in the UK. The second and clearly relevant comparison is with the OTC market, which again had helped to prompt the foundation of the USM as well as that of the Stock Exchange Third Market. The French experience demonstrates the scope for regeneration of new issue markets following structural reform. The most notable difference between the USM and the Second Marché is in their relationship to regional equity markets. While the trend within the UK has been to emphasize the advantages of greater market centralization, this has not been the case in France. In both countries the second-tier markets have been viewed as a means towards regeneration of quotation in smaller, often regionally specialized, businesses, but in France it has also been regarded as a means towards revitalization of regional exchanges themselves.

Examination of the performance of Britain's OTC market indicates a number of salient differences. The undeniably smaller scale and relatively insignificant business history of many of its entrants inevitably entailed larger elements of risk. Clearly it would be wrong to expect an 'unregulated' market like the OTC to conform with standards of the 'regulated' markets of the Stock Exchange. But the problem of illiquidity of share-trading in such a market is undeniably compounded by the combination of firm characteristics with those of the market itself. In particular, the reduced minimum requirements on proportions of equity to be made available, together with the dependence on matching transactions, means that liquidity is the fundamental problem and one whose prospects are unlikely to be assuaged by a sustained bear market. This failure, inevitably endemic to a varying extent in 'junior' markets, is likely to serve as a continuing constraint upon innovations such as the Stock Exchange's Third Market.

9

Firms' Quotation Experience: The Implications for Corporate Policy

Introduction

This research has concentrated on what may be termed the *channelling efficiency* of the new issue market. The process by which firms gain quotation, raise new equity, and, for that matter, enable existing shareholders to liquidate their portfolios, is a matter of vital concern for economic growth. The fact of quotation allows firms access to capital—debt as well as equity—so that the terms on which such capital is available, the efficiency of the market mechanism, merits detailed consideration in its own right. Such analysis necessarily embraces the success of the USM in opening access to firms which might otherwise have been barred, or deterred, from entry to quotation, a feature which, as we have seen, characterized the new issue market of the 1960s and 1970s. Once quotation has been obtained, several interesting questions arise, beyond the scope of this study, as to how the USM may be used by companies quoted on the Exchange. The market may be used to finance subsequent growth, whether by the issue of new equity for acquisitions, or rights issues to fund direct investment. But there are also potential advantages for marketing and strategic development which accrue from enhanced public status, which have so obviously benefited such household names as Body Shop or Tie Rack. This, however, is critically dependent upon access to the new issue market in the first instance, and it is upon this specific aspect of market performance, and the structural reform which the USM so conspicuously embodies, that this research has focused.

In Section I of this chaper we are concerned first to draw together our various findings from preceding chapters, primarily in terms of the impact of the USM upon access and experience of the firms themselves. In Section II we develop an integrated analysis of issuing costs, both administrative and market pricing, and their implications for corporate policy. We consider the benefit of quotation in relation to the overall transfer of wealth involved in market pricing as well as deadweight issue costs. We complete this section by discussion of the implications for companies of transfer from the USM to the Official List, primarily in terms of the impact upon total costs of securing a full listing. Experience of the transfer process in the USA has generated a not insignificant debate upon such firms' resultant stock market valuation.

I Access to the USM and the Experience of Firms

The Stock Exchange established the USM in response to the stagnation of quotations business during the 1970s and in response to potential competitors in less formalized or regulated equities trading. The scarcity of new business during the period of recession following the oil shock of 1973/4, reopened discussion of a financing 'gap' for small, growing firms. Without access to secondary markets in their equity, such firms have restricted access to the volumes of both equity and lending required for their independent growth.

The first seven years of the USM were accompanied by a general resurgence in both UK and world equities markets. This backdrop is necessary in order to frame the USM's own success; and the resurgence of quotations business into the Official List is as remarkable as has been the rapid growth of new quotes of USM companies.

Chapter 4 examined some of the features of USM entrants. Businesses quoted there are generally smaller, newer, faster-growing. They have been successful in terms of sustaining their quotations during their early years on the market, with relatively few failures, suspensions, or takeovers by other firms. In contrasting the industrial classification of USM firms with those entering the Official List, however, it has been seen that USM firms are not radically different. There is no evidence from this research to suggest that the USM, by contrast with the Official List, is associated to a greater extent with new technology industries. But access has been afforded to firms which previously either could not or would not have obtained quotation on the Official List. The relaxation of requirements with respect to trading history and the reduction in the minimum proportion of equity to be issued to 10% have undeniably encouraged the growth of the USM, as a substantial number of USM new entrants have taken advantage of the relaxation in the requirement for a five-year record. While it is apparent from Chapter 4 that USM firms are, generally, of a size and history which could qualify them for Official List entry, it is nevertheless possible for (extremely) small issues to be floated on the USM, issues which otherwise would not have been able to obtain a quotation. Beyond this we can note the relatively greater incidence of new money issues raised by USM entrants by contrast with new entrants to the Official List. The significance of this lies not just in the shift from a relatively passive role for the new issue market—that of providing liquidity for executors and representatives of deceased shareholders—to a more pro-active role of generating new capital, whether for expansion or the transformation of firms' financial structure.

The popularity of the new USM amongst aspiring entrants, the use of USM status to raise new money and to make acquisitions, and the continued presence in the USM of the great majority of entrants suggest that it offers considerable benefits. The attitudinal research of studies such as that of Ransley (1984) would also confirm that: 80% or more of responding entrants perceived advantages in trading status, capital availability, or strategic outlook, or a combination of these factors (as reported in Bannock and Doran 1987: Table 3.7).

The impact of administrative expenses

The administrative costs of entry were analysed in Chapter 5. Barriers to entry for prospective newly quoted firms seeking admission to the USM were found to have been significantly reduced, with percentage costs for obtaining a placing on the USM being significantly lower than on the Official List, even allowing for the effects of firm/issue size. This research confirms the known influence of the method of issue upon relative costs, but highlights the major cost disadvantage experienced in the 1980s by the use of the Placing for direct entry to the Official List. The existence of scale economies in the new issue market was subjected to a comprehensive re-examination in terms both of administrative expenses and, in Chapter 7, market pricing costs, and found to exhibit a classic size effect in relation to the size of issue involved, among several variables considered (through means and correlation analysis) as likely to produce this effect.

This is the first study to provide a detailed analysis of the relative costs incurred by progression from the USM to the Official List. In terms of the cost of progression to the ultimate destination of the Official List, it seems clear that as far as administrative expenses alone are concerned, smaller firms would still benefit by deferring entry until able to take advantage of scale economies available to Placings on the USM and then to proceed to the Official List by way of Introduction: while the USM has undeniably facilitated the entry of smaller firms to quotation, and has restored costs of quotation to the levels prevailing between 1967 and 1973, it has not altered the fact of significant economies of scale in the issuing process. The threat moved the Stock Exchange in 1986 to relax its rules for listing on the Official List. In regard to Placings it has ruled that, providing prior authorization is gained from shareholders, a company will be allowed to set aside the pre-emption rules and to place as much equity as it chooses, without offering any to existing shareholders (Stock Exchange 1986a). This move seems likely to improve the attractiveness of the main market for entrants and advisers, but may, by further reducing the number of public offers, destabilize the market for Offers for Sale and Tenders.

The relationship with suppliers of debt: firms adherence to target gearing ratios

In our original objectives for this research we sought to develop a model with which to obtain further insights into the decisions behind firms' wishes to seek a market quotation, with specific reference to their financial structure. The relationship between suppliers of debt, particularly the banking system, has long been canvassed as posing a problem in the UK in comparison with other countries. The long-standing complaint, investigated by the Bolton Committee, was that smaller firms, in particular, were more dependent upon bank finance, and that this could put them at a disadvantage due to the alleged conservatism of such lenders. Specific arguments have been examined on the extent to which access to the new equity market was sought by firms faced with capital rationing. This might apply either from evidence of constraints on borrowing pre-quotation which are eased by access to the new equity market, or evident changes, in either direction, of firms' debt ratios.

The financing norms of business

Implicit in any notion of a 'distortion' of the debt ratio of the pre-quotation business is the belief that there are optimal or target levels of gearing which the firm would prefer and which would benefit the shareholder through a lower average cost of capital for the business. The literature suggests that there may be 'target' levels of the debt ratio (as in Marsh 1982): clearly, a rational destination is a prerequisite for finding rational, systematic debt behaviour in entrants. We find that firms do appear to be working towards target debt ratios.

However, in the extensive empirical literature on determinants of debt there are few signs that firms' choice of debt levels have economically relevant and significant causes (see, again, Marsh 1982). In analysis of this data on debt levels, debt behaviour, and firm characteristics, we have found little evidence in support of hypotheses which would link gearing to industry, riskiness, yields, or other factors. Firm size is associated with significantly higher debt ratios in the USM, but newly quoted firms' behaviour and levels of gearing reveal no patterns of targets for the gearing ratio. The fact that firms involved are at critical stages of economic development and are likely to have different organizational structures and managerial processes may help to explain the lack of evidence regarding a common or optimal debt structure. We do however find that firms are moving towards something which they see as a target, by their choice of the method of entry and the raising of new money. That the destination is largely obscure would suggest that the selection and pursuit of a debt ratio by firms, which forms such an important aspect of their entry to quoted status, is an informational or signalling medium as much as an optimization process. Or, it may be that these firms' managers exercise wide discretion in selecting some financial structure which is appropriate to their own culture and their attitudes towards risk, control, and earnings.

The operation of markets

The conclusions and practical implications to be drawn from this analysis concern advisers' treatment of entrants, the regulation of entrants' prospectus disclosure, and, of course, entrants' use of the USM and Official List. The particular financial structure adopted by firms which become quoted does not appear to be of much significance and is likely to be an accident of the past access of the firm to financing sources, not a product of good or poor past management. Hence entrants should be encouraged to use quotation as an opening for restructuring their finances, when the costs of doing so can be shared with the costs of quotation. On the other hand, it would be difficult to justify any particular structure more rational than the one with which it happens to arrive initially.

One unanticipated feature of the data is the extent to which the UK USM has been characterized by entrants with little or no debt rather than over-extension in debt. In contradiction of the argument, advanced on the basis of a small sample by Hutchinson *et al.* (1988), that USM entrants were small firms in financial distress through over-borrowing, we find here that it is more characteristic of the USM that its entrants have been debt free, that their growth as unquoted businesses has been largely equity financed. This remains an instance of a financing 'gap' occasioned by any unjustified barriers to becoming quoted, but the nature of that gap is not associated only with debt. The larger incidence of low-geared entrants within the USM firms when compared with the Official List entrants may well suggest that the USM, in lowering the entry barriers to quotation, has been of great importance in opening up the access to debt financing for these growing, independent businesses.

The pricing of new issues

In Chapter 7 we addressed the question of the USM's efficiency as a new issue market and the extent to which, and how, it has altered the policy options open to firms. The scale of discounting on USM issues has been established through this work, with questions raised about the efficiency of a market which generated large premiums on such issues. Chapter 7 gives rise to several key conclusions.

First, by comparison with previous research, we found that during the first five years of the USM there seems to have been a shift in new entrant pricing, reinforcing the presumed 'conventions' of the Official List—past growth signals, yields, and variability—towards an emphasis on company size, security of information, and a reflection of the equity's specific risk. Comparison of USM new issues with those on the Official List suggests that higher average discounts are associated with missing or otherwise inexact forecasts.

Second, we were able to provide conclusive tests of the price:pressure hypothesis both in the USM and in the contemporary Official List markets. In sum there is no evidence of this hypothesis having an effect on discounts, and there is no support for the hypothesis that larger issues either required, or receive, higher introductory discounts for flotation in the UK (a finding not without relevance for the government's privatization issues). Further, rather than confirming any positive association, multiple regression analysis confirmed the contrary hypothesis—that, in the USM, the smallest issues are marketed at the highest discounts. In Table 7.11 we reproduced the results for the statistically best-performing regression model on USM discounts. Both issue size and its square root are significant independent variables, and the sign of the square root of issue size is significantly negative. These size effects in the USM survived any alternative model structure, suggesting that size is not standing in for any other variable. The effects echoed the findings for the 1960s Official List, viz. that smaller issues by smaller firms attract disproportionately high levels of discount (Davis *et al.* 1974).

Third, it is also quite clear that USM discounts are erratic, that systematic influences are minor, and in particular that they are small in relation to the general uncertainty over pricing. The initial price 'performance' of a USM entrant is a poor guide to even first-year returns, and they are set apart from Official List entrants by their levels of specific risk as much as by any other criterion.

Fourth, the influence of the method of issue upon discounting is clear. The general use of the Placing involves significantly higher discounting for USM entrants: it is the single most important reason why USM discounts have been, on average, higher than those in the Official List. These discounts are wealth transfers which are much higher than underwriting charges. They impose costs upon vendor shareholders in the USM which may well be avoidable by a change of issue method, a change of timing, or a reduction in the price incentives offered to broker's and sponsors' clients.

II USM Costs and Corporate Policy

In this section we are concerned with three crucial matters: how beneficial to capital-raising costs and capacity is the quotation; how much do shareholders lose by their firm's equity entering the secondary market; and does a segmented secondary market promote or inhibit movement of equities from one market-place to another.

In contemplating the move to quoted status, shareholders require management to balance the benefits of quoted status against the costs of entering secondary markets. The success of the USM can thus be measured by the degree to which it lowers and restructures entry costs in order that more businesses benefit from secondary tradability and that they do so earlier in their life cycles. In Chapter 5 the 'deadweight' entry costs of administrative expenses were analysed, and it was found that the USM's utilization of simpler, cheaper issuing procedures has considerably lowered the price of quoted status on the USM from the Official List levels applicable to entrants of similar size and history. This reduction in costs was most marked for smaller businesses using the Placing method.

Shareholders of unquoted businesses face additional costs during entry, however. Whenever shares are sold at a discount, there is a transfer of wealth from existing to new shareholders. When new money is raised, that transfer is effectively shared amongst all 'old' shareholders of the unquoted business; when existing shares are sold, the vendors of those shares bear the incidence of the transfer.

Clearly, where such transfers are non-trivial in scale, investors will be inhibited from investment in unquoted businesses, and the availability and cost of equity capital to such businesses will deteriorate. In addition, the relative attractions of merger or takeover in preference to an independent, quoted future will increase where wealth transfers at entry to quoted markets are sizeable. Third, businesses will choose a time and method of market entry according not only to the direct, deadweight costs of administration of the issue, but also to the size and incidence of the transfer costs to existing shareholders.

Conversely, purchasers in new issue markets will be influenced by their perceptions of wealth transfers during the issue process. Discounting will be attractive, but negative discounts (transferring wealth from applicants to vendors), will depress applicants' interest. In this section, the data on discounts is used to explore the impact of the USM on wealth transfers and the links with company strategy and investors' attitudes to prospective entrants are drawn out. The overall costs of the market—wealth transfers and deadweight issue costs—are combined in order to compare and contrast the new USM with the existing Official List market; and the evidence relating to those companies transferring between markets is examined to complete the picture.

The scale of transfers during entry

The scale of entry transfer is decided by three factors. First, whether any issue of shares needs to be made at entry; second, the size of the discount given in order to market any such issue; and third, the proportion of the business' equity which is involved in the sale. For Introductions, therefore, the extent of such transfers is zero. For other entrants, it can be derived from measures of discount (as above in Chapter 7) and the proportion of equity involved, as follows:

$$\text{Transfer} = \frac{\text{Discount percentage} \times \text{proportion issued} \times 100}{100 + \text{discount percentage}}$$

with 'Transfer' being the percentage of the company's market capitalization given by vendors to the new owners of the issued shares. Thus, for example, if an entrant to the Official List sells 30% of the company's equity and if the market price is 20% above the issue price, the amount of wealth transferred to new shareholders is 5% of the company's capitalization.[1] If a USM issue could be effected on the same terms, but involved a sale of only 10% of the equity, the costs of the transfer would be reduced to 1.67%.[2] The USM therefore has the potential to encourage quotation and to encourage investment in businesses prior to quotation by prospects of minimizing the costs to shareholders imposed by transfers of wealth as well as in deadweight costs.

In Table 9.1 it can be seen that, overall, sellers of USM shares bear smaller burdens than do sellers of Official List entrants. The average transfer, of 3.01% of company capitalization, is appreciably smaller than that for the Official List (3.77%). We must hedge this comparison around with caveats, however. First, Table 9.1 shows that there are wide variations in the wealth transferred. These vary greatly between methods of issue. We note in particular that USM Placings—the biggest group, and of the smallest issues—involve transfers which are on average substantially higher than for the Official List Placings

TABLE 9.1 Wealth Transferred on Entry, by Market Status and Method of Sale

Mean (%) No. of firms SD	USM entrant	OL entrant	Row total
Placing	3.29 205 8.25	1.55 9 3.32	3.22 214 8.10
Offer for Sale	0.91 21 3.77	5.14 35 6.58	3.55 56 6.02
Tender	1.50 10 4.60	2.50 22 6.14	2.19 32 5.65
Column total	3.01 236 7.85	3.77 66 6.20	3.17 302 7.52

Note: 'Wealth' is measured as the percentage of equity capitalization transferred from vendor shareholders to new shareholders.
Chi square = 134.41 with 2 degrees of freedom; significance = 0.0000.

[1] That is, $\frac{20}{120} \times 0.3 \times 100 = 5\%$.

[2] That is, $\frac{20}{120} \times 0.1 \times 100 = 1.67\%$.

and they are very variable. Indeed, in 4 out of 10 USM Placings, the transfer is not from vendor to new shareholders, but is the reverse, with shares trading in the market at values below those received in the sale.

This is, of course, the result of the high but very variable discounts observed on USM Placings. In terms of Offers for Sale (both fixed price and by Tender), the USM demonstrates its anticipated lowering of transfer costs. The only caveat to be made here is that the Official List entrants include seven of the government's issues of privatization equities. These involve both higher-than-average proportions of equity sold and higher-than-average discounts, making their wealth transfers nearly double that of the typical private sector offering on the Official List (the average privatization issue transfers 6.6% of company capitalization, as opposed to only 3.4% for a typical private sector issue).

These figures suggest that it would be in the interests of vendors either to use Offers for Sale more in the USM context, or to relax the proportion issued where Offers for Sale are made by the Official List entrants. USM Offers for Sale would seem to have been managed at relatively low costs to vendors in terms of transfers of their corporate wealth, whereas the Placing—now favoured by the Stock Exchange community, for more and larger entrants and issues—appears relatively expensive and erratic in its impact on the wealth of companies' owners.[3]

In looking simply at issue methods one can of course hide other systematic forces influencing wealth transfers. When comparing issues according to their industry class, as in Table 9.2, it is apparent that there are strong industry effects as well as, perhaps even in place of, the impact of method. The combination of discounting and issue proportion accentuates the disparities between sectors such as energy and minerals—with considerable wealth transfers from buyer to vendors in the USM—and those of management services, or of communications and leisure industries, where transfers towards new USM owners were double those experienced by Official List entrants.

For substantial numbers of USM entrants, there was no option of a quotation on the Official List. These companies were too young, too small in profits or experience, incapable of making the commitment to accurate forecasts or of satisfying requirements for wide shareholding. This research has shown that the costs to such businesses of gaining a USM quote have been commensurate with the costs that would have been faced if they had waited for eventual Official List eligibility. Deadweight, administrative costs, as demonstrated in Chapter 5, have been contained within the limits familiar from Official List experience. Discounting transfers, as seen in the preceding section, have been very variable but, due to the smaller proportions of equity

[3] One must, in fairness, note that in the USM, Offers for Sale are likely to be reserved for the most secure and easiest valuation problems; the distinctions between methods, transfers, and variability stemming from the entrants as well as, or rather than, the methods.

TABLE 9.2 Wealth Transferred on Entry, by Market Status and Industry Group

Mean (%) No. of firms SD	USM entrant	OL entrant	Row total
Distribution and other	2.59 72 4.68	4.38 16 4.15	2.92 88 4.62
Communication and leisure	5.42 25 8.38	1.49 3 3.32	5.00 28 8.05
Traditional manufacturing	2.87 16 3.89	4.01 10 9.32	3.31 26 6.38
Electronic and process industry	3.52 46 4.74	5.01 20 6.68	3.97 66 5.39
Energy and mineral exploration	−15.94 6 29.33	2.28 3 9.95	−9.87 9 25.41
Management services	3.87 71 6.88	1.95 14 4.68	3.56 85 6.59
Column total	3.01 236 7.85	3.77 66 6.20	3.17 302 7.52

Note: Wealth is measured as the percentage of equity capitalization transferred from vendor shareholders to new shareholders.
Chi square = 11.82 with 5 degrees of freedom; significance = 0.0373.

issued, have involved transfers which are on average comparable with Official List norms.

The total cost barrier faced by entrants' shareholders can, crudely, be found by adding the deadweight losses of issue administration to the wealth transfers of discounting. On such a basis, the average USM share sale incurred total costs of 5.49%: in the Official List total costs averaged 6.15%. The USM, therefore, has offered businesses earlier quotation at the same or lower costs of entry when compared to the Official List.

Two groups of issues remain to be considered. First, we must note that, for USM Introductions, quoted status was acquired both earlier and with lower entry costs than for Official List entrants. Paradoxically, however, few USM entrants, and especially USM Introductions, have transferred onto the Official List. Given the considerable overlap between the two samples' characteristics (size, industry, profitability, post-quotation behaviour), the question arises as to why—if a full, Official List quotation is more valuable than one on the USM—have more USM entrants not shifted to the main market.

Transfer to the Official List: the effect upon market valuation

This brings us neatly to the second 'missing' group of issues: those 41 companies which *do* transfer. In Chapter 5 it was noted that these companies were typically reaching the Official List by an Introduction, but subsequent to a share sale, by Placing, on the USM. Such a combination accelerated the breadth of shareholding required for Introduction status and brought forward the benefits of quotation while maintaining aggregate administrative costs at levels similar to those for direct Official List entrants. However, only a small minority (12%) of USM entrants had so far opted to make the transfer, although changes in the listing rules introduced at the beginning of 1985, with the effect of making transfer from the USM to the Official List more expensive, may encourage a shift towards direct entry to the latter (Unsworth 1986). When we examined the impact of shifting from USM to the Official List, one reason was readily apparent. Where USM firms have moved to the Official List, their share price has dropped rather than risen. On average, and after adjustments for rights and bonus issues during the transfer, prices of shares fell by 7.79% from the last-quoted USM levels. The majority of these 41 transferring Official List entrants were medium to large businesses with capitalization above £7.5m (in 1980); and, if anything, the larger transferees displayed higher falls in capitalization (−9% for the 26 of above £7.5m capitalization).

The size and consistency of these adjustments in company capitalization are surprising, not only in the context of a hypothesis that USM trading will be, *ceteris paribus*, less valuable than Official List trading, but also in the light of the extensive US literature on trading location and capitalization. In repeated and detailed US studies on the price and liquidity effects of changing location—between NASDAQ and Big Board (Baker and Spitzfaden 1982; Phillips and Zecher 1982; Dhaliwal 1980), and variously from OTC to Big Board and between the Boards (Dubofsky and Groth 1984), it has been concluded that 'listing status does not affect risk or the cost of capital for companies of similar asset size' (Phillips and Zecher 1982: Abstract). The debate has been a long one in the US, from Furst's original sceptical studies (Furst 1970), through the equivocal results of Merjos (1963) and Dhaliwal (1980), who found OTC securities rated lower than equivalent Big Board stocks, to the contemporary consensus that the specific trading location within the US is of no discernible advantage (Baker and Spitzfaden 1982;

Cooper, Groth and Avera 1983; Dubofsky and Groth 1984). There is, in contrast, US evidence from McConnell and Sanger (1987), of a price shift (they call it a 'puzzle') consistent with that found here.

In this context the finding that UK companies' capitalization fell when transferring from the USM to the Official List requires explication: if both markets are efficient, the change in location should, by hypothesis and US experience, be seamless; if the USM is, as designed, a 'junior' market, the Official List rating should, by hypothesis, be higher than that of the USM

There might be several explanations for this phenomenon. First, it may be that the USM is more efficient than the Official List and thus supports a higher price for assets of equivalent status. Given the known characteristics of the two markets in information, liquidity, and the thinness of trading, this can be dismissed as absurd. Alternatively, there may be technical considerations connected with the transfer. It is, however, hard to construct sustainable factors which would produce the required fall across the transfer.

One possibility is that USM equities benefit in value and liquidity from institutional practices. Thus, many funds operate percentage rules as to their weight in USM equities. In this context when a strong USM equity transfers to the Official List, into a peer group of strong quoted shares, it may lose substantial institutional support into the medium term. Without detailed attention to such institutional practices and reactions, to announcement effects, and to the analysis of pricing both prior to USM suspension and subsequent to Official List dealing, we can neither confirm nor exclude such technical factors.

Again, it might be argued that increased competition from jobbers (now market-makers) in the Official List will secure efficient trading at more competitive, lower, bid prices: but it stretches credibility that this could account for an average drop of some 8%. Of more appeal is the hypothesis that transferred shares are rerated, downward, by analysts when they join the Official List. That is, that brokers' and analysts' signals are conditioned by location in addition to fundamentals; and that equities' rating *vis-à-vis* their peers in their particular location has a systematic effect on their price. Indeed, attention has been drawn to the fact that USM companies on the whole receive more attention than the smaller but otherwise similar companies on the main market, through specialist USM analysts and press comment, which contributes to their superior rating on the USM.[4]

Such a crude signal from market location would account for the observed drop in values but would reflect poorly upon the efficiency of the USM (or of the Official List, of course). It is, however, a consistent and plausible explanation of the phenomenon. Certainly it is necessary that more detailed

[4] Thus USM businesses receive frequent publicity through promotional activity by sponsors, accountants, brokers, and the media. The point is taken up by Unsworth (1986) and *Investors Chronicle* (1986).

analysis is undertaken of these transfers, in order to tease out the hypothesis and to determine whether, in the UK, exchange location is a determinant of equity costs and values.

This hiatus in valuation, with USM entrants facing downwards rerating as they join the Official List, leads to increased segmentation of the market. At one level, the OTC markets are fuelled by the equities of BES-supported businesses, where transfer to USM or Official List is inhibited for tax reasons. This has trapped firms and investors in relatively thin, unstable, and uncertain markets, with little competition among market-makers and large dealing spreads. At another level, firms are joining the USM and experiencing higher capitalization, with lower equity costs of capital, than they would if they were joining or transferring to the Official List.

From the data here, we cannot tell whether this novel barrier to Official List entry is offset by the prospects of the larger volumes of financing, or by the systematic impact of listing on other capital costs and volumes. It is readily apparent that a minority of USM entrants do wish to 'progress' to the Official List, and that they have done so in the past despite the fall in the value of their business' equity.

Conclusion

The most obvious yardstick for assessment of the significance of the USM is whether it has opened up opportunities for firms which previously had been denied access to the new issue market. We have found that access has been made available for newer, smaller firms with more irregular profit records and indeed unconventional financing experience. Given that formal opportunities for entry have been relaxed, the next matter for concern is the cost at which entry is attainable. In this chapter we have integrated the burden of deadweight, administrative expenses with that of market pricing costs to assess the overall burden on entry to the USM or Official List. For firms whose 'status' would have warranted direct entry to the Official List in the period considered it would have been cheaper to have obtained quotation on the USM. But for those firms which did not meet the more exacting requirements for quotation on the Official List, it is clear that although the USM has enabled them to obtain quotation, the terms on which they have done so have inevitably been subject to scale economies.

10
Epilogue

In our concluding chapter we seek first of all to round off our analysis by a brief consideration of two main factors which must inevitably impact upon the future performance of the USM. Deregulation of financial services—the 'Big Bang'—had important implications not just for 'secondary' transactions in equities but for 'primary' new issues as well; and particularly for those of smaller firms. Response by the Stock Exchange to allow greater competition, in particular access to its markets for international financial institutions, inevitably bringing with it large firms of US and Japanese brokers (and investment bankers) has served to emphasize a competitive response based on the efficiency of large volume transactions. To this may be linked a second factor—the October 1987 collapse in share prices, and the inevitable reinforcement of attitudes disposed towards greater discrimination by investors and brokers. How this might impact upon the USM (or, for that matter, the Third Market), is a matter which we must also consider. Finally we need to stand off from this statistically based survey of firm and market behaviour to speculate on broader implications.

The Stock Exchange, Financial De-regulation, and the USM

Further important influences upon the USM and the Third Market arise from the revolution in security trading occasioned by the deregulation of financial services. The traditional *modus operandi* of the City had been that of a series of relatively segmented financial markets. So, for example, equity markets on the Stock Exchange had been essentially markets in the securities of British companies, albeit with some foreign representation. In the United States and Japan, large international securities firms had developed from an original basis of stockbroking to provide a comprehensive range of financial services. Such competition reflected in part the massive advance in information technology which has sharply reduced the costs of international transactions and limited the extent to which these need to be bounded by any particular location. The threat to the traditional monopoly of the Stock Exchange emphasized the importance of a competitive response embodying significant structural reform.

The catalyst was the opening up by the Stock Exchange of its facilities for membership. From March 1986 the Exchange allowed 100% ownership of existing member firms by outside organizations. This in turn has prompted a series of mergers between Stock Exchange member firms, traditionally based on personal membership through partnerships, and companies outside the Stock Exchange, largely British and overseas banks with joint-stock structures. The entry of Merrill Lynch from the USA and Nomura Securities from Japan marked the physical presence in the UK of world competition from overseas securities houses, much larger than their UK counterparts, whose growth, and participation in all financial markets, had been constrained by the rigidities of the British financial system. The outcome of this process, compounded by the abolition of single capacity (i.e. the strict separation of broker and jobber) together with the removal of minimum fixed commission on share transactions, is that of a financial revolution in which differences in financial markets, whether of historical accident or by virtue of location, are likely to be subsumed within an international arena.

Following deregulation, equities listed on the various Stock Exchange markets have been divided into four categories, each of which determines the obligations of the competing market-makers. The most actively traded equities, representing in the first instance 62 major UK companies, have been designated as Alpha securities. These represent 56% of the 1986 UK market capitalization and approximately 50% of turnover value. The Beta category is represented by somewhat less actively traded securities, embracing initially 453 stocks, including some USM stocks. The Gamma category requires market-makers to maintain indicative two-way prices and to make a firm price on enquiry. The final category, Delta, carries the least requirement upon market makers. The Gamma and Delta categories are likely to involve the most substantial proportion of USM and Third Market securities. Here we may note preliminary Stock Exchange research findings arising from an investigation of the effect of deregulation upon security trading. They find that, corresponding with greater competition in the market making for Alpha securities, there is a reduction in market-making capacity at the lower end of the scale. While the Stock Exchange has always sought to ensure that securities quoted on its Exchanges were dealt in by at least two jobbers, it finds that the obligation on market-makers to run a book in unprofitable stocks cannot be sustained after Big Bang, with an implicit reduction in the depth of market-making available to smaller firms. It notes, however, that the reduction may be more illusory than real, in that for these very inactive stocks the system could in fact only operate on an order-matching service, similar to that offered on the OTC market (Stock Exchange 1987).

As part of its investigation of the preliminary effects of deregulation, the Stock Exchange also conducted research into the costs of dealing, as represented by the differences between the best bid and best offer price of a security (the 'touch'), which is used as a measure of the cost of the market-making service to the investor. The Stock Exchange found that Alpha shares recorded the lowest touches, followed by Betas, with Gammas, the thinnest market, having the highest touch (*Investors Chronicle* 1986). While in a market-based dealing system the market-maker carries the cost (and attempts to recover this by quoting a two-way price), in markets without market-makers, as characterized by Delta securities, the investors themselves bear the risk and cost of waiting and searching. As Chapter 3 indicated, such privately borne search and transactions costs lie at the heart of the secondary exchanges' advantage for investors, and the size of the market makers' touch is critical in the markets' attractiveness to investors and entrants.

Just as the Stock Exchange itself has recognized the underlying reality of illiquidity in some of its smaller company shares, so this factor is likely to be the chief distinguishing feature of substance in the future, rather than any formal distinction between second or third markets. 'Larger' USM companies, perhaps the top third, may benefit from deregulation by becoming more marketable, as jobbers continue to make markets and are joined by the firm's issuing brokers as well as by other dealers. But it is perhaps likely that many USM shares could find themselves relegated to the Delta division in which shares are dealt on only an infrequent bargain-matching basis, with the eventual implication for many such companies that the benefits of a public quotation become largely illusory. A by-product of the cessation of the stock jobbers' monopoly will be a correspondingly greater selectivity in the shares in which they deal with the result of a less liquid, even stagnant, market in trading in smaller, lesser-known companies. For smaller USM or Third Market companies with prospective market capitalizations of less than £5m, the principal hope may be the generation of continued financial intermediation through the emergence of specialist, small-company brokers from the ranks of venture capitalists. Here, for the smaller, regional-based company in particular, market-making may have to depend on regional brokers willing to make a market in their shares on a matching basis. By comparison we may note how the innovation of the French Second Marché has been responsible for a remarkable regional emphasis on equity trading in contrast to the fundamentally London-based activity of the USM.

The Advent of a Bear Market: The Implications for Second-tier Markets

Throughout most of their history, both the USM and the OTC have had the benefit of a long sustained equity bull market. Previous experience has suggested that the securities of smaller firms, by virtue both of their greater intrinsic riskiness together with their relative illiquidity, would suffer more in the advent of a bear market. We could therefore hardly expect the USM to be immune from fundamental structural change affecting world stock markets. The events of autumn 1987 confirmed this. We can distinguish between short-run and long-term effects, and the immediate consequences are clear.

Investors seeking cash liquidated holdings of small-company securities in narrow markets, inevitably incurring subtantial losses. Whereas in the first nine months of 1987, the closing phase of the bull market, the USM substantially out-performed the Official List, its fall, after the Stock Market collapse, exceeded that of the plunging FT All Share index. The Third Market, particularly characterized by thinness of trading, fared even worse, forfeiting all the gains of its first year of operation. In the short term, the emphasis by investors on 'defensive' investment, with greater weight attached to good profit records, a strong balance sheet, and sound management, does not favour investment in USM firms, let alone Third Market or OTC companies, many of which had excessively optimistic stock market ratings.

In the longer term, however, it is likely that smaller companies on the USM, with intrinsically greater flexibility than larger firms, should generate greater earnings per share than the average company quoted on the Official List. Indeed, it is not unreasonable to suppose that, despite a greater short-term volatility in share price, over the longer term the smaller company should out-perform larger firms, even in a sustained bear market. In terms of the effect upon firms' performance, as distinct from the interests of shareholders and potential investors, a depressing effect appears probable on use of the market, whether for new issues by previously unquoted firms or for rights issues. We should not exaggerate this, however, for the fact that over this period the USM effectively displaced the Official List as the main vehicle for a first quotation means that, on the assumption of continuing economic growth, it is to this market that firms will come.[1] In doing so, however, they may encounter a market likely to be more discriminating in its effective (as distinct from formal) requirements, with rather more emphasis on evidence of past performance and greater information disclosure and a probable shift towards standards effectively required for a full listing.

Small Firms and the Capital Market

Another dimension which we should note in any assessment of the USM is the way in which it has contributed to the promotion of the concept of successful entrepreneurship in the UK. From Chapter 2 we know that many firms enter the market to float shares on behalf of shareholders. At the same time the regular publication in the press of Touche Ross's features on USM millionaires has served to demonstrate success in an obvious way. All this must be seen in the overall context of a much more sympathetic climate for small firms in general, and of a public capital market process with a role for individual as well as institutional investors.

[1] Although the relaxation of restrictions on Official List Placings has revived the popularity of that market since 1986 (see Fig. 2.1).

For the companies themselves, as distinct from their present or potential shareholders, quotation on the USM can serve as a vehicle for the promotion of their image. In strategic terms this may have as much, if not more, value than that simply provided through access to a larger source of capital. Indeed, it is perhaps this feature which many firms' managers, interviewed after quotation, consider to be the most important benefit of the quotation process (see e.g. Binder Hamlyn, 1986; Bradley-Jones and Hussey 1985).

The events of the autumn of 1987 may be said to have concluded the first phase of the USM's development. It has emerged as the major innovation of the new issue market in this century, generating an example of structured reform to be followed by other countries. It has shifted the role of the stock market towards an emphasis on greater risk and return associated with investment in relatively small and relatively new companies, with potentially superior growth prospects. While the experience of a bear market may shift the parameters within which the USM operates, it is in the longer term likely to strengthen its position.

Appendix

Table 1 New Money Raised, by Entry Status

Count Row % Column % Total %	USM entrant	OL entrant	Row total
Under £200,000	86 80.4 34.1 26.7	21 19.6 30.0 6.5	107[a] 33.2
£200th–£400,000	68 93.2 27.0 21.1	5 6.8 7.1 1.6	73 22.7
£400th–£1m	57 87.7 22.6 17.7	8 12.3 11.4 2.5	65 20.2
£1–£5m	36 61.0 14.3 11.2	23 39.0 32.9 7.1	59[b] 18.3
Over £5m	5 27.8 2.0 1.6	13 72.2 18.6 4.0	18[c] 5.6
Column total	252 78.3	70 21.7	322 100.0

Chi square = 50.47 with 4 degrees of freedom. Significance = 0.0000. Missing = 12.

Note: Excluding all market transfers and Introductions.

[a] There were also 32 USM Introductions, 30 USM transfers by Introduction, 11 Official List Introductions and 33 transfers to the Official List by Introduction: all of which involved no new money for entrants.

[b] There were 2 issues involving new money in this band within transfer into the USM and 2 more within transfers into the Official List.

[c] There was 1 issue involving new money in this band within transfers into the Official List.

TABLE 2 Proportion of New Money in Issues, by Entry Status

Count Row % Column % Total %	USM entrant	OL entrant	Row total
None	49 71.0 19.6 15.3	20 29.0 28.6 6.3	69[a] 21.6
Under 30%	54 77.1 21.6 16.9	16 22.9 22.9 5.0	70 21.9
30–60%	60 74.1 24.0 18.8	21 25.9 30.0 6.6	81 25.3
Over 60%	87 87.0 34.8 27.2	13 13.0 18.6 4.1	100[b] 31.3
Column total	250 78.1	70 21.9	320 100.0

Chi square = 7.47 with 9 degrees of freedom. Significance = 0.0584. Missing = 14.

Average Proportion of New Money in Issues

Mean (%)	43.59	33.14	41.30
Count	250	70	320
SD	33.72	31.14	31.18

$F = 5.42$. Significance = 0.0205.
K–W chi square = 15.53, significance = 0.0014[a].

Note: Excluding all market transfers and Introductions.
[a] Plus Introductions as in n.[a] to Appendix Table 1.
[b] All five transfers in which sales were involved generated new money in this band.

TABLE 3 Correlation Matrix for Financial Structure Variables and Entrants' Size, Yield, Profitability, Risk and Issue Performance Measures

	1	2	3	4	5	6	7	8	9	10	11	12	13	14	15	16	17	18	19	20
Opening	—	0.44†	0.04	−0.62†	0.04	0.23†	0.56†	0.33†	−0.17†	−0.04	0.24†	−0.06	0.33†	0.09	−0.05	−0.16†	0.16†	0.24†	0.05	0.02
gearing		302	194	301	295	325	310	303	324	324	323	201	325	321	320	247	225	255	30	261
1st year	0.57†	—	0.21†	0.44†	0.32†	0.06	0.42†	0.03	0.23†	−0.03	0.06	−0.28†	0.13*	0.09	−0.23†	−0.16†	0.3	−0.09	−0.36*	0.01
gearing	110		191	301	295	302	287	281	301	301	300	189	302	301	300	231	210	241	29	247
3rd year	0.47†	0.68†	—	0.43†	0.01	0.03	0.26†	0.02	0.13†	0.17†	−0.02	−0.14*	−0.09	0.06	0.01	0.04	0.14	0.06	−0.25	0.31†
gearing	84	86		191	187	194	185	180	194	194	195	114	195	194	193	148	133	142	18	149
Change in	−0.26†	0.54†	0.27†	—	0.25†	−0.49†	−0.21†	−0.30†	0.33†	−0.02	−0.20	−0.19†	−0.23*	−0.05	−0.17†	0.02	−0.17†	−0.30†	−0.42†	−0.02
gearing	110	110	84		295	302	287	281	301	301	300	189	302	301	300	231	210	241	29	247
B:S	0.9	0.31†	0.32†	0.24†	—	0.10*	−0.03	0.11*	0.27†	−0.27†	−0.09	0.10	−0.15†	0.06	0.06	−0.04	−0.06	−0.35†	−0.51†	−0.07
ratio	106	109	83	106		295	280	274	295	294	293	187	295	295	294	226	206	237	29	242
Long-term	0.19*	−0.11	−0.29†	−0.32†	−0.02	—	−0.26†	−0.03	0.02	−0.02	−0.06	0.15*	−0.07	0.01	0.11*	0.02	0.01	−0.02	−0.36*	0.01
debt ratio	111	108	82	108	104		310	303	325	325	324	202	326	322	321	248	226	255	30	262
Creditors	0.50†	0.48†	0.49†	−0.03	0.01	−0.32†	—	−0.06	−0.08*	0.07	0.13*	−0.09	0.27†	0.15†	−0.03	0.02	0.00	0.14*	0.15	0.06
ratio	109	106	81	106	102	109		304	310	310	309	193	311	307	306	239	214	246	28	248
Overdraft	0.32†	0.19*	0.25*	−0.14	0.09	−0.00	−0.06	—	0.01	−0.07	0.04	0.21†	0.12*	−0.02	−0.01	0.06	0.10	−0.04	0.22	−0.01
ratio	108	105	80	105	101	108	107		303	303	302	190	304	300	299	233	208	243	28	248
Total	−0.03	−0.12	−0.10	−0.11	0.14	0.23†	−0.25†	−0.06	—	0.51†	0.10*	−0.05	−0.24†	−0.11*	−0.17†	−0.25†	−0.19†	−0.48†	−0.25	−0.10
assets	114	113	86	110	109	111	109	108		325	324	202	326	322	321	249	226	255	30	262
Equity	0.05	−0.05	−0.08	−0.12	−0.31†	0.12	−0.17*	−0.03	0.74†	—	0.34†	−0.03	−0.01	0.11*	−0.02	0.01	0.03	0.35†	−0.04	0.11*
capitalization	112	111	84	108	109	109	107	106	116		324	203	326	322	321	248	225	255	30	263

TABLE 3 Correlation Matrix for Financial Structure Variables and Entrants' Size, Yield, Profitability, Risk and Issue Performance Measures

	1	2	3	4	5	6	7	8	9	10	11	12	13	14	15	16	17	18	19	20
Issue size	0.24†	−0.01	−0.01	−0.27†	−0.05	0.09	−0.07	−0.01	0.71†	0.67†	—	−0.32†	0.60†	0.12*	−0.05	0.06	0.15*	0.24†	−0.20	−0.09
	114	113	86	110	109	111	109	108	118	116		203	325	321	320	248	225	253	30	261
Proportion	0.10	−0.25*	−0.27*	−0.34†	0.11	0.39†	−0.30*	0.27*	0.26*	0.16	0.17	—	−0.03	−0.05	0.13*	0.10	−0.09	−0.10	−0.28	0.03
new money	53	51	40	51	50	52	51	52	53	52	53	203		201	201	161	149	193	22	201
Proportion	0.32†	0.02	0.04	−0.32†	−0.25†	0.06	0.15	0.29*	0.16*	0.29†	0.35†	−0.01	—	0.07	−0.19†	−0.03	0.09	0.02	0.02	−0.13*
equity issued	113	112	85	109	109	110	108	107	117	116	117	52		323	322	249	226	255	30	263
Beta risk	−0.03	−0.08	−0.06	−0.04	−0.03	0.07	−0.21*	0.11	0.23†	0.25†	0.14	0.04	0.09	—	0.38†	0.02	0.08	0.19†	0.13	0.05
	113	112	85	109	108	110	108	107	117	115	117	52	116		322	245	223	253	30	261
Specific	−0.09	−0.14	−0.09	−0.06	0.00	−0.03	−0.18*	0.10	−0.15	−0.12	−0.13	0.20	−0.18*	0.15	—	0.12*	0.04	0.23†	0.02	0.13*
risk	113	112	85	109	108	110	108	107	117	115	117	52	116	117		237	249	249	26	209
Profits	0.23†	−0.06	−0.03	−0.30†	−0.03	0.31†	−0.06	0.19*	−0.05	−0.04	−0.04	0.16	0.06	−0.00	0.05	—	0.10	0.31†	−0.16	−0.00
variability	105	105	80	102	103	103	101	101	109	109	109	50	109	108	108		179	206	21	209
Profits	0.26†	0.28†	0.21*	0.00	0.18*	−0.04	0.25*	0.09	−0.12	0.05	−0.06	0.08	−0.08	0.04	0.06	0.10	—	0.31†	0.04	0.09
growth	87	88	68	85	86	86	85	86	91	91	91	41	91	90	90	91		188	24	189
Value:asset	0.26*	0.11	0.11	−0.12	−0.47†	−0.16	0.26*	0.11	−0.53†	0.03	−0.24*	−0.27*	−0.32†	−0.12	0.16	0.03	0.39†	—	0.17	−0.09
ratio	71	69	53	69	69	70	69	69	71	71	71	52	71	70	70	67	56		35	263
Subscription	0.01	−0.10	−0.11	−0.12	−0.13	0.01	0.09	0.23*	−0.07	0.15	0.16*	−0.08	0.01	0.04	−0.22	−0.00	0.11	0.02	—	0.20
ratio	48	49	38	48	48	47	46	46	49	48	49	40	48	48	48	45	36	47		30
Discount	0.20*	0.02	−0.11	−0.18*	−0.13	0.01	0.09	0.23*	−0.07	0.15	0.16*	0.02	0.46†	−0.11	−0.04	−0.06	0.09	0.43†	0.19†	—
on entry	102	102	77	100	98	100	99	99	105	103	105	52	104	104	104	96	84	70	48	

Figures are: Pearson's product-moment correlation coefficient
No. of valid pairs of observations
Coefficients significant at better than 5% are marked *; better than 1% marked †
USM results are reported above the diagonal, Official List below.

TABLE 4 Regression Analyses, Opening Gearing Regressed on Industry Sectors and Transformed Variables (dependent variable: gearing from prospectus)

	USM					Official List				
	Step	Change in R^2	t	Significant t	Beta	Step	Change in R^2	t	Significant t	Beta
Stepwise[a]										
Energy/minerals	1	0.11	−4.67	0.000**	−20.96					
PC—Risk	2	0.03	3.48	0.001**	3.82	2	0.05	2.41	0.018*	3.91
PC—Yields	3	0.03	3.45	0.001**	4.40	1	0.10	3.88	0.000**	5.30
Forced entry[b]										
PC—Yields			3.58	0.000**	4.71			3.33	0.001**	4.96
PC—Size			−0.84	0.399	−1.65			−0.84	0.404	−1.00
PC—Risk			3.36	0.001**	3.89			2.45	0.016*	4.22
Industry sector dummies[c]										
Communications/leisure			−0.27	0.790	−1.13			−0.74	0.459	−5.21
Manufacturing			0.71	0.476	3.16			−0.27	0.789	−1.41
Electronics/processing			−0.65	0.514	−2.32			−1.18	0.243	−5.36
Energy and minerals			−4.44	0.000**	−22.76			−0.99	0.323	−6.62
Management services			−0.36	0.719	−1.11			0.33	0.743	1.46
Consistent motive dummy[d]			−0.54	0.591	−3.63					

Note: Coefficients significant at better than 5% are marked *; better than 1%**.

[a] For USM, $R^2=17.2\%$, $F=22.25$, significance = 0.000**. For Official List, $R^2=14.3\%$, $F=9.28$, significance = 0.000**.

[b] For USM, $R^2=17.8\%$, $F=7.59$, significance = 0.000**. For Official List, $R^2=17.8\%$, $F=2.84$, significance = 0.007**.

[c] Leaving Distribution and Miscellaneous as the reference sector.

[d] = 1 if repay motive not followed; no inconsistent cases in Official List.

TABLE 5 Multiple Discriminant Analysis: Functions Estimated to Separate Entrants which Reduce Gearing from Those which Increase Gearing

	Eigen-value	Canonical correlation	Wilk's lambda	% correctly estimated	% improvement on random
USM: random allocation implies 50.00% *correct*					
Opening gearing	0.27	0.47	0.78**	71.52	43.04
+Industry dummies	0.31	0.49	0.76**	74.50	49.00
+Principal components	0.30	0.48	0.77**	72.52	45.04
+Inds and PCs	0.33	0.50	0.75**	73.51	47.02
+Inds and transforms[a]	0.36	0.52	0.73**	75.17	50.34
Official List: random allocation implies 50.15% *correct*					
Opening gearing	0.09	0.29	0.92**	70.00	39.58
+Industry dummies	0.16	0.37	0.86**	68.18	36.36
+Principal components	0.12	0.33	0.89**	67.27	34.54
+Inds and PCs	0.20	0.41	0.83**	65.45	30.90
+Inds and transforms	0.19	0.40	0.83**	74.55	49.10

[a] Total assets, profits variability, value:assets ratio, beta, specific risk, forecast yield, subscription ratio.

TABLE 6 Standardized Canonical Correlation Coefficients for MDA Analyses: Functions Estimated with Opening Gearing, Industry Dummies and Principal Component Scores

	Grouped on gearing change		Grouped on repayment declaration	
	USM	OL	USM	OL
Opening gearing	0.97*	0.67*	0.40*	0.10
PC—Forecast P:E/cover	0.26*	0.15	0.15	0.09
PC—Issue characteristics	0.05	0.38*	0.77*	0.58*
PC—Market risk	−0.14	0.23	0.23	0.17
PC—Firm size	0.19	−0.46*	0.32*	−0.25*
PC—New money	0.03	0.08	0.31*	0.36*
PC—Issue reception	−0.07	0.39*	0.14	0.55*
PC—Profits growth	−0.10	0.17	0.07	0.57*
Industry sector dummies[a]:				
Management services	−0.11	0.16	−0.26*	0.18
Communications/leisure	−0.15	−0.17	0.01	0.27*
Electronics/process ind.	−0.04	0.16	−0.32*	0.26*
Manufacturing	−0.12	0.26*	−0.01	0.22
Energy	−0.12	0.10	−0.20	0.06

Note: Coefficients over 0.25 are marked*.
[a] Leaving 'Distribution and Miscellaneous' as the reference sector.

TABLE 7 Mean Subscription Levels, by Method of Issue and Market Status

Mean No. of firms SD	Non-linear measure of subscription[a]			Linear measure of subscription[b]		
	USM entrant	OL entrant	Row total	USM entrant	OL entrant	Row total
Offer for Sale	0.84 19 0.96	1.19 31 0.70	1.06 50 0.82	22.71 19 25.46	36.35 31 37.52	31.17 50 33.83
Tender	0.47 7 0.39	0.34 22 0.45	0.37 29 0.44	4.41 7 4.85	3.32 22 2.88	3.58 29 3.39
Column total	0.74 26 0.85	0.84 53 0.74	0.81 79 0.78	17.78 26 23.25	22.64 53 32.95	21.04 79 30.04

[a] Measured by $\text{Log}_{10} \frac{\text{(Applications)}}{\text{Shares issued}}$.

Thus 0 denotes full subscription, positives denote oversubscription.
Chi square = 1.99 with 1 degree of freedom, significance = 0.1581.

[b] Measured by $\frac{\text{Applications}}{\text{Shares issued}}$.

Thus, 1 denotes full subscription, 10 denotes 10 × oversubscription, etc.
Chi square = 1.60 with 1 degree of freedom, significance = 0.2063.

TABLE 8 USM Share Issues: Average Discount, by Industry Sector and Method of Issue

Mean (%) No. of firms SD	Placing[a]	Offer for Sale	Tender	Other	Row total
Distribution and other	20.26 59 31.10	11.80 11 19.55	−9.92 2 6.44	22.83 4 45.00	18.38 76 30.20
Communication and leisure	43.01 23 44.71	20.37 2 5.36		14.17 3 13.57	38.30 28 41.84
Traditional and manufacturing	24.40 15 30.84		0.00 1 0.00	15.37 5 66.61	21.09 21 39.90
Electronic and process industry	26.22 36 33.60	2.52 5 9.99	25.04 5 34.61	60.80 8 76.98	29.04 54 43.03
Energy and mineral exploration	−21.86 4 39.38	−22.92 2 11.50		−7.50 2 32.66	−18.53 8 29.71
Management services	34.07 68 74.59	−20.00 1 0.00	7.99 2 17.31	39.99 3 77.83	32.88 74 73.04
Column total	27.92 205 52.01	5.59 21 19.46	12.13 10 28.12	32.08 25 61.74	25.92 261 50.78

13 out of 24 (54.2%) of the valid cells have expected cell frequency less than 5.0. Minimum expected cell frequency = 0.307. Chi square = 34.32 with 15 degrees of freedom. Significance = 0.0031.

[a] The differences in mean discounts for USM Placings grouped by industry sector are not statistically significant, with $F = 1.61$ for 5 degrees of freedom, significance = 0.1586.

TABLE 9 Official List Share Issues, Average Discount, by Industry Sector and Method of Issue

Mean (%) No. of firms SD	Placing	Offer for Sale[a]	Tender	Other	Row total
Distribution and other	14.95	26.61	2.35	8.49	17.78
	3	9	4	1	17
	18.79	16.52	12.21	0.00	17.86
Communication and leisure		0.59	33.43		11.53
		2	1		3
		6.26	0.00		19.47
Traditional and manufacturing	4.66	10.49	2.58		8.32
	1	7	2		10
	0.00	17.23	5.74		14.63
Electronic and process industry	−7.29	23.88	23.55		20.65
	2	11	7		20
	3.40	33.55	11.13		26.90
Energy and mineral exploration		43.87	−5.45		27.43
		2	1		3
		85.52	0.00		66.84
Management services	13.73	24.06	3.85	8.41	10.89
	3	4	8	2	17
	13.10	22.00	17.84	19.55	18.60
Column total	8.46	21.74	10.36	8.43	15.72
	9	35	23	3	70
	14.92	28.22	16.74	13.82	23.46

17 out of 24 (70.8%) of the valid cells have expected cell frequency less than 5.0. Minimum expected cell frequency = 0.129. Chi square = 11.10 with 15 degrees of freedom. Significance = 0.7454. Missing = 3.

[a] The differences in mean discounts for Official List Offers for Sale, grouped by industry sector are not statistically significant, with $F = 0.735$ for 5 degrees of freedom, significance = 0.6031.

TABLE 10 Regression Analysis, USM Sample

Order of entry	Independent variable	Coefficient	t	Sig. t	95% confidence interval	
					Low	High
Information states[a]						
	Constant	28.55	1.987	0.048*	0.2488	56.85
2	Precise profits record	−15.58	−1.254	0.211	−28.89	6.413
—	Precise forecast provided	−11.24	−2.097	0.037*	−30.21	−0.9516
	Placing dummy	21.03	2.374	0.018*	3.588	38.47
	Fixed price offer dummy	10.05	0.700	0.485	−18.22	38.32
3	Energy sector	29.33	−1.844	0.066*	−60.67	2.001
—	Management services sector	8.216	1.183	0.238	−5.463	21.90
—	Electronics sector	4.823	0.595	0.552	−11.13	20.77
—	Communications/leisure sector	17.23	1.756	0.080*	−2.094	36.54
6	Issue size	0.00307	1.989	0.048*	0.3046E-4	0.00611
1	Root issue size	−0.6982	−2.585	0.010**	−1.230	−0.1664
4	Specific risk	0.3939	2.194	0.029*	0.7475	0.1349
—	Forecast yield	−1.802	−1.470	0.143	−4.215	0.6113

TABLE 10 Regression Analysis, USM Sample

Order of entry	Independent variable	Coefficient	*t*	Sig. *t*	95% confidence interval	
					Low	High
Company structure[2]						
—	Constant	19.75	2.801	0.007**	5.687	33.81
—	Placing dummy	−9.286	−1.109	0.271	−25.98	7.410
—	Issue size	0.3008E-4	1.143	0.257	−0.2278E-5	0.8253E-4
—	Root issue size	−0.04162	−0.967	0.337	−0.1275	0.04421
—	Debt Ratio	0.1225	0.687	0.495	−0.2332	0.4782
—	Forecast yield	−0.7787	−0.720	0.474	−2.934	1.377
—	Proportion equity issued	5.117	0.291	0.772	−30.00	40.24
—	Proportion new money	0.0069	0.068	0.946	−0.1941	0.2079
Motive[c]						
—	Constant	42.12	6.497	0.000**	29.36	54.89
—	Loan repayment	6.097	0.771	0.441	−9.469	21.66
—	Acquisition	−2.708	−0.396	0.692	−16.16	10.75
—	Shareholder realization	−3.766	−0.594	0.553	−16.26	8.724
—	Issue size	0.00229	1.570	0.1177	−0.5812E-3	0.00515
—	Root issue size	−0.6303	−2.673	0.000**	−1.095	−0.1659

Note: '—' under Order of Entry indicates that these variables were not included in stepwise designs. All designs utilize a mean substitution method for missing values.

[a] $R^2=0.12249$; $F=2.97787$; significance $=0.0007$.**

[b] $R^2=0.04779$; $F=0.509$; significance $=0.8248$.

[c] $R^2=0.0379$; $F=2=072$; significance $=0.0693$.

TABLE 11 Regression Analysis: Market Reception

Order of entry	Independent variable	Coefficient	*t*	Sig. *t*	95% confidence interval	
					Low	High
Pooled sample of offers for sale [a]						
—	Constant	−11.42	−0.875	0.386	−37.60	14.77
—	Log (applications ratio)	17.76	4.523	0.000*	9.876	25.64
—	Index change	−66.60	−0.896	0.375	−215.9	82.67
—	Time lapse	0.1203	0.140	0.889	−1.607	1.848
—	Official List dummy	11.42	1.806	0.077*	−1.273	24.11
Tender issues [b]						
—	Constant	11.48	4.237	0.001**	6.082	16.88
—	Log (applications ratio)	−1.905	−0.317	0.752	−13.87	10.06
—	Index change	−59.96	−1.246	0.217	−154.8	35.66
All placings [c]						
—	Constant	72.12	4.317	0.000**	39.19	105.1**
—	Official List dummy	−18.20	−1.029	0.305	−53.33	16.75
—	Issue size	0.00551	2.592	0.010*	0.00212	0.00132*
—	Root issue size	−1.398	−3.094	0.002**	−2.288	−0.5070**
—	Index change prior to dealing	−136.15	−1.702	0.090**	79.98	−293.8*
—	Time lapse issue to dealing	−0.3152	−0.359	0.720	−2.046	1.415
—	Time trend	−0.2207	−0.954	0.341	0.2356	−0.06721
—	P:E ratio	0.2495	0.391	0.696	−1.009	1.508

Note: '—' under Order of Entry indicates that these variables were not included in stepwise designs. All designs utilize a mean substitution method for missing values.

[a] $R^2 = 0.360$; $F = 7.156$; significance $= 0.0001$.**

[b] $R^2 = 0.0276$; $F = 1.048$; significance $= 0.356$.

[c] $R^2 = 0.07140$; $F = 2.2784$; significance $= 0.0299$.

TABLE 12 Regression Analysis: Tender Issues

Order of entry	Independent variable	Coefficient	t	Sig. t	95% confidence interval Low	High
Risk and yield[a]						
—	Constant					
—	Official List dummy	−0.9156	−0.274	0.785	−7.576	5.745
—	Index change	−68.15	−1.455	0.150	−161.5	25.21
—	Specific risk	0.03762	0.430	0.667	−1.368	0.2120
—	Forecast yield	0.4060	0.550	0.584	−1.064	1.876
Structure and profits[b]						
—	Constant	13.87	3.319	0.0014**	5.537	22.20
—	Official List dummy	−1.734	−0.536	0.594	−8.191	4.723
—	Debt ratio	−0.00942	−0.087	0.931	−0.2256	0.2067
—	Proportion new money	−0.0204	−0.231	0.818	−0.1968	0.1559
—	Profits growth	−0.0231	−1.358	0.179	−0.05709	0.01083
—	Profits variability	−0.5932	−0.216	0.829	−6.058	4.871

Note: '—' under Order of Entry indicates that these variables were not included in stepwise designs. All designs utilize a mean substitution method for missing values.

[a] $R^2 = 0.0342$; $F = 0.6369$; significance = 0.6379.

[b] $R^2 = 0.0287$; $F = 0.420$; significance = 0.833.

TABLE 13 Administrative Costs for OTC Companies, by Grouped Capitalization

Grouped market capitalization	No. of firms	Mean capitalization (£000)	Mean cost (£000)	Mean cost as % market capitalization
Placings				
Under £1m	29	718	58	8.1
£1–2m	21	1,497	83	6.2
£2–3m	14	2,501	66	2.6
£3–4m	7	3,519	79	2.2
£4–5m	—	—	216	—
Over £5m	5	11,261	170	1.5
Offers for sale				
Under £1m	28	719	46	6.4
£1–2m	24	1,476	78	5.3
£2–3m	22	2,542	147	5.8
£3–4m	15	3,552	205	5.8
£4–5m	5	4,692	228	4.9
Over £5m	14	9,233	289	3.1

References

ALEXANDER, J. (1987), 'Another Share of the Risks', *The Times*, Jan. 31: 28.

ANSARI, S. L. (1977), 'An Integrated Approach to Control Systems Design', *Accounting, Organization and Society*, 2/2: 101–12.

ANTHONY, R. N. and DEARDEN, J. (1980), *Management Control Systems*, 4th edn. (Homewood, Ill.: R. D. Irwin).

BAKER, H. K. and SPITZFADEN, J. (1982), 'The Impact of Exchange Listing on the Cost of Equity Capital', *Financial Review*, 17: 128–38.

BANNOCK, G. and DORAN, A. (1987), *Going Public*. (London: Harper & Row). (Previously published (1985) as *Going Public*. London: Economist Publications.)

BAXTER, N. (1967), 'Leverage, Risk of Ruin and the Cost of Capital', *Journal of Finance*, 22/4: 395–403.

BERRY, R. and NIX, S. (1988), 'The Role of Ratios in Financial Statement Analysis', paper to the European Accounting Association, Nice, April.

BHAGAT, S., MARR, M. W., and THOMPSON, G. R. (1985), 'The Rule 415 Experiment: Equity Markets', *Journal of Finance*, 60/5: 1385–401.

BINDER HAMLYN (1986), *Going to the Market: A Survey of Businessmen's Experience of the U.S.M.* (London).

BLAZENKO, G. W. (1987), 'Managerial Preference, Asymmetric Information and Financial Structure', *Journal of Finance*, 42/4: 839–62.

BOLTON (1971), *Report of The Committee of Enquiry into Small Firms*. Cmnd 4811 (London: HMSO).

BRADLEY-JONES, R. and HUSSEY, R. (1983), *The U.S.M. Experience* (London: Spicer and Pegler).

—— and —— (1985), *The U.S.M. Experience: A Survey of Companies' Opinions* (London: Spicer and Pegler).

BRISCOE, G. and HAWKE, G. (1976), 'Long Term Debt and Realizable Gains in Shareholder Wealth: An Empirical Study', *Journal of Business Finance and Accounting*, 3/1: 125–35.

BREALEY, R. A., HODGES, S. D., and CAPRON, D. (1976), 'The Return on Alternative Sources of Finance', *Review of Economics and Statistics*, 58/4: 469–77.

BUCKLAND, R. (1982), 'Post-quotation Performance of New Issues', Management Centre Working Paper no. 230, Aston University, Birmingham.

—— (1987), 'The Costs and Returns of the Privatisation of Nationalised Industries', *Public Administration*, 65/3: 241–57.

BUCKLAND, R. and DAVIS, E. W. (1984), 'The Unlisted Securities Market', *Lloyds Bank Review*, 154: 32–43.

—— and —— (1987), 'Barriers to Entry in the Unlisted Securities Market: The Significance of Administrative Expenses', *Accounting and Business Research*, 17/68: 301–10.

BUCKLAND, R., HERBERT, P. H., and YEOMANS, K. A. (1981), 'Price Discount on New

Equity Issues in the UK and Their Relationship to Investor Subscription', *Journal of Business Finance and Accounting*, 8/1: 79–96.

CBI (1987), *Investing in Britain's Future: Report of the CBI City/Industry Task Force* (London: Confederation of British Industry).

COB (1985*a*), *Frais d'introduction au second marché*, January bulletin (Paris: Commission d'Operation de Bourse.)

—— (1985*b*), *L'Année boursière*. (Paris: Commission d'operation de bourse).

—— (1986), *L'Année boursière*. (Paris: Commission d'operation de bourse).

COLLIER, P. and DAVIS, E. W. (1985), 'The Management of Currency Transaction Risk by UK Multinational Companies', *Accounting and Business Research*, 15/60: 327–34.

COOPER, K., GROTH, J. C., and AVERA, W. E. (1983), 'Liquidity, Exchange Listing and Common Stock Performance', unpublished working paper. Texas A&M University (mimeo).

COUTTY, A., LAMBERT, F., PETTELAT, F., and MOLLIER-CARROZ, L. (1984),'Rush sur la bourse bis: Le second marché', ESC, Dijon (mimeo).

CURRAN, J. (1986), *Bolton Fifteen Years On: A Review and Analysis of Small Business Research in Britain 1971–1986* (London: Small Business Research Trust).

DAVIDSON, J. H. (1987), *Offensive Marketing*, 2nd edn. (London: Penguin Books).

DAVIS, E. W. and YEOMANS, K. A. (1976), 'Market Discount on New Issues of Equity: The Influence of Firm Size, Method of Issue and Market Volatility', *Journal of Business Finance and Accounting*, 3/4: 27–42.

DAVIS, E. W., YEOMANS, K. A., and BUCKLAND, R. (1974), *Company Finance and the Capital Market: The Effects of Firm Size*. Department of Applied Economics Occasional Paper No. 39 (Cambridge: Cambridge University Press).

DERMER, J. (1977), *Management Planning and Control Systems: Advanced Concepts and Cases* (Homewood, Ill.: R. D. Irwin).

DHALIWAL, D. S. (1980), 'The Effect of Exchange-Listing on a Firm's Cost of Equity Capital', *Securities and Exchange Commission Capital Market Working Papers* (Washington D.C.: SEC).

DIMSON, E. (1979), 'The Efficiency of the British New Issue Market for Ordinary Shares', thesis, London Business School.

DOWNES, D. H. and HEINKEL, R. (1982), 'Signalling and the Valuation of Unseasoned New Equities', *Journal of Finance*, 37/1: 1–10.

DUBOVSKY, D. A. and GROTH, J. C. (1984), 'Exchange Listing and Stock Liquidity', *Journal of Financial Research*, 7/4: 291.

ERNST, M. (1984), 'Le second marché boursier français: Fonctionnement et evaluation', Faculty of Social Sciences, University of Notre Dame de la Paix, Namur (doctoral thesis: mimeo).

Financial Times (1986), Editorial, May 29.

FIRTH, M. (1977), *The Valuation of Shares and the Efficient Markets Theory* (London: Macmillan).

FRANKE, G. (1987), 'Costless Signalling in Financial Markets', *Journal of Finance*, 42/4: 809–22.

FURST, R. (1970), 'Does Listing Increase the Price of Common Stocks?' *Journal of Business*, 49/2: 174–80.

GHANDHI, J. K. (1964), 'Some Aspects of the Provincial New Issue Market', *Bulletin of the Oxford Institute of Statistics*.
GROSSMAN, S. J. and HART, O. D. (1982), 'Corporate Financial Structure and Managerial Incentives', in J. J. McCall (ed.), *The Economics of Information and Uncertainty* (Chicago, Ill.: University of Chicago Press).
GUPTA, M. K. (1969), 'The Effect of Size, Growth and Industry on the Financial Structure of Manufacturing Companies', *Journal of Finance*, 24/3: 517–29.
HEDDERSON, J. (1987), *SPSSX Made Simple* (Belmont, Calif.: Wadsworth Publishing).
HEINKEL, R. and SCHWARTZ, E. (1986), 'Rights versus Underwritten Offerings: An Asymmetric Information Approach', *Journal of Finance*, 41/1: 1–18.
HENDERSON, R. F. (1950), *The New Issue Market and the Finance of Industry* (Cambridge: Cambridge University Press).
HUTCHINSON, P., MERIC, I., and MERIC, G. (1988), 'The Financial Characteristics of Small Firms which Achieve Quotation on the UK Unlisted Securities Market', *Journal of Business Finance and Accounting*, 15/1: 1–20.
IBBOTSON, R. G. (1975), 'Price Performance of Common Stock New Issues', *Journal of Financial Economics*, 2: 235–72.
Investors' Chronicle (1986), Editorial, Aug. 8.
JOHN, K. (1987), 'Risk-shifting Incentives and Signalling through Corporate Capital Structure', *Journal of Finance*, 42/3: 623–42.
KEANE, S. M. (1983), *Stock Market Efficiency: Theory, Evidence, Implications* (London: Phillip Allan).
KEELEY, M. (1986), 'Raising Equity: The Problem of Setting the Issue Price', in M. Firth and S. M. Keane (eds.), *Issues in Finance* (Oxford: Phillip Allan).
KEENAN, M. (1970), 'The Great SERM Bubble', *Journal of Finance*, 25/(papers and proceedings): 243–73.
KELLAWAY, L. (1986), 'Criticism as Expenses Increase', *Financial Times Unlisted Securities Market Supplement*, 27 Jan., p. 3.
KNOWLMAN, N., POINTON, G., and WATKINS, D. (1985), *The Operation and the Effectiveness of the Business Expansion Scheme* (London: Small Business Research Trust).
LEE, C. (1985), 'Stochastic Properties of Cross-sectional Financial Data', *Journal of Accounting Research*, 23/1: 213–27.
LELAND, H. and PYLE, D. (1977), 'Information Asymmetries, Financial Structure and Financial Intermediation', *Journal of Finance*, 32/2: 261–75.
MCCONNELL, J. J. and SANGER, G. D. (1987), 'The Puzzle in Post-listing Common Stock Returns', *Journal of Finance*, 42/1: 119–40.
MCDONALD, B. and MORRIS, M. H. (1984), 'The Statistical Validity of the Ratio Method in Financial Analysis: An Empirical Investigation', *Journal of Business Finance and Accounting*, 11/1: 89–98.
MCKENNA, C. J. (1985), *Uncertainty and the Labour Market* (Brighton: Wheatsheaf).
MACMILLAN (1931), *Report of the Committee on Finance and Industry*, Cmd 3897 (London: HMSO).
MARSH, P. (1982), 'The Choice Between Equity and Debt: An Empirical Study', *Journal of Finance*, 37/1: 121–44.
MERJOS, A. (1963), 'Like Money in the Bank: Big Board Listing is a Valuable Asset', *Barrons*, 43: 2.

MERRETT, A. J., HOWE, M., and NEWBOULD, G. D. (1964), *Equity Issues and the London Capital Market* (London: Longmans).

MILES, R. E. and SNOW, C. C. (1977), *Organisational Strategy, Structure and Process* (New York: McGraw-Hill).

MILLER, M. and ROCK, K. (1985), 'Dividend Policy under Asymmetric Information', *Journal of Finance*, 40/4: 1031–51.

MODIGLIANI, F. and MILLER, M. (1958), 'The Cost of Capital, Corporation Finance and the Theory of Investment', *American Economic Review*, 48/2: 261–97.

NASDAQ (1986), *1986 Fact Book* (New York: National Association of Securities Dealers).

NEWELL, R. (1985), 'The USM: A Little Less Glamour', *Money Management*, June.

PEAT, MARWICK, MITCHELL (1985), *Entering the Unlisted Securities Market* (London).

—— (1986*a*), *Going Public* (Birmingham).

—— (1986*b*), *OTC Market Survey* (London).

PHILLIPS, S. M. and ZECHER, J. R. (1982), 'Exchange Listing and the Cost of Equity Capital', *Securities and Exchange Commission Capital Market Working Papers* (Washington DC: SEC).

RADCLIFFE (1959), *Report of the Committee on the Working of the Monetary System*, Cmnd 827. (London: HMSO).

RANSLEY, R. (1984), 'The Operation and Development of the Unlisted Securities Market', London Business School (mimeo).

RAY, G. and HUTCHINSON, P. (1983), *The Financing and Financial Control of Small Enterprise Development* (London: Gower).

ROLL, R. (1981), 'A Possible Explanation of the Small Firm Effect', *Journal of Finance*, 36/4: 879–88.

ROSS, S. A. (1977), 'The Determination of Financial Structure: The Incentive Signalling Approach', *Bell Journal of Economics*, 8/1: 23–40.

SCHOLES, M. S. (1972), 'The Market for Securities: Substitution versus Price Pressure and the Effects of Information on Share Prices', *Journal of Business*, 45/2: 179–211.

STOCK EXCHANGE (1979), *The Stock Exchange Unlisted Securities Market, A Document for Discussion* (London).

—— (1986), 'Flotations and Preemption' Discussion Paper from the Committee on Quotations (London, Jan.; reprinted in *Stock Exchange Quarterly* March).

—— (1987), *Quality Markets* (London).

—— (1988), *Quality Markets* (London).

STOLL, H. R. and CURLEY, A. J. (1970), 'Small Business and the New Issue Market for Equities', *Journal of Financial and Quantitative Analysis*, 5: 309–22.

STOLL, H. R. and WALEY, R. E. (1983), 'Transaction Cost and the Small Firm Effect', *Journal of Financial Economics*, 12: 57–9.

TAIT, N. (1986), *Investors' Chronicle*, 15 Nov.

TAUB, A. (1975), 'The Determinants of the Firm's Capital Structure', *Review of Economics and Statistics*, 57: 410–16.

TOUCHE ROSS (1986), *The Unlisted Securities Market: An Opportunity for Growing Companies*, 7th edn. London.

UNSWORTH, I. (1986), *The Times USM Review*. Times Newspapers: London, May 27.

VAUGHAN, G. D., GRINYER, P., and BIRLEY, S. (1977), *From Private to Public* (London: Woodhead-Faulkner).

WHITTINGTON, G. (1980), 'Some Basic Properties of Accounting Ratios', *Journal of Business Finance and Accounting*, 7/2: 219–23.

WILSON, LORD (1978), *Committee to Review the Functioning of the Financial Institutions*. Vol. 3, *Evidence on the Financing of Industry and Trade* (London: HMSO).

—— (1979), *Committee to Review the Functioning of Financial Institutions: Interim Report*. Cmnd 7503. (London: HMSO).

—— (1980), *Committee to Review the Functioning of Financial Institutions: Report*. Cmnd 7937. (London: HMSO).

Index

acquisitions 26
actions françaises 113, 116, 117; *see also* French Bourse
administrative expenses 12, 13, 17, 20, 53–63, 135, 137, 143, 147
  economies of scale in 9, 11, 13, 14–15, 20, 53, 58–9, 63, 116, 124, 127, 137, 147
  influence of scale on 57–60
  see also deadweight costs; transfer of wealth
agency theory *see* debt
Alexander, J. 131
Ansari, S. L. 67
Anthony, J. 131
Apricot Computers plc 127
asset composition (intangible assets)
  and corporate debt 66, 78, 87
  and discounts at entry 97
  and firm size 87
authority of the Exchange *see* London Stock Exchange
Avera, W. E. 146

Baker, H. K. 145
bank borrowing *see* debt
Bannock, G. 40, 49, 53, 57, 137
barriers to entry *see* new issue market (London); French Second Marché
Baxter, N. 65
bear market 16, 17, 134, 150–1, 152
Berry, R. 35
Bhagat, S. 29, 122
'Big Bang' 148, 149, 152
Big Board 145; *see also* stock exchanges (American)
Binder Hamlyn 152
Birley, S. 16, 53, 55, 67, 91
Blazenko, G. W. 65, 68
Body Shop International plc 135
Bolton Committee 3, 10, 16, 27, 63, 64, 138; *see also* small firms: financing problems
Bradley-Jones, R. 53, 67, 152
Brealey, R. A. 66
Briscoe, G. 66
British Institute of Dealers in Securities 131; *see also* Over-The-Counter Markets
brokers 12, 17–19, 30–2, 121, 149–50
  and administrative expenses 54
  and issue pricing 103–4
  see also issuing houses; market makers
Buckland, R. 10, 13, 15, 16, 17, 18, 29, 31, 32, 35, 36, 49, 53, 55, 57, 59, 62, 67, 73, 91, 92, 94, 101, 103, 104, 105, 110, 111, 122, 140
bull market 17, 101, 133, 150, 151
Business Expansion Scheme 123–4, 130, 131, 133, 147
Business Monitor MA3 69, 70, 77

Capron, D. 66
Confederation of British Industry 10
centralization *see* stock exchanges
channelling efficiency 24, 92, 135; *see also* equity values: market efficiency
Collier, P. 66
Commission d'Operation de Bourse 112, 114–18, 122
Companies Act (1948) 130
contingency theory *see* debt
Cooper, K. 146
corporate gearing *see* debt
cost of disposal 23; *see also* equity values
cost of financial assets 22
cost of transfer 60–3; *see also* administrative expenses
Cote Officiel 113, 114, 117; *see also* French Bourse
Coutty, A. 114, 117
Curley, A. J. 10
Curran, J. 10

Davis, E. W. 10, 13, 15, 16, 17, 29, 31, 32, 35, 36, 49, 53, 57, 59, 62, 66, 67, 73, 91, 94, 105, 110, 111, 122, 140
deadweight costs 135, 140–4, 147; *see also* administrative expenses; transfer of wealth
Dearden, J. 66
death duties and quotation 50; *see also* new issue market (London): motives for entering
debt
  and agency theory 63, 65–7
  bank borrowing 3, 7, 32, 65, 138
  capital 21, 32
  and contingency theory 66
  corporate gearing 33, 35, 66, 69–70, 73; 77, 89, 97, 137, 138
  debt to assets ratio 72, 75, 77, 83, 87, 89
  debt to equity ratio 66, 68, 77, 87, 90

debt—(*cont.*)
long-term 68, 69, 72
management 3, 33, 64–90, 138, 139
measurement of gearing ratio 68, 70, 73, 77
trade creditors 69, 70, 76
Department of Trade and Industry 130, 131
deregulation *see* London Stock Exchange
Dermer, J. 66
Dhaliwal, D. S. 145
Dimson, E. 30, 92
discounts 15, 17, 29–30, 31, 33, 91–111, 122, 139–40, 141, 143
influence of firm size 97–8, 99, 105
influence of issue size 98, 105–7, 111
influence of prospectus information 93–6, 98, 107
influence of risk measures 97, 98, 101, 107
method of issue and 91, 92, 93, 95–6, 99–104, 105–7, 108, 109, 111, 140, 143
models of discounting 91, 92
price: pressure hypothesis 29, 139
disposal times 24; *see also* equity values
distress sales 26; *see also* new issue market (London): motives for entering
Doran, A. 40, 49, 53, 57, 137
Downes, D. H. 29
Dubofsky, D. A. 145, 146

economies of scale *see* administrative expenses
effect of quotation *see* equity values
entrants' behaviour 65–7, 73, 74
entrepreneurial behaviour 151–2
equity values 3, 21–5, 28, 33
effect of quotation 21, 23–4
market clearing price 28, 30
market efficiency 2, 29, 30, 33
options theory 30
unquoted shares 24
see also disposal times; secondary trading

finance gap *see* small firms; Macmillan Gap
Financial Services Act (1987) 133
financial structures 3, 65–9, 70, 71, 73–7, 78–90; *see also* debt
Financial Times 133
Financial Times All-Share index 151
financing acquisitions 21
financing problems *see* small firms
firm size 114, 138
see also administrative expenses: influence of scale; discounts: influence of firm size; small firms
Firth, M. 2, 28
forecast profits 47–9; *see also* prospectus information

Franke, G. 29, 66
French Bourse 116, 119–22
French Second Marché 3, 112, 115–17, 133, 150
barriers to entry 113, 114, 122
comparison with USM 112, 113–17, 121–3, 133
disclosure requirements 113
regional exchanges 116, 117, 122, 133
and regionalization 115–17
Furst, R. 145

gearing *see* debt: corporate gearing
General Undertaking 11; *see also* London Stock Exchange: Listing Agreement
Ghandhi, J. K. 7
Granville and Co. 1, 131, 132; *see also* Over-The-Counter Market (OTC UK)
Grinyer, P. 16, 53, 55, 67, 91
Grossman, S. J. 65
Groth, J. C. 145, 146
Gupta, M. K. 64

Hart, O. D. 65
Harvard Securities 131; *see also* Over-The-Counter Market (OTC UK)
Hawke, G. 66
Hedderson, J. 88
Heinkel, R. 29
Henderson, J. 91
Herbert, P. J. 16, 31, 36, 91, 101, 122
Hodges, S. D. 66
Howe, M. 91, 111
Hussey, R. 53, 67, 152
Hutchinson, P. 7, 33, 66, 67, 78, 82, 139

Ibbotson, R. G. 29
industrial classification of new issues 37, 39–43, 69, 136
influence of scale *see* administrative expenses; *see also* discounts: influence of firm/issue size
insider knowledge 29; *see also* signalling; debt and agency theory
institutional investors 14, 146
Introduction *see* methods of issue
introductory discount *see* methods of issue; discounts
Investors Chronicle 150
irrelevance hypothesis 65; *see also* debt management
issuing houses 12, 16, 17–18, 31, 53, 63
Issuing Houses Association 18
see also brokers; USM: fee income from
issuing process *see* new issue market

John, K. 66

Keane, S. M. 2
Keeley, M. 30
Keenan, M. 91
Kellaway, L. 62
Kleinwort Benson 18
Knowlman, N. 123

Lambert, F. 114, 117
Lee, C. 35
Leland, H. 29, 49, 66, 68
liquidity 7, 64, 117, 121–2, 123, 130–1, 134, 145, 146
Listing Agreement 9, 11; *see also* London Stock Exchange
London Stock Exchange 2, 137, 147
  access to markets 1, 148–9
  authority of the exchange 1, 131, 133
  deregulation 4, 121, 148–9, 150
  market categories 149–50
  new entrants 3, 7, 136, 144
  Official List 2, 3, 11, 12, 18, 23, 24, 28, 33, 114, 116, 136, 137
  quotation requirements 5, 11, 17; *see also* General Undertaking; Listing Agreement
  Rule 163(2) (now Rule 535(2)) 1, 24, 40–7, 55, 123, 130
  rules 92, 113
  see also methods if issue; USM; Third Market

McConnell, J. J. 146
MacDonald, B. 35
McKenna, C. J. 23
Macmillan Committee 3, 27, 63
  Macmillan gap 11, 64, 67
market efficiency *see* equity values
market makers 26, 27, 123, 130–1, 132, 146, 147, 149–50
  NASDIM 130–1
  OTC Trading 131
  size of 'touch' 149–50
  see also Granville and Co.; Harvard Securities; Merrill Lynch; Nomura Securities
market pricing costs *see* small firms
Marr, M. W. 29, 122
Marsh, P. 33, 36, 67, 69, 78, 82, 89, 138
Meric, G. 33, 67, 78, 139
Meric, I. 33, 67, 78, 139
Merjos, A. 145
Merrett, A. J. 91, 111
Merrill Lynch 149
methodology 34–6
methods of issue 10–13, 31, 53, 54–61
  fixed price 12, 15–16
  introductory discount 15, 16
  Offer for Sale 9–10, 12, 31, 39, 55, 56, 57, 58, 143
  Offer for Sale by Tender 12, 31, 55, 56, 58, 137
  Private Placing 12, 31
  Stock Exchange Introduction 7, 11, 54, 55–7, 60–2, 63, 70, 73, 137, 141, 144–5
  Stock Exchange Placing 9–10, 12, 39, 55–8, 59–60, 61–2, 63, 137, 141, 143
  transfers between markets 142–3
  see also Over-The-Counter Market (UK)
Miller, M. 65, 66, 88
M. J. H. Nightingale and Co. *see* Granville and Co.
Modigliani, F. 65, 66, 88
Mollier-Carroz, L. 114, 117
Morris, M. H. 35
motives for entry *see* new issue market

NASDAQ *see* stock exchanges
NASDIM *see* market makers
Newbould, G. D. 91, 111
Newell, R. 13, 53, 55
new issue market (London) 5, 152
  barriers to entry 2, 3, 9, 11, 13–14, 16, 24, 28, 37–9, 43, 52, 53, 57, 58, 62, 64, 67, 88, 91, 137, 139, 140–1, 147, 151
  issuing process 5, 7–9, 11–20, 53
  motives for entering 6–7, 67, 70, 72, 73; *see also* death duties; distress sales
  pricing 3, 29–30, 91–111, 139–40
  reasons for decline 9, 20
  subscription levels 13, 15, 16, 31, 59, 91, 97, 103, 104, 105, 108, 111, 113, 130
new money 5, 32, 37, 49–52, 69, 73, 75, 95, 99, 136, 138, 141
new technologies 40, 42–3, 52, 113, 136; *see also* industrial classification of new issues
Nix, S. 35
Nomura Securities 149; *see also* market makers

Offer for Sale *see* methods of issue
Offer for Sale by Tender *see* methods of issue
Office of Fair Trading 28; *see also* London Stock Exchange: deregulation
Official List *see* London Stock Exchange
OTC Trading *see* market makers
overseas securities houses 148–9
Over-The-Counter Market (OTC UK) 4, 43, 44, 47, 48, 112, 121, 123–30, 133–4, 150–1
  comparison with USM entrants 112, 124, 130, 133
  growth 123–31
  methods of issue 124, 127–8

Over-The-Counter-Market—(*cont.*)
performance 124
regulation 130
tax benefits 123–4
see also market makers; Third Market
Over-The-Counter Market (OTC US) 1, 4, 112, 123, 131, 133

Peat Marwick Mitchell (now Peat Marwick McLintock) 13, 16, 18, 40, 49, 53, 116, 124
Pettelat, F. 114, 117
Phillips, S. M. 145
Placing *see* methods of issue
Pointon, G. 123
predators 25, 30
price: pressure hypothesis 29, 139, 140
pricing efficiency *see* equity values: market efficiency
pricing of new issues *see* new issue market (London)
Private Placing *see* methods of issue
privatization 18, 29, 31, 40, 49, 95, 140, 143
proportion of equity issued 49–51
prospectus information 5, 11, 18, 28–30, 34, 45–7, 49, 54, 55, 61, 68, 69, 91, 92–4, 139
profit performance 37, 43–7
see also discounts; General Undertaking
Pyle, D. 29, 49, 66, 68

quotation *see* London Stock Exchange

Radcliffe Committee 63, 64
Ransley, R. 43, 137
Ray, G. 7, 66, 67, 82
regionalization *see* French Second Marché; USM
regulation of exchanges 2, 28; *see also* London Stock Exchange; Over-The-Counter Market; Financial Services Act (1987)
reporting requirements 1; *see also* London Stock Exchange: quotation requirements
requirements for admission *see* London Stock Exchange: quotation requirements
risk capital 32
risk measures 79, 83, 97, 98, 101, 107; *see also* discounts
Rock, K. 68
role of advisers *see* brokers; issuing houses; USM
Roll, R. 10
Ross, S. A. 29
Rule 163(2) *see* London Stock Exchange
Rule 535(2) *see* London Stock Exchange

Sanger, G. D. 146
Scholes, M. S. 29
Schwartz, E. 29
secondary trading 2, 21–4, 25–8, 33, 59, 64, 65, 81, 112–34, 136, 140; *see also* equity values
share register management 30
'short-termism' 10; *see also* Confederation of British Industry
signalling 66, 67, 92, 102, 138, 146
information as signals 28, 29, 68, 105
price as a signal 30
see also insider knowledge
size of entrants *see* USM
small firms 7, 9–10, 49, 52, 59, 63–5, 67, 100, 105, 130, 136–8, 148, 151–2
finance gap 10, 11, 24, 27, 63, 65, 75, 77, 82, 89, 136, 139
financing problems 27, 150
high growth 32
market pricing costs 13, 20
see also administrative expenses: influence of scale on; discounts: influence of firm size
Smith, Keen, Cutler 116
Spicer and Pegler 53
Spitzfaden, J. 145
stags 31; *see also* new issue market (London): subscription levels
status *see* new issue market (London): motives for entering
Stock Beech 116
stock exchanges
American 1, 145; *see also* Big Board
centralization 115–16, 133
European 112; *see also* French Bourse; French Second Marché
Irish 115, 117
NASDAQ 1, 131, 145
New York 1, 145
regionalization *see* French Second Marché
Stock Exchange *see* London Stock Exchange
see also London Stock Exchange; USM
Stoll, H. R. 10
subscription levels *see* new issue market (London); stags
syndicat de liquidité 114, 121

Tait, N. 24, 123, 130
take-overs 26
Taub, A. 66, 82
Third Market 1, 123, 131, 133–4, 151
and OTC 131–3
and USM 131–3, 148, 150

see also London Stock Exchange
Thompson, G. R. 29, 122
Tie Rack plc 135
Touche Ross and Co. 16, 53, 62, 151
transactions costs 10, 24–5, 26, 27, 28, 66; *see also* administrative expenses; equity value
transfer of wealth during entry 15, 16, 140, 141–3, 144
cost of transfer 141–3
scale of transfer 141–5
see also deadweight costs; discounts
transfers between markets
OTC to USM 44–48, 61, 55, 56
USM to Official List 34, 39, 46, 53, 61, 62, 135, 137, 145–7

underwriting 14, 16, 101–3
discounts and issue underwriting 103–4
Placings as underwritten offers 102–3
USM 2
access 136–140
entrants 3, 8, 121, 127, 136–7, 139, 143, 144–5
fee income from 18–19
market efficiency 2, 29, 30; *see also* channelling efficiency
origins and growth 2, 7–8, 112, 136
and regional firms 116, 122
role of advisers 5, 17–19, 90, 139
size of entrants 37–9, 51
see also debt: corporate gearing; discounts; French Second Marché; London Stock Exchange; Third Market
unquoted shares *see* equity value
Unsworth, I. 145, 146

Vaughan, G. D. 16, 53, 55, 67, 91
venture capital 12, 24, 27

Waley, R. E. 10
Watkins, D. 123
Whittington, G. 35
Wilson Committee 1, 2, 7, 8, 10, 13, 53, 64, 65, 75; *see also* small firms: financing problems

Yeomans, K. A. 10, 13, 15, 16, 17, 18, 29, 31, 32, 35, 36, 49, 53, 55, 57, 59, 67, 73, 91, 94, 101, 103, 105, 110, 111, 122, 140

Zecher, J. R. 145